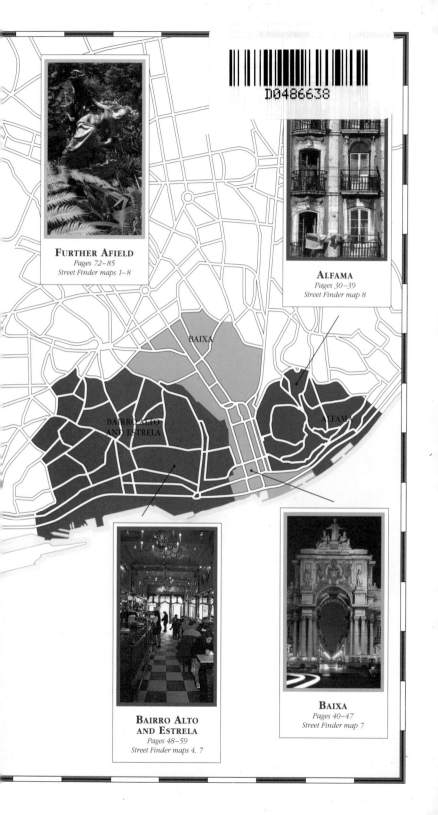

FURTHER AFIELD
Pages 72–85
Street Finder maps 1–8

ALFAMA
Pages 30–39
Street Finder map 8

BAIXA

BAIRRO ALTO
AND ESTRELA

ALFAMA

**BAIRRO ALTO
AND ESTRELA**
Pages 48–59
Street Finder maps 4, 7

BAIXA
Pages 40–47
Street Finder map 7

D0486638

EYEWITNESS *TRAVEL GUIDES*

LISBON

EYEWITNESS TRAVEL GUID·ES

LISBON

Main contributor: SUSIE BOULTON

DK

LONDON, NEW YORK,
MELBOURNE, MUNICH AND DELHI
www.dk.com

PROJECT EDITORS Claire Folkard, Ferdie McDonald
ART EDITORS Jim Evoy, Vanessa Hamilton
EDITORS Francesca Machiavelli, Rebecca Miles,
Alice Peebles, Alison Stace
DESIGNERS Anthea Forlee, Carolyn Hewitson,
Nicola Rodway, Dooty Williams

CONTRIBUTORS AND CONSULTANTS
Clive Gilbert, Peter Gilbert, Sarah McAlister, Norman Renouf,
Joe Staines, Martin Symington, Tomas Tranæus

PHOTOGRAPHERS
Linda Whitwam, Peter Wilson

ILLUSTRATORS
Isidoro González-Adalid Cabezas/Acanto Arquitectura y Urbanismo S.L.,
Paul Guest, Claire Littlejohn, John Woodcock, Martin Woodward

Reproduced by Colourscan (Singapore)
Printed and bound by L. Rex Printing Company Limited, China

First American Edition, 1997
6 8 10 9 7

Published in the United States
by DK Publishing, Inc., 375 Hudson Street,
New York, New York 10014

Reprinted with revisions 1999, 2000, 2001, 2002, 2003

Copyright 1997, 2003 © Dorling Kindersley Limited, London
A Penguin Company

Published in Great Britain by Dorling Kindersley Limited.

ISSN 1542-1554
ISBN 0-7894-9566-X

FLOORS ARE REFERRED TO THROUGHOUT IN ACCORDANCE WITH EUROPEAN
USAGE, I.E., THE "FIRST FLOOR" IS ONE FLIGHT UP

**The information in this
Dorling Kindersley Travel Guide is checked annually.**
Every effort has been made to ensure that this book is as up-to-date
as possible at the time of going to press. Some details, however,
such as telephone numbers, opening hours, prices, gallery hanging
arrangements and travel information, are liable to change. The
publishers cannot accept responsibility for any consequences arising
from the use of this book, nor for any material on third party
websites, and cannot guarantee that any website address in this
book will be a suitable source of travel information. We value the
views and suggestions of our readers very highly. Please write to:
Publisher, DK Eyewitness Travel Guides,
Dorling Kindersley, 80 Strand, London, Great Britain WC2R 0RL.

◁ **View of the Castelo de São Jorge at night**

CONTENTS

HOW TO USE THIS
GUIDE 6

**Manueline vaulting in the cloister
in the Mosteiro dos Jerónimos**

INTRODUCING
LISBON

PUTTING LISBON ON
THE MAP 10

THE HISTORY OF
LISBON 12

LISBON THROUGH
THE YEAR 22

**A statue of St Antony, dressed up
for his feast day celebrations**

View to the Sé across the Baixa from the Elevador de Santa Justa

LISBON AREA BY AREA

LISBON AT A
GLANCE 28

ALFAMA 30

BAIXA 40

Porco à alentejana, a popular dish in Lisbon

TRAVELLERS' NEEDS

WHERE TO STAY 112

RESTAURANTS, CAFÉS AND BARS 120

SHOPS AND MARKETS 136

Atmospheric houses in the old Moorish district of Alfama

BAIRRO ALTO AND
ESTRELA 48

BELÉM 60

FURTHER AFIELD 72

THE LISBON COAST 86

ENTERTAINMENT IN
LISBON 140

SURVIVAL GUIDE

PRACTICAL
INFORMATION 146

GETTING TO LISBON
154

GETTING AROUND
LISBON 156

LISBON STREET
FINDER 164

GENERAL INDEX 178

The Monument to the Discoveries

ACKNOWLEDGEMENTS
189

PHRASE BOOK 191

Palácio da Pena, Sintra

HOW TO USE THIS GUIDE

THIS GUIDE helps you get the most from a visit to Lisbon, providing expert advice as well as detailed practical information. The opening chapter *Introducing Lisbon* maps the city and sets it in its historical and cultural context. Each of the five area chapters, plus *The Lisbon Coast*, describe important sights, using maps, pictures, and illustrations. Hotel and restaurant recommendations plus features on subjects like entertainment, food, and drink can be found in *Travelers' Needs*. The *Survival Guide* contains practical information on everything from transportation to personal safety.

LISBON

Lisbon has been divided into five main sightseeing areas. Each of these areas has its own chapter, which opens with a list of the major sights described. All sights are numbered and plotted on an *Area Map*. Information on the sights is easy to locate as the order in which they appear in the chapter follows the numerical order used on the map.

Sights at a Glance lists the chapter's sights by category: Churches, Museums and Galleries, Historic Buildings, Parks and Gardens.

1 Area Map
For easy reference, the sights covered in the chapter are numbered and located on a map. The sights are also marked on the Street Finder *maps on pages 164–77.*

A locator map shows clearly where the area is in relation to other parts of the city.

Each area is indicated by a color-coded thumb tab (see inside front cover).

2 Street-by-Street Map
This gives a bird's-eye view of the heart of each of the sightseeing areas.

A suggested route for a walk is shown in red.

Stars indicate the sights that no visitor should miss.

3 Detailed Information
All the sights in Lisbon are described individually. Addresses and practical information are provided. The key to the symbols used in the information block is shown on the back flap.

1 Introduction to The Lisbon Coast

The Lisbon Coast has its own introduction, which provides an overview of the history and character of the coast and countryside around Lisbon, and it outlines what is has to offer the visitor today. The area covered by this section is highlighted on the map of Portugal shown on page 89. It covers coastal resorts and local wildlife, as well as beautiful palaces and historic towns.

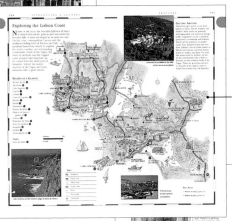

2 Pictorial Map

This shows the main road network and gives an illustrated overview of the region. All entries are numbered, and there are also useful tips on getting around the region.

The Lisbon Coast chapter is indicated by a green thumb tab.

3 Detailed Information

All the important towns and other places to visit are described individually. They are listed in order, following the numbering given on the Pictorial Map. Within each entry, there is more detailed information on important buildings and other sights.

Story boxes explore specific subjects further.

For all the top sights, a Visitors' Checklist provides the practical information you need to plan your visit.

4 The Top Sights

These are given two or more full pages. Historic buildings are dissected to reveal their interiors; museums and galleries have color-coded floor plans to help you locate the most interesting exhibits.

INTRODUCING
LISBON

PUTTING LISBON ON THE MAP 10-11
A HISTORY OF LISBON 12-21
LISBON THROUGH THE YEAR 22-25

Putting Lisbon on the Map

L ISBON, the capital of Portugal, is situated on the
Atlantic coast, in the southwest of the country.
It is approximately 300 km (180 miles) from the
Algarve in the south and around 400 km (250 miles)
from the Minho in the north. The political, economic
and cultural centre of Portugal, the city lies on the
steep hills on the north bank of the Tagus. The
greater Lisbon area occupies around 1,000 sq km
(300 sq miles) and has a population of 3.3 million.
The city has become increasingly popular as a holiday
destination and its proximity to the coast makes it an
ideal choice for both sightseeing and sunbathing.

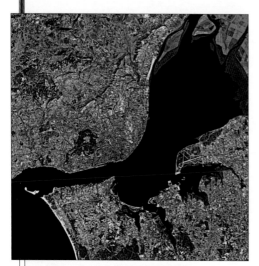

Aerial view of Lisbon, showing the Tagus river

| 0 kilometres | | 100 |
| 0 miles | 50 | |

KEY

✈	Airport
⚓	Port
═	Motorway
▬	Major road
═	Minor road
—	Main railway line
– ·	National boundary

ATLANTIC

OCEAN

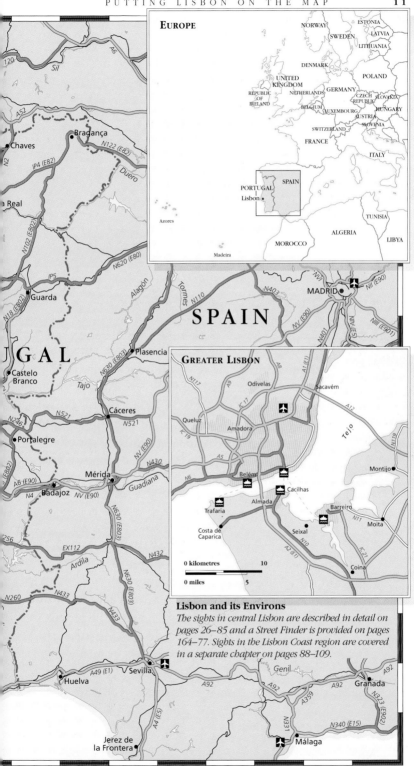

EUROPE

NORWAY
SWEDEN
ESTONIA
LATVIA
LITHUANIA
DENMARK
UNITED KINGDOM
REPUBLIC OF IRELAND
NETHERLANDS
GERMANY
POLAND
BELGIUM
LUXEMBOURG
CZECH REPUBLIC
SLOVAKIA
HUNGARY
AUSTRIA
SLOVENIA
SWITZERLAND
FRANCE
ITALY
PORTUGAL
Lisbon
SPAIN
TUNISIA
MOROCCO
ALGERIA
LIBYA
Azores
Madeira

Bragança
Chaves
N122 (E82)
N2
IP4 (E82)
120
Sil
Duero
a Real
A52
N102 (E802)
Guarda
IP18 (E802)
IP5
Alagón
Tormes
N110
MADRID
N403
A1 (E1)
NI (E90)
NII (E90)
NIV (E5)
NIII (E901)
N401
NV (E90)

SPAIN

JGAL
GAL
Castelo Branco
Tajo
Plasencia
N630 (E803)
N630 (E803)
Cáceres
N521
N521
NV (E90)
N246
Portalegre
N430
Mérida
Guadiana
A6 (E90)
Badajoz
N4
NV (E90)
256
Ardila
EX112
N432
N630 (E803)
N260
N433
N433
Huelva
A49 (E1)
Sevilla
A4 (E5)
Jerez de la Frontera
Genil
A92
A92
A92
A359
Granada
N323 (E902)
N331
N340 (E15)
Málaga

GREATER LISBON

N117
Odivelas
Sacavém
A9
IC17
A8
Queluz
A12
Amadora
IC19
Teio
A5
N6
Belém
Montijo
Trafaria
Cacilhas
Almada
N119
Costa de Caparica
Seixal
Barreiro
N11
Moita
A2 (E1)
N10
IC21
Coina

0 kilometres 10
0 miles 5

Lisbon and its Environs
The sights in central Lisbon are described in detail on pages 26–85 and a Street Finder is provided on pages 164–77. Sights in the Lisbon Coast region are covered in a separate chapter on pages 88–109.

Rolloguo defegido ao ferenisſimo i muito pode
roſo primçipe elſrey dom manuell noſſo ſeñoz ſobre
as bydas i excellentes, feitos dos Reis de portugall
ſeue amteçesſozes, hordenados, i eſcepto per ſeu
mandado per duarte galluam fidallguo de ſua
caſa do ſeu cosſelho noquall falla do grande lou
uoz da preſemte materia que he o pzopio i bdadei
ro louuoz deſtes meſmos Reys de portugall :·

Uito deuem ſerenisſimo ſeñoz trabalhar os homēes poz
emſua uida obzazem uirtudes, poz que mereçã a ds, no ou
tro mũdo i neſte leixem de ſeu tempo memozia. Nam ſoo
mēte que uiuesam o que as annmallias tem per Jguall
com nosco. Mas que bem i louuadamēte byuam que he pzopio do
homem O quall teeindo auida em dias bzeue com auiſtude a faz

THE HISTORY OF LISBON

O VER THE CENTURIES, *Lisbon has both flourished and suffered. The city is most famous for its history of maritime successes, in particular the voyages of Vasco da Gama, who first navigated a sea route to India. In recent years the city has flourished again, and is now a major European center of commerce.*

According to myth, the Greek hero Odysseus (also known as Ulysses) founded Lisbon on his journey home from Troy. The Phoenicians are known to have established a trading post on the site in around 1200 BC. From 205 BC the town was in Roman hands, reaching the height of its importance when Julius Caesar became the governor in 60 BC.

St. Vincent

overran the peninsula and occupied the city for some 450 years. Lisbon was an important trading center under the Moors and their legacy is evident today in the Castelo de São Jorge and the streets of the Alfama district.

The first king of Portugal, Afonso Henriques, finally ousted the Moors from Lisbon in 1147. Among those who helped was the English Crusader Gilbert of Hastings, who became Lisbon's first bishop. A new cathedral was built below the castle, and shortly afterward, the remains of St. Vincent, the patron saint of Portugal, were brought there. Lisbon received its charter early in the 13th century, but it was not until 1256, under Afonso III, that it became the capital.

With the collapse of the Roman Empire, barbarian tribes invaded from northern Europe. The Alans, who conquered the city in around AD 409, were superseded by the Suevi who in turn were driven out by the Visigoths. None of these tribes were primarily town-dwellers, and Lisbon began to decline. In 711 North African Muslim invaders, the Moors,

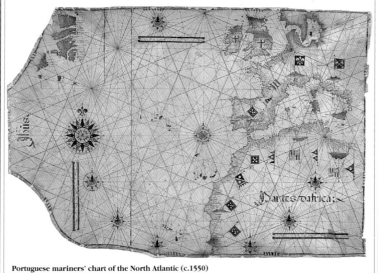

Portuguese mariners' chart of the North Atlantic (c.1550)

◁ **Illuminated page from the *Chronica de Dom Afonso Henriques*, showing Lisbon in the 16th century**

THE REIGN OF KING DINIS

Under King Dinis, the son of Afonso III, the court at Lisbon became a centre of culture and in 1290 the University of Lisbon was founded. Dinis extended the city away from the castle, developing the Baixa, and Lisbon flourished as trade with Europe grew.

In the 14th century, the city continued to expand westwards along the river, despite the ruin caused by the Black Death, which spread throughout Portugal from Lisbon. In 1373, after Lisbon was sacked by Enrique II of Castile, Fernando I built a new line of fortifications to protect his 40,000 citizens and to redefine the boundaries of the growing city. When Fernando died without an heir, the throne was claimed by his illegitimate half brother, João of Avis, who defeated Juan of Castile, in 1385.

Statue of Manuel I and St Jerome on the Mosteiro dos Jerónimos

Musicians at the court of King Dinis

THE DISCOVERIES

Periodic outbreaks of plague continued to destabilize the economy and led to riots in Lisbon over grain shortages. Prosperity returned during the Age of Discovery *(see pp18–19)* when Vasco da Gama, setting out from Belém in 1497, successfully navigated a sea route to India. The resulting wealth from the spice trade made Lisbon the mercantile centre of Europe. In gratitude for this newfound prosperity, Manuel I ordered the building of the Torre de Belém *(see p70)* and the magnificent Mosteiro dos Jerónimos in Belém *(see pp66–7)*; their ornate late-Gothic style, known as Manueline after the king, reflects the Discoveries in the exotic and nautical nature of the detailed sculpture on the two monuments.

The 16th century saw major developments: a new square, the Terreiro do Paço (now the Praça do Comércio), was built on the waterfront, and a new district, the Bairro Alto, sprang up to house the many merchants drawn to Lisbon. The Inquisition, a Catholic movement which persecuted heretics and non-believers, began a reign of terror. Mass trials and executions of those that were condemned took place regularly in the Terreiro do Paço.

SPANISH CONTROL

The young King Sebastião I was killed at the battle of Alcácer-Quibir in a doomed attempt to invade Morocco in 1578. The lack of an heir led to conquest by Spain in 1580. Ignoring his advisers, Philip II of Spain refused to make Lisbon the capital of his extended kingdom and left the government of Portugal to a viceroy. The Spanish were ousted in 1640 and the Duke of Bragança crowned João IV.

With the discovery of Brazilian gold in 1697, Lisbon enjoyed a new wave of prosperity. From 1706, João V began an ambitious building programme in the city. The most valuable addition to Lisbon at this time was the Águas Livres aqueduct *(see p84)*,

The battle of Alcácer-Quibir in Morocco, where 8,000 men were killed and 15,000 captured

which was carrying water across the Alcântara valley just a few years before the devastating earthquake struck the city in 1755 *(see pp20–21)*.

POMBAL'S VISION

Responsibility for rebuilding the ruined city fell to José I's chief minister, the Marquês de Pombal. Engineers drew up a plan that re-aligned Lisbon on a north–south axis and created a grid of streets with the Baixa at its heart. Pombal's vision was not continued by his successors; when the royal family fled to Brazil in 1807, ahead of Napoleon's invading army, Rio de Janeiro temporarily became the capital of the Portuguese empire, and Lisbon began to decline.

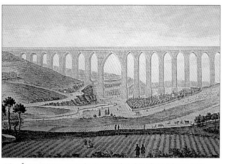

The Águas Livres aqueduct, completed in the 19th century

The Marquês de Pombal pointing to the new Lisbon

REGENERATION

In the second half of the 19th century a period of economic revival and industrialization commenced. Railways and new roads were built, trams were introduced, modern drains and sewers were constructed and work began on the embankment of the Tagus. In 1908 the king was assassinated and two years later the monarchy was overturned. Under António Salazar's lengthy dictatorship (1926–68), Lisbon's modernization continued at the expense of the rest of the country.

Soldiers in the Carnation Revolution of 1974 which ended the dictatorship

A suspension bridge across the Tagus was completed in 1966. Initially called the Ponte Salazar, it was later renamed Ponte 25 de Abril in commemoration of the peaceful Carnation Revolution in 1974 which finally ended the totalitarian regime instituted by Salazar.

MODERN LISBON

The years following the Revolution were a period of both euphoria and political chaos. Then, in 1986, Portugal joined the European Community and foreign companies began to set up in Lisbon. Under the leadership of the Social Democratic prime minister, Aníbal Cavaco Silva, Lisbon's economy recovered. Even the disastrous fire which swept through the Chiado district in 1988 failed to dampen the general optimism. To mastermind the rebuilding of this historic district, the city appointed Portugal's most prestigious architect, Álvaro Siza Vieira. Since then, Lisbon has enjoyed much prestige, and was voted European City of Culture in 1994. In 1998 the city hosted a World Exposition on the theme of the Oceans, in celebration of its maritime history. Today, Lisbon is a cosmopolitan city where the influence of its previous African and South American and colonies is still widely evident.

The Rulers of Portugal

AFONSO HENRIQUES declared himself Portugal's first king in 1139, but his descendants' ties of marriage to various Spanish kingdoms led to dynastic disputes. João I's defeat of the Castilians in 1385 established the House of Avis which presided over the golden age of Portuguese imperialism. Then in 1580, in the absence of a direct heir, Portugal was ruled by Spanish kings for 60 years before the Duke of Bragança became João IV. A Republican uprising ended the monarchy in 1910. However, in the first 16 years of the Republic there were 40 different governments, and in 1926 Portugal became a dictatorship under the eventual leadership of Salazar. Democracy was restored by the Carnation Revolution of 1974.

1481–95 João II

1438–81 Afonso V

1211–23 Afonso II

1185–1211 Sancho I

1248–79 Afonso III

1279–1325 Dinis

1100	1200	1300	1400	1500
HOUSE OF BURGUNDY			**AVIS**	
1100	1200	1300	1400	1500

1325–57 Afonso IV

1357–67 Pedro I

1223–48 Sancho II

1367–83 Fernando I

1139–85 Afonso Henriques (Afonso I)

1433–8 Duarte

1521– João III

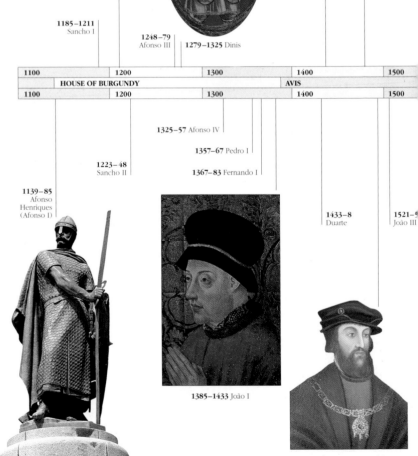

1385–1433 João I

1495–1521 Manuel I

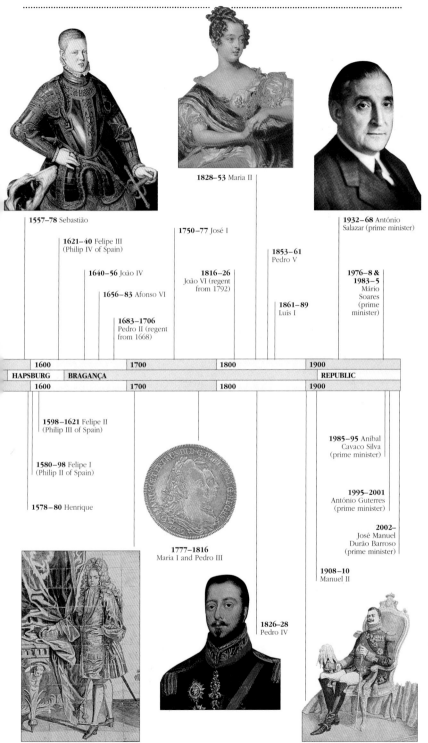

1828–53 Maria II

1557–78 Sebastião

1621–40 Felipe III
(Philip IV of Spain)

1640–56 João IV

1656–83 Afonso VI

1683–1706
Pedro II (regent
from 1668)

1750–77 José I

1816–26
João VI (regent
from 1792)

1853–61
Pedro V

1861–89
Luís I

1932–68 António
Salazar (prime minister)

1976–8 &
1983–5
Mário
Soares
(prime
minister)

1600	1700	1800	1900
HAPSBURG	BRAGANÇA		REPUBLIC
1600	1700	1800	1900

1598–1621 Felipe II
(Philip III of Spain)

1580–98 Felipe I
(Philip II of Spain)

1578–80 Henrique

1985–95 Aníbal
Cavaco Silva
(prime minister)

1995–2001
António Guterres
(prime minister)

2002–
José Manuel
Durão Barroso
(prime minister)

1908–10
Manuel II

1777–1816
Maria I and Pedro III

1826–28
Pedro IV

1706–50 João V

1889–1908 Carlos I

The Age of Discovery

PORTUGAL'S ASTONISHING PERIOD of conquest and exploration began in 1415 with the capture of the North African city of Ceuta. Maritime expeditions into the Atlantic and along the West African coast followed, motivated by conflict between Christianity and Islam and the desire for commercial gain. Great riches were earned from the gold and slaves taken from the Guinea coast, but the real breakthrough for Portuguese imperialism occurred in 1498 when Vasco da Gama *(see p68)* reached India. Portugal soon controlled the Indian Ocean and the spice trade, and established an eastern capital at Goa. With Pedro Álvares Cabral's "discovery" of Brazil, Portugal became a mercantile super-power rivalled only by her neighbour Spain.

Portuguese padrão

Armillary Sphere
This celestial globe with the earth in its centre was used by navigators for measuring the positions of the stars. It became the personal emblem of Manuel I.

Magellan (c.1480–1521)
With Spanish funding, Portuguese sailor Fernão de Magalhães, known as Magellan, led the first circumnavigation of the globe (1519–22). He was killed in the Philippines before the voyage's end.

1500–1501 Gaspar Corte Real reaches Newfoundland.

1427 Diogo de Silves discovers the Azores.

1434 Gil Eanes rounds Cape Bojador (Western Sahara).

1460 Diogo Gomes discovers the Cape Verde archipelago.

1470s Discovery of island of São Tomé.

1482 Diogo Cão reaches the mouth of the Congo.

1485 On his third voyage Diogo Cão reaches Cape Cross (Namibia).

1488 Bartolomeu Dias rounds Cape of Good Hope.

1500 Pedro Álvares Cabral reaches Brazil.

The Adoration of the Magi
Painted for Viseu Cathedral shortly after Cabral returned from Brazil in 1500, this panel is attributed to the artist Grão Vasco (c.1475–1540). King Baltazar is depicted as a Tupi Indian.

African Ivory Salt Cellar
This 16th-century ivory carving shows Portuguese warriors supporting a globe and a ship. A sailor peers out from the crow's nest at the top.

Japanese Screen (c.1600)
This screen shows traders unloading a nau, *or great ship. Between 1575 and their expulsion in 1638, the Portuguese monopolized the carrying trade between China and Japan.*

HENRY THE NAVIGATOR

Although he did not sail himself, Henry (1394–1460), the third son of João I, laid the foundations for Portugal's maritime expansion that were later built upon by João II and consolidated by Manuel I. As Master of the wealthy Order of Christ and Governor of the Algarve, Henry was able to finance expeditions along the African coast. By the time he died he had a monopoly on all trade south of Cape Bojador. Legend tells that he founded a school of navigation in the Algarve, at either Sagres or Lagos.

KEY

- - -   Discoverers' routes

1543 Portuguese arrive in Japan.

1513 Trading posts set up in China at Macau and Canton.

1510 Capture of Goa.

1498 Vasco da Gama reaches Calicut in India.

1518 Fortress built in Colombo (Sri Lanka).

1512 Portuguese reach Ternate in the Moluccas (Spice Islands).

Cloves
Pepper
Nutmeg
Cinnamon

The Spice Trade
Exotic spices were a great source of wealth for Portugal. The much-disputed Moluccas, or Spice Islands, were purchased from Spain in 1528.

PORTUGUESE DISCOVERIES

The systematic attempt to find a sea route to India, which led to a monopoly of the spice trade, began in 1482 with the first voyage of Diogo Cão, who planted a *padrão* (stone cross) on the shores where he landed.

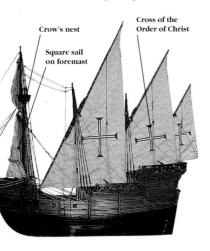

Cross of the Order of Christ

Crow's nest

Square sail on foremast

Lateen-rigged Caravel
These ships with three triangular sails were favoured by the first Portuguese explorers who sailed close to the African coast. For later journeys across the open ocean, square sails were found more effective.

The 1755 Lisbon Earthquake

Votive tile panel offered by survivors

THE FIRST TREMOR of the devastating earthquake was felt at 9:30am on 1 November. A few minutes later there was a second, far more violent shock, reducing over half the city to rubble. Although the epicentre was close to the Algarve, Lisbon, as the most populated area, bore the worst. Over 20 churches collapsed, crushing the crowds who had assembled for All Saints' Day. A third shock was followed by fires which quickly spread. An hour later, huge waves came rolling in from the Tagus and flooded the lower part of the city. Most of Portugal suffered damage and the shock was felt as far away as Italy. Perhaps 15,000 people lost their lives in Lisbon alone.

***This anonymous painting** of the arrival of a papal ambassador at court in 1693 shows how Terreiro do Paço looked before the earthquake.*

Some buildings that might have survived an earthquake alone were destroyed by the fire that followed.

The old royal palace, the 16th-century Paço da Ribeira, was utterly ruined by the earthquake and ensuing flood.

***The royal family** was staying at the palace in Belém, a place far less affected than Lisbon, and survived the disaster unscathed. Here the king surveys the city's devastation.*

Ships crammed full of people fleeing the fire were wrecked and anchors thrown up to water level.

***This detail is** from a votive painting dedicated to Nossa Senhora da Estrela, given by a grateful father in thanks for the sparing of his daughter's life in the earthquake. The girl was found miraculously alive after being buried under rubble for seven hours.*

THE RECONSTRUCTION OF LISBON

Marquês de Pombal (1699–1782)

No sooner had the tremors abated than Sebastião José de Carvalho e Melo, chief minister to José I and later to become Marquês de Pombal, was outlining ideas for rebuilding the city. While philosophers moralized, Pombal reacted with practicality. "Bury the dead and feed the living" is said to have been his initial response. He then began a progressive town-planning scheme. His efficient handling of the crisis won him almost total political control.

REACTIONS TO THE DISASTER

French author, Voltaire

The earthquake had a profound effect on European thought. Eyewitness accounts appeared in the papers, many written by foreigners living in Lisbon. A heated debate developed over whether the earthquake was a natural phenomenon or divine wrath. Pre-earthquake Lisbon had been a flourishing city, famed for its wealth – also for its Inquisition and idolatry. Interpreting the quake as punishment, preachers prophesied further catastrophes. Famous literary figures debated the significance of the event, among them the French writer Voltaire, who wrote a poem about the disaster, propounding his views that evil exists and man is weak and powerless, doomed to an unhappy fate on earth.

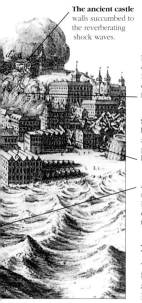

The ancient castle walls succumbed to the reverberating shock waves.

Flames erupted as the candles lit for All Saints' Day ignited the city's churches. The fire raged for seven days.

Some of Lisbon's finest buildings were destroyed, along with gold, jewellery, priceless furniture, archives, books and paintings.

At 11am, tidal waves rolled into Terreiro do Paço. The Alcântara docks, to the west, bore the brunt of the impact.

Churches, homes and public buildings all suffered in the disaster. The Royal Opera House, here shown in ruins, was only completed in March the same year.

A CONTEMPORARY VIEW OF THE EARTHQUAKE

This anonymous German engraving of 1775 gives a vivid picture of the scale of the disaster. Many who fled the flames made for the Tagus, but were washed away in the huge waves which struck the Terreiro do Paço. The human and material losses were incalculable.

The reconstruction of the centre of Lisbon took place rapidly. By the end of November the Marquês de Pombal had devised a strikingly modern scheme for a grid of parallel streets running from the waterfront to Rossio. The new buildings are shown in yellow.

Modern-day Lisbon holds many reminders of the earthquake. Pombal's innovative grid system is clearly visible in this aerial view of the Baixa (see pp40–47). The scheme took many years to complete, and the triumphal arch that spans Rua Augusta was not finished until over a century later, in 1873.

LISBON THROUGH THE YEAR

WHILE THE SUMMER MONTHS are the most popular for visiting Lisbon and have many events on the calendar – the Festas dos Santos Populares, in June, are one of the highlights of the year – spring and autumn can also be rewarding if you want to tour the Lisbon Coast. In late winter, the colourful Carnaval celebrations attract many visitors to Lisbon. Other events during the year include music festivals, sporting fixtures and the many religious *festas*, which are great times of celebration for the Portuguese people.

SPRING

WITH THE ARRIVAL of spring-time in Lisbon, the café and restaurant terraces begin to fill with people. Many events, such as concerts and markets, start to take place in the open air again as the weather improves. At the weekends the coastal resorts of Cascais and Estoril become livelier when on warm, bright days local people take day trips there to enjoy the seaside.

MARCH

Festa da Primavera
(25 Mar). Music, theatre and dance performances, including many open-air events, are held at the Centro Cultural de Belém. The festival offers rock and pop as well as classical music.
Procissão dos Terceiros Franciscanos *(4th Sun before Easter)*. The colourful

João Moura, one of Portugal's top bullfighters *(cavaleiros)*

procession through the streets of Mafra *(see p92)* starts at the convent. The ceremonial robes worn in the procession were given to the church by João V, in the 18th century.

APRIL

Lisbon's Half Marathon *(1 Apr)*. One of the city's most popular sporting events, the race crosses the Ponte 25 de Abril *(see p74)* and draws international runners .
Festa dos Merendeiros *(7 Apr)*. A traditional festival and procession held in Santo Isidoro, near Mafra *(see p92)*. There is a ceremony to bless the bread and the fields in the hope of a successful harvest later on in the year.
Estoril Open Tennis Championship *(early April)*. International players compete in Portugal's top tennis competition, held at the Jamor Tennis Courts.

Liberty Day *(25 Apr)*. The annual celebration of the Carnation Revolution that ended 48 years of dictatorship in 1974 *(see p15)* is also known as the Dia da Revoluçaõ. A public holiday throughout Portugal, commemorations include a military parade and political speeches at the Praça do Império. The unions organize festivities that take place all over the city.
Beginning of the bull-fighting season *(Apr– Sep)*. The Campo Pequeno bullring in Lisbon is the usual venue for this traditional entertainment. However, the ring is being currently refurbished and is now scheduled to re-open in 2003. Bullfights may be seen at rings in Cascais *(see p102)* and Montijo.
Moda Lisboa *(April)*. This biannual fashion show attracts designers from all over the world, and is Portugal's principal fashion event.

MAY

Dia do Trabalhador *(1 May)*. Protest marches and political speeches throughout Lisbon are organized by the unions on Labour Day.
Gulbenkian Contemporary Music Encounters *(21 May–1 Jun)*. A forum for conferences, debates and performances by lesser-known composers and musicians.
Feira do Livro *(May–Jun)*. One of the main literary events in Lisbon, this book fair offers numerous bargains, such as second-hand books and signed copies. The event takes place at the Parque Eduardo VII, the city's largest park *(see p75)*.
Feira do Mar *(May–Jun)*. Held in Sesimbra *(see p106)*, this festival promotes the town's artists and local food.

Formal military parades are held in Lisbon in celebration of Liberty Day

AVERAGE DAILY HOURS OF SUNSHINE

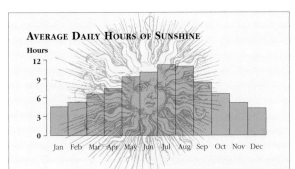

Hours

12 · 9 · 6 · 3 · 0

Jan Feb Mar Apr May Jun Jul Aug Sep Oct Nov Dec

Sunshine Chart
Although Lisbon enjoys a moderate amount of sunshine all year, the days are particularly hot and sunny in the summer months. Care should be taken to protect the skin against the sun, both when walking around Lisbon itself and when sunbathing along the coast on the beaches of Estoril or Cascais.

SUMMER

THE SUMMER MONTHS are a major holiday time in Lisbon, especially August when many Lisboetas retire to the coastal resorts, in particular Costa da Caparica and Cascais.

JUNE

Festas da Cidade *(throughout Jun)*. A celebration of the city of Lisbon itself, that includes all sorts of events from rock concerts to drive-in films. The streets are all lit up and decorated for the event.

Troia Internationl Film Festival *(throughout Jun)*. This small festival based at Setúbal, south of Lisbon is aimed at countries with an annual production of less than 21 feature films.

Santo António *(12–13 Jun)*. A major festival in Lisbon, honouring the city's patron saint, and the beginning of the Festas dos Santos Populares (Feasts of

The beach at Estoril, just one of the many popular bays along the Lisbon Coast

the People's Saints). Locals put up lanterns and streamers in the Alfama and bring out chairs for the hundreds who come for the wine and sardines.

São João *(23–24 Jun)*. A similar festival to that of Santo António, forming part of the Festas dos Santos Populares.

Arraial Gay e Lésbico *(late Jun)*. Up to a week of events and celebrations held in one of Lisbon's parks or squares.

Festival de Música de Sintra *(mid-Jun–mid-Jul)*. A series of classical music concerts held in the parks and palaces of Sintra and Queluz. *(see pp96–9)*.

São Pedro *(25 Jun–1 Jul)*. The end of the Festas dos Santos Populares. The fishing boats are blessed in Montijo, on the south bank of the Tagus.

JULY

Festival Internacional de Teatro (FIT) *(early–mid-July)*. This international festival is held in venues across Lisbon, and is one of Portugal's main theatrical events.

FIA-Lisbon International Handicraft Exhibition *(early Jul)*. This huge display of arts and crafts is held in the Parque de Nações.

Festival Estoril Jazz *(early Jul)*. A series of jazz concerts, lasting about a week, takes place in locations in and around Lisbon.

Feira de Artesanato *(Jul–Aug)*. This craft fair is held in Estoril *(see p102)*, and features folk music and dance performances.

Feira dos Alhos *(3rd Sun in Jul)*. Annual market of crafts, delicacies and wine- and cheese-tasting, near the Convent of Mafra *(see p92)*.

Feira Grande de São Pedro *(31 Jul)*. A market of crafts, antiques and local delicacies, in Sintra *(see pp96–9)*.

Capuchos Music Festival *(Jul–Aug)*. Centred on the Capuchos Monastery on the south side of the Tagus.

Verão Em Sesimbra *(Jul–Sep)*. Popular entertainment festival held in the coastal town of Sesimbra *(see p106)*.

AUGUST

Jazz em Agosto *(early Aug)*. Jazz music is performed in the gardens of the Calouste Gulbenkian Cultural Centre.

Noites de Bailado em Seteais *(weekends throughout Aug)*. Ballet performances are held in the Seteais palace gardens, near Sintra *(see pp96–7)*.

Romaria de São Mamede *(14–22 Aug)*. Farmers lead their animals around the chapel of Janas, north of Colares *(see p93)*, to be blessed. The tradition originates in the fact that the site of the church was once that of a Roman temple dedicated to Diana, goddess of hunting and animals.

Celebrating Santo António, one of Lisbon's most important festivals

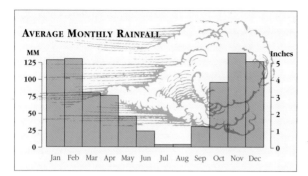

AVERAGE MONTHLY RAINFALL

| MM | | | | | | | | | | | | Inches |

Rainfall Chart
Rainfall is fairly heavy in the winter months in Lisbon, and then drops steadily until the height of summer, when there is almost no rain at all. The autumn, although still warm, can produce some wet days, the wettest month on average being November.

AUTUMN

IN MANY WAYS, this is the best season for touring and sightseeing. The strong heat of the summer has passed but the weather is still pleasantly warm. The countryside around Sintra is particularly beautiful with the changing colours of the trees.

SEPTEMBER

Avante! *(1st weekend in Sep).* This lively *festa* in Seixal, south of the Tagus, attracts large crowds. It includes national and international music shows, exhibitions and cultural events.
Nossa Senhora da Luz *(2nd weekend of Sep).* A religious *festa* held in honour of Our Lady of Light in Sampaio, near Sesimbra *(see p106).*
Festa das Vindimas *(early Sep).* At the foot of Palmela's medieval castle *(see p106),* the first grape harvest is blessed, amid traditional entertainment, wine- and cheese-tasting and fireworks.

Nossa Senhora do Cabo Espichel *(last Sun of Sep).* Local fishermen honour the Virgin Mary with a procession up to the church at Cabo Espichel *(see p103).*
Feira da Luz *(throughout Sep).* This event focuses on arts and crafts, especially pottery. It takes place in the Carnide district of Lisbon.
Festa de Senhora da Consolação *(throughout Sep).* This festival in the Assafora area of Sintra *(see p96–101)* celebrates Portugal's patron saint with a month of parties, music and food.
Encontros ACARTE *(throughout Sep).* Organized by the Gulbenkian Foundation, this is a programme of activities designed to promote new talent in the arts. It runs all year round but a show is held in September. *Acarte* is an acronym standing for Animation, Creativity, Art and Education.

OCTOBER

Republic Day *(5 Oct).* The revolution that brought the monarchy to an end in 1910 *(see p15),* is commemorated annually in Lisbon with military parades.
Estoril Golf Open *(late Oct).* A major golf tournament, in Estoril *(see p102).*

An old lady laying flowers at a cemetery in Lisbon in honour of All Saints' Day

NOVEMBER

All Saints' Day *(1 Nov).* An important festival in the Portuguese religious calendar, many families light candles and lay flowers in local cemeteries throughout the area, in honour of their dead relatives.
Feira de Todos os Santos *(1 Nov).* Also known as the Dried Fruits' Market, this is a lively fair held in Azureira, near Mafra *(see p92).*
Dia do Magusto e de São Martinho *(11 Nov).* The celebration of Roast Chestnut Day is based on the tradition of preparing for winter.
Circus *(late Nov–early Jan).* Before Christmas, circuses arrive in Lisbon. Check venues and dates with tourist offices.
Lisbon Marathon *(end Nov).* Festive celebrations in the city as the runners compete.

Blessing the grape harvest at the Festa das Vindimas in Palmela

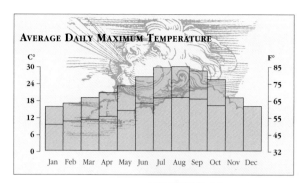

AVERAGE DAILY MAXIMUM TEMPERATURE

Temperature Chart
Lisbon is rarely very cold, and maintains a pleasantly mild climate, even during the winter months, making it a good city to visit in any season. However, the summer months bring days of consistent heat, and although the city is quiet in high summer, it can become humid and stifling.

WINTER

THOSE SEEKING MILD, sunny climes and an escape from the winter cold, will find this a good time of year to visit Lisbon. The nightlife is very lively and continues until the early hours, especially at weekends. Christmas is a time of great celebration and an important occasion for families to reunite and enjoy long meals together.

Colourful parades during the annual Carnaval celebrations in Lisbon

DECEMBER

Festa de Imaculada Conceição *(8 Dec).* This festival of the Immaculate Conception is a national holiday throughout Portugal. There are special church services and Lisbon's population celebrate with their usual festive spirit.

Christmas *(24–25 Dec).* Throughout the Lisbon area, churches and shops display nativity scenes and cribs. The main celebrations take place on Christmas Eve, when families get together and go to midnight mass. They then return home for a large traditional meal of *bacalhau* (salted dried cod) and *sonhos* (small fried cakes similar to doughnuts, usually flavoured with pumpkin or orange).

Nossa Senhora da Conceição *(26 Dec).* A traditional religious procession held in honour of Our Lady of the Immaculate Conception, the saint protector of Alfarim, near Sesimbra *(see p106).*

The celebratory cake, *bolo rei*

JANUARY

New Year *(31 Dec–1 Jan).* In Lisbon, a spectacular firework display is held in Praça do Comércio to welcome the New Year.

Epiphany *(6 Jan).* The traditional cake baked for the Epiphany is *bolo rei* (king's cake), a small fruit cake made with a lucky charm and a bean inside. Crown-shaped, it is topped with crystallized fruit, resembling gems. The person who gets the bean must then buy the next cake. *Bolo rei* is also made at Christmas time.

Opera season *(Jan–Nov).* The opera season starts at the Teatro Nacional de São Carlos *(see p53).*

FEBRUARY

Carnaval *(date varies).* This is celebrated throughout Portugal with spectacular costumes and floats; there is an especially colourful parade in Sesimbra *(see p106).*

Procissão do Senhor dos Passos da Graça *(second Sun in Lent).* The figure of Christ *(Senhor dos Passos)* is taken out of the Igreja da Graça *(see p37)* and carried through the streets of Graça, in Lisbon. The procession dates back to the 16th century.

PUBLIC HOLIDAYS

New Year's Day (1 Jan)
Carnaval (Feb)
Good Friday (Mar or Apr)
Dia 25 de Abril, *commemorating 1974 revolution* (25 Apr)
Dia do Trabalhador, *Labour Day* (1 May)
Corpus Christi (6 Jun)
Camões Day (10 Jun)
Assumption Day (15 Aug)
Republic Day (5 Oct)
All Saints' Day (1 Nov)
Dia da Restauração, *commemorating Independence from Spain, 1640* (1 Dec)
Immaculate Conception (8 Dec)
Christmas Day (25 Dec)

LISBON AREA
BY AREA

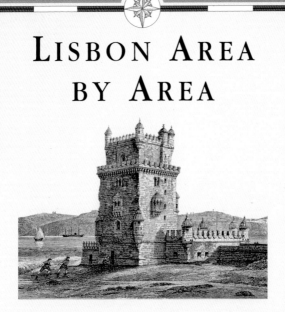

ALFAMA 30-39
BAIXA 40-47
BAIRRO ALTO AND ESTRELA 48-59
BELÉM 60-71
FARTHER AFIELD 72-85

Lisbon at a Glance

PORTUGAL'S CAPITAL, a city of about 550,000 people, sits on the north bank of the Tagus estuary, 17 km (10 miles) from the Atlantic. Razed to the ground by the devastating earthquake of 1755 *(see pp20–21)*, the city centre, the Baixa, is essentially 18th century, with a carefully planned grid of elegant streets. On the hills on either side of the centre, the narrow streets of the Alfama and Bairro Alto make it a personal, approachable city. Since the construction of the bridge, Ponte 25 de Abril, in the 1960s, it has been possible for the city to expand to the Outra Banda (the other bank). Since its days of glory during the Age of Discovery, when Lisbon was at the forefront of world trade, the city has been an important port. Today the docks have moved, but in Belém, 6 km (4 miles) west along the river from the city centre, the Mosteiro dos Jerónimos and the Torre de Belém still bear witness to the city's maritime past.

The Museu Nacional de Arte Antiga houses paintings and sculpture. There are notable Flemish-influenced Portuguese works such as Jorge Afonso's Apparition of Christ to the Virgin *(see pp56–7).*

The Mosteiro dos Jerónimos is a magnificent 16th-century monastery. Commissioned by Manuel I, much of it is built in the peculiarly Portuguese style of architecture, known as Manueline. The extravagantly sculpted south portal of the church with its minute detailing was designed by João de Castilho in 1516. It is one of the finest examples of the style (see pp66–7).

BELÉM
(See pp60–71)

The Torre de Belém was a beacon for navigators returning from the Indies and the New World and a symbol of Portuguese naval power (see p70).

◁ **View from the Tagus of Praça do Comércio with the statue of José I at the centre**

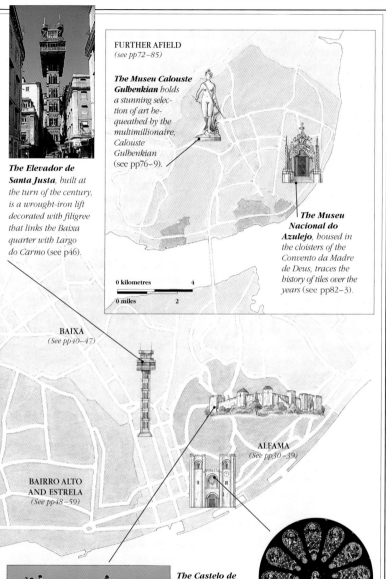

The Elevador de Santa Justa, built at the turn of the century, is a wrought-iron lift decorated with filigree that links the Baixa quarter with Largo do Carmo (see p46).

FURTHER AFIELD
(see pp72–85)

The Museu Calouste Gulbenkian holds a stunning selection of art bequeathed by the multimillionaire, Calouste Gulbenkian (see pp76–9).

The Museu Nacional do Azulejo, housed in the cloisters of the Convento da Madre de Deus, traces the history of tiles over the years (see pp82–3).

0 kilometres 4

0 miles 2

BAIXA
(See pp40–47)

BAIRRO ALTO AND ESTRELA
(See pp48–59)

ALFAMA
(See pp30–39)

The Castelo de São Jorge, once a Moorish castle and then the abode of the Portuguese kings, was transformed in the 1930s into tranquil public gardens. The battlements afford spectacular views of the city (see pp38–9).

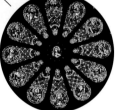

The Sé, the city's greatly restored cathedral, is a sturdy Romanesque building noted for its beautiful rose window. Ornate silver and ecclesistical robes are among the many religious objects on display in the treasury (see p36).

0 metres 500

0 yards 500

ALFAMA

T IS DIFFICULT TO BELIEVE that this humble neighbourhood was once the most desirable quarter of Lisbon. For the Moors, the tightly packed alleyways around the fortified castle comprised the whole city. The seeds of decline were sown in the Middle Ages when wealthy residents moved west for fear of earthquakes, leaving the quarter to fishermen and paupers. The buildings survived the 1755 earthquake *(see pp20–21)* and, although there are no Moorish houses still standing, the quarter retains its kasbah-like layout. Compact houses line steep streets and stairways, their façades strung with washing.

Portugal's coat of arms in the treasury of the Sé

Long-overdue restoration is under way in the most dilapidated areas, but daily life still revolves around local grocery stores and small, cellar-like tavernas.

Above the Alfama, the imposing Castelo de São Jorge crowns Lisbon's eastern hill. This natural vantage point, a defensive stronghold and royal palace until the 16th century, is today a popular promenade, with spectacular views from its greatly restored ramparts.

West of the Alfama stand the proud twin towers of the Sé. To the northeast, the domed church of Santa Engrácia and the white façade of São Vicente de Fora dominate the skyline.

SIGHTS AT A GLANCE

Museums and Galleries
Museu de Artes Decorativas ②
Museu Militar ⑥

Historic Buildings
Casa dos Bicos ⑦
Castelo de São Jorge pp38–9 ⑩

Churches
Santo António à Sé ⑨

Santa Engrácia ⑤
São Vicente de Fora ③
Sé ⑧

Belvederes
Miradouro da Graça ⑪
Miradouro de Santa Luzia ①

Markets
Feira da Ladra ④

GETTING THERE

The 12 and 28 trams rattle up the narrow streets of the Alfama from the Baixa. Bus 37 does a circuit from the Castle to Rossio. Many buses run east along Avenida Dom Infante Henrique to Santa Apolónia station, and west to Belém.

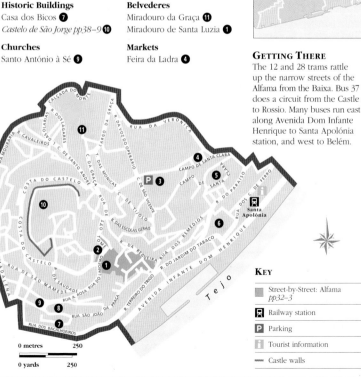

KEY

Street-by-Street: Alfama *pp32–3*

🚉 Railway station

🅿 Parking

ℹ Tourist information

— Castle walls

0 metres　　　250
0 yards　　　250

◁ **Ironwork balconies on a house in Rua dos Bacalhoeiros, beside the Casa dos Bicos**

Street-by-Street: Alfama

A FASCINATING QUARTER at any time of day, the Alfama comes to life in the late afternoon and early evening when the locals emerge at their doorways and the small tavernas start to fill. Many African immigrants live here and several venues play music from Mozambique and the Cape Verde Islands. Given the steep streets and steps of the quarter, the least strenuous approach is to start at the top and work your way down. A walk around the maze of winding alleyways will reveal picturesque corners and crumbling churches as well as panoramic views from the shady terraces, such as the Miradouro de Santa Luzia.

On Largo das Portas do Sol, café tables look out over the Alfama towards the Tagus estuary. Portas do Sol was one of the entrance gates to the old city.

The church of Santa Luzia has 18th-century blue and white *azulejo* panels on its south wall.

Statue of St. Vincent

Largo das Portas do Sol has its own terrace viewpoint on a converted rooftop on the east side of the Santa Luzia church.

Castelo de São Jorge

★ Museu de Artes Decorativas
Set up as a museum by the banker Ricardo do Espírito Santo Silva, the 17th-century Palácio Azurara houses fine 17th- and 18th-century Portuguese furniture and decorative arts ❷

KEY

– – – Suggested route

0 metres 25
0 yards 25

STAR SIGHTS

★ Miradouro de Santa Luzia

★ Museu de Artes Decorativas

★ Miradouro de Santa Luzia
The view from this bougainvillea-clad terrace spans the tiled roofs of the Alfama toward the Tagus. This is a pleasant place to rest after a walk around the area's steep streets ❶

Beco dos Cruzes, like most of the alleyways *(becos)* that snake their way through the Alfama, is a steep cobbled street. Locals often hang washing between the tightly packed houses.

LOCATOR MAP
See Lisbon Street Finder map 8

Rua de São Pedro is the scene of a lively early-morning fish market where the *varinas* sell the catch of the day. *Peixe espada* (scabbard fish) is one of the fish sold here.

Largo do Chafariz de Dentro is named after the 17th-century fountain *(chafariz)* that was originally placed within *(dentro)* rather than outside the 14th-century walls.

BECO DAS CRUZES

BECO DA CARDOSA

RUA DE SÃO MIGUEL

BECO DO MEXIAS

LARGO DO CHAFARIZ DE DENTRO

BECO DO POCINHO

RUA DE SÃO PEDRO

Sé

The church of Nossa Senhora dos Remédios was rebuilt after the 1755 earthquake *(see pp20–21)*. The pinnacled Manueline portal is all that remains of the original building.

São Miguel was rebuilt after it was damaged in the 1755 earthquake. It retains a few earlier features, including a fine ceiling of Brazilian jacaranda wood.

Popular restaurants hidden in the labyrinth of alleyways spill out onto open-air patios. The Lautasco *(see p128)*, in Beco do Azinhal, serves excellent Portuguese food.

Tile panel showing pre-earthquake Praça do Comércio, Santa Luzia

Miradouro de Santa Luzia ❶

Rua do Limoeiro. **Map** 8 D4. 🚌 28.

THE TERRACE by the church of Santa Luzia provides a sweeping view over the Alfama and the River Tagus. Distinctive landmarks, from left to right, are the cupola of Santa Engrácia, the church of Santo Estêvão and the two startling white towers of São Miguel. While tourists admire the views, old men play cards under the bougainvillea-clad pergola. The south wall of Santa Luzia has two modern tiled panels, one of Praça do Comércio before it was flattened by the earthquake, the other showing the Christians attacking the Castelo de São Jorge (see pp38–9) in 1147.

Museu de Artes Decorativas ❷

Largo das Portas do Sol 2. **Map** 8 D3.
📞 21-888 19 91 or 881 46 00. 🚌 37.
🚌 12, 28. 🕐 10am–5pm Sun–Fri.
⬤ 1 Jan, Easter, 1 May, 25 Dec. 📷 ♿

ALSO KNOWN AS the Ricardo do Espírito Santo Silva Foundation, the museum was set up in 1953 to preserve the traditions and increase public awareness of the Portuguese decorative arts. The foundation was named after a banker who bought the 17th-century Palácio Azurara in 1947 to house his fine collection of furniture, textiles, silver and

ceramics. Among the 17th- and 18th-century antiques displayed in this handsome four-storey mansion are many fine pieces in exotic woods, including an 18th-century rosewood backgammon and chess table. Also of note are the collections of 18th-century silver and Chinese porcelain, and the Arraiolos carpets. The spacious rooms still retain some original ceilings and *azulejo* panels.

18th-century china cutlery case, Museu de Artes Decorativas

Workshops are housed in the adjoining building, where visitors can watch artisans preserving the techniques of cabinet-making, gilding, bookbinding and other traditional crafts. Temporary exhibitions, lectures and concerts are also held in the palace.

Stone figure of a woman praying by the tomb of Carlos I in São Vicente de Fora

São Vicente de Fora ❸

Largo de São Vicente. **Map** 8 E3.
📞 21-882 44 00. 🚌 12. 🚌 28.
🕐 9am–6pm Tue–Fri, 9am–7pm Sat, 9am–12:30pm & 3–5pm Sun.
📷 to cloisters.

ST VINCENT was proclaimed Lisbon's patron saint in 1173, when his relics were transferred from the Algarve, in southern Portugal, to a church on this site outside *(fora)* the city walls. Designed by Italian architect Filippo Terzi, and completed in 1627, the off-white Italianate façade is sober and symmetrical, with towers either side and statues of saints Augustine, Sebastian and Vincent over the entrance.

Inside, one is drawn immediately to Machado de Castro's Baroque canopy over the altar, flanked by life-size wooden statues.

The adjoining former Augustinian monastery, retains its 16th-century cistern and vestiges of the former cloister but is visited for its 18th-century *azulejos*. Among the panels in the entrance hall off the first cloister there are lively, though historically inaccurate, tile scenes of Afonso Henriques attacking Lisbon and Santarém. Around the cloisters, the tiled rural scenes are surrounded by floral designs and cherubs, illustrating the fables of La Fontaine. A passageway leads behind the church to the old refectory, transformed into the Bragança Pantheon in 1885. The stone sarcophagi of almost every king and queen are here, from João IV, who died in 1656, to Manuel II, last king of Portugal. Only Maria I and Pedro IV are not buried here. A stone mourner kneels at the tomb of Carlos I and his son Luís Felipe, assassinated in Praça do Comércio in 1908.

Feira da Ladra ❹

Campo de Santa Clara. **Map** 8 F2. ◯
7:30am–1pm Tue & Sat. 🚌 12. 🚋 28.

THE STALLS of the so-called "Thieves' Market" have occupied this site on the edge of the Alfama for over a century, laid out under the shade of trees or canopies. As the fame of this flea market has grown, bargains are increasingly hard to find amongst the mass of bric-a-brac, but a few of the vendors have interesting wrought-iron work, prints and tiles, as well as second-hand clothes. The influence of the African colonies can be seen in some of the stalls selling statuary, masks and jewellery. Fish, vegetables and herbs are sold in the nearby wrought-iron marketplace.

Bric-a-brac for sale in the Feira da Ladra

Santa Engrácia ❺

Campo de Santa Clara. **Map** 8 F2.
📞 21-885 48 20. 🚌 12. 🚋 28.
◯ 10am–5pm Tue–Sun; 10am–7pm Sun. ◯ public hols. 🅿 ♿

ONE OF LISBON'S most striking landmarks, the soaring dome of Santa Engrácia punctuates the skyline in the east of the city. The original church collapsed in a storm in 1681. The first stone of the new Baroque monument, laid in 1682, marked the beginning of a 284-year saga which led to the invention of a saying that a Santa Engrácia job was never done. The church was not completed until 1966.

The interior, paved with coloured marble and crowned by a giant cupola, emanates a feeling of space. As the National Pantheon, it houses cenotaphs of heroes of Portuguese history, such as Vasco da Gama *(see p68)* and Afonso de Albuquerque, Viceroy of India (1502–15) on the left, and on the right Henry the Navigator *(see p19)* and Luís de Camões *(see p23)*. On request you can take the lift up to the dome and enjoy a 360-degree panorama of the city.

Museu Militar ❻

Largo dos Caminhos de Ferro. **Map** 8 D3. 📞 21-884 25 69. 🚌 9, 12, 25, 28, 35, 39, 46. 🚋 28. ◯ 10am–5pm Tue–Sun. ◯ public hols. 🅿

APTLY LOCATED on the site of a 16th-century cannon foundry and arms depot, the military museum contains an extensive display of arms, uniforms and historical military documents. Visits begin in the Vasco da Gama Room with a collection of old cannons and modern murals depicting the discovery of the sea route to India. The Salas da Grande Guerra, on the first floor, display World War I related exhibits. Other rooms are devoted to the evolution of weapons in Portugal, from primitive flints through spears to rifles. The large courtyard, flanked by cannons, tells the story of Portugal in tiled panels, from the Christian Reconquest to World War I. The Portuguese artillery section in the oldest part of the museum displays the wagon used to transport the triumphal arch to Rua Augusta *(see p47)*.

The multicoloured marble interior beneath Santa Engrácia's dome

Casa dos Bicos ❼

Rua dos Bacalhoeiros. **Map** 8 D4.
📞 21-881 09 00. 🚌 9, 28, 46, 59.
🚋 18, 25. ◯ 9:30am–5:30pm Mon–Fri (ground floor only). ◯ public hols.

THIS CONSPICUOUS house, faced with diamond-shaped stones *(bicos)*, was built in 1523 for Brás de Albuquerque, illegitimate son of Afonso, Viceroy of India and conqueror of Goa and Malacca. The façade is an adaptation of a style popular in Europe during the 16th century. The two top storeys, ruined in the earthquake of 1755, were restored in the 1980s, recreating the original from old views of Lisbon in tile panels and engravings. In the interim the building was used for salting fish (Rua dos Bacalhoeiros means street of the cod fishermen). The modern interior of the lower floors is used for temporary exhibitions.

The curiously faceted Casa dos Bicos, and surrounding buildings

The façade of the Sé, the city's cathedral

Sé **8**

Largo da Sé. **Map** 8 D4. 🕻 *21-886 67 52.* 🚊 *37.* 🚋 *12, 28.* ○ *9am–7pm Tue–Sat (cloister & treasury 10am–5pm), 9am–5pm Sun, Mon & public hols.* 🕇 🄾 🄰 *to cloister & treasury.*

I N 1150, THREE YEARS after Afonso Henriques recaptured Lisbon from the Moors, he built a cathedral for the first bishop of Lisbon, the English crusader Gilbert of Hastings, on the site of the old mosque. Sé is short for Sedes Episcopalis, the seat (or see) of a bishop. Devasted by three earth tremors in the 14th century, as well as the earthquake

of 1755, and renovated over the centuries, the cathedral you see today blends a variety of architectural styles. The façade, with twin castellated belltowers and a splendid rose window, retains its solid Romanesque aspect. The gloomy interior, for the most part, is simple and austere, and hardly anything remains of the embellishment lavished upon it by King João V in the first half of the 18th century. Beyond the renovated Romanesque nave the ambulatory has nine Gothic chapels. The Capela de Santo Ildefonso contains the 14th-century sarcophagi of Lopo Fernandes Pacheco, companion in arms to King Afonso IV, and his wife, Maria Vilalobos. The bearded figure of the nobleman, sword in

Tomb of the 14th-century nobleman Lopo Fernandes Pacheco in the ambulatory

Detail of the Baroque nativity scene by Joaquim Machado de Castro

hand, and his wife, clutching a prayer book, are carved onto the tombs with their dogs sitting faithfully at their feet. In the adjacent chancel are the tombs of Afonso IV and his wife Dona Beatriz.

The Gothic **cloister**, reached via the third chapel in the ambulatory, has elegant double arches with some finely carved capitals. One of the chapels is still fitted with its 13th-century wrought-iron gate. Archaeological excavations in the cloister have unearthed various Roman and other remains.

To the left of the cathedral entrance the Franciscan chapel contains the font where the saint was baptized in 1195 and is decorated with a charming tiled scene of St Antony preaching to the fishes. The adjacent chapel contains a Baroque nativity scene made of cork, wood and terracotta by Machado de Castro (1766).

The **treasury** is at the top of the staircase on the right. It houses silver, ecclesiastical robes, statuary, illustrated manuscripts and a selection of relics associated with St Vincent which were transferred to Lisbon from Cape St Vincent in southern Portugal in 1173. Legend has it that two sacred ravens kept a vigil over the boat that transported the relics; the raven became the symbol of Lisbon's liberation from Muslim rule used on the city's coat of arms. The ravens' descendants used to dwell in the cloisters of the cathedral.

SANTO ANTÓNIO (C.1195–1231)

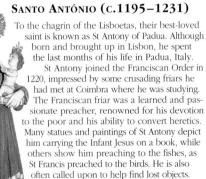

To the chagrin of the Lisboetas, their best-loved saint is known as St Antony of Padua. Although born and brought up in Lisbon, he spent the last months of his life in Padua, Italy.

St Antony joined the Franciscan Order in 1220, impressed by some crusading friars he had met at Coimbra where he was studying. The Franciscan friar was a learned and passionate preacher, renowned for his devotion to the poor and his ability to convert heretics. Many statues and paintings of St Antony depict him carrying the Infant Jesus on a book, while others show him preaching to the fishes, as St Francis preached to the birds. He is also often called upon to help find lost objects.

In 1934 Pope Pius XI declared St Antony a patron saint of Portugal. The year 1995 saw the 800th anniversary of his birth – a cause for major celebrations throughout the city.

Santo António à Sé **9**

Largo Santo António à Sé, 24. **Map**
7 C4. 21-886 91 45. 37.
12, 28. 8am–7:30pm daily.
public hols. **Museu Antoniano**
21-886 04 47. 10am–1pm,
2–6pm Tue–Sun.

The Miradouro and Igreja da Graça seen from the Castelo de São Jorge

THE POPULAR LITTLE church of Santo António allegedly stands on the site of the house in which St Antony was born. The crypt, reached via the tiled sacristy on the left of the church, is all that remains of the original church destroyed by the earthquake of 1755. Work began on the new church in 1757 headed by Mateus Vicente, architect of the Basílica da Estrela *(see p55)* and was partially funded by donations collected by local children with the cry "a small coin for St Antony". Even today the floor of the tiny chapel in the crypt is strewn with escudos and the walls are scrawled with devotional messages from worshippers.

The church's façade blends the undulating curves of the Baroque style with Neo-Classical Ionic columns on either side of the main portal. Inside, on the way down to the crypt, a modern *azulejo* panel commemorates the visit of Pope John Paul II in 1982. In 1995 the church was given a facelift for the saint's eighth centenary. It is traditional for young couples to visit the church on their wedding day and leave flowers for St Antony who is believed to bring good luck to new marriages.

Next door the small **Museu Antoniano** houses artefacts, relating to St Antony, as well as gold and silverware which used to decorate the church. The most charming exhibit is a 17th-century tiled panel of St Antony preaching to the fishes.

Castelo de São Jorge **10**

See pp38–9.

Miradouro da Graça **11**

Map 8 D2. 37. 12, 28.

THE WORKING-CLASS quarter of Graça developed at the end of the 19th century. Today, it is visited chiefly for the views from its *miradouro* (belvedere). The panorama of rooftops and skyscrapers is less spectacular than the view from the castle, but it is a popular spot, particularly in the early evenings when couples sit at café tables under the pines. Behind the *miradouro* stands an Augustinian monastery, founded in 1271 and rebuilt after the earthquake. Once a flourishing complex, the huge building is nowadays used as barracks but the church, the **Igreja da Graça**, can still be visited. Inside, in the right transept, is the *Senhor dos Passos*, a representation of Christ carrying the cross on the way to Calvary. This figure, clad in brilliant purple clothes, is carried on a procession through Graça on the second Sunday in Lent. The *azulejos* on the altar front, dating from the 17th century, imitate the brocaded textiles usually draped over the altar.

Tiled panel recording Pope John Paul II's visit to Santo António à Sé

Castelo de São Jorge ⑩

Stone head of Martim Moniz

FOLLOWING THE RECAPTURE of Lisbon from the Moors in 1147, King Afonso Henriques transformed their hilltop citadel into the residence of the Portuguese kings. In 1511 Manuel I built a more lavish palace in what is now the Praça do Comércio and the castle was used variously as a theatre, prison and arms depot. After the 1755 earthquake the ramparts remained in ruins until 1938 when Salazar *(see p15)* began a complete renovation, rebuilding the "medieval" walls and adding gardens and wild-fowl. The castle may not be authentic but the gardens and the narrow streets of the Santa Cruz district within the walls make a pleasant stroll and the views are the finest in Lisbon.

Torre de Ulisses camera obscura projects views of Lisbon onto the inside walls of the tower.

RUA DAS COZINHAS

★ Battlements
Visitors can climb the towers and walk along the reconstructed ramparts of the castle walls.

Casa do Leão Restaurant
Part of the former royal residence can be booked for evening meals and parties (see p128).

A multimedia exhibit called Olisipónia recreates 16th-century Lisbon here.

★ Observation Terrace
This large shaded square affords spectacular views over Lisbon and the Tagus. Local men play backgammon and cards under the trees.

KEY

— — — Suggested route

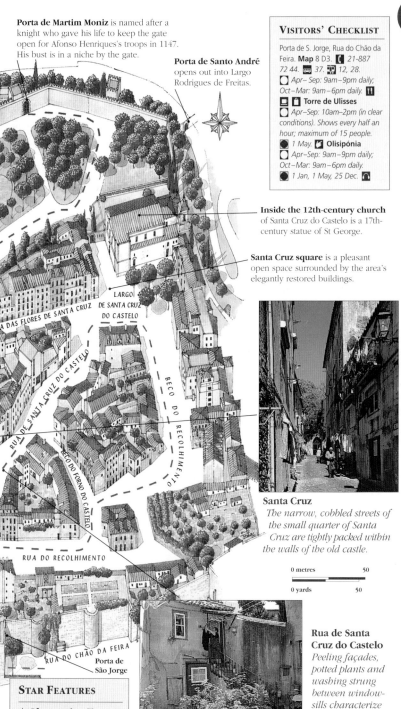

Porta de Martim Moniz is named after a knight who gave his life to keep the gate open for Afonso Henriques's troops in 1147. His bust is in a niche by the gate.

Porta de Santo André opens out into Largo Rodrigues de Freitas.

VISITORS' CHECKLIST

Porta de S. Jorge, Rua do Chão da Feira. **Map** 8 D3. 21-887 72 44. 37. 12, 28.
Apr– Sep: 9am–9pm daily; Oct–Mar: 9am–6pm daily.
Torre de Ulisses
Apr–Sep: 10am–2pm (in clear conditions). Shows every half an hour; maximum of 15 people.
1 May. **Olisipónia**
Apr–Sep: 9am–9pm daily; Oct–Mar: 9am–6pm daily.
1 Jan, 1 May, 25 Dec.

Inside the 12th-century church of Santa Cruz do Castelo is a 17th-century statue of St George.

Santa Cruz square is a pleasant open space surrounded by the area's elegantly restored buildings.

LARGO DE SANTA CRUZ DO CASTELO

RUA DAS FLORES DE SANTA CRUZ

RUA DE SANTA CRUZ DO CASTELO

BECO DO FORNO DO CASTELO

BECO DO RECOLHIMENTO

RUA DO RECOLHIMENTO

RUA DO CHÃO DA FEIRA

Porta de São Jorge

Santa Cruz
The narrow, cobbled streets of the small quarter of Santa Cruz are tightly packed within the walls of the old castle.

| 0 metres | 50 |
| 0 yards | 50 |

Rua de Santa Cruz do Castelo
Peeling façades, potted plants and washing strung between window-sills characterize the pretty streets south of the Castelo de São Jorge.

STAR FEATURES

★ **Observation Terrace**

★ **Battlements**

BAIXA

Detail on statue of José I
in Praça do Comércio

FROM THE RUINS of Lisbon, devastated by the earthquake of 1755 *(see pp20–21)*, the Marquês de Pombal created an entirely new centre. Using a grid layout of streets, he linked the stately, arcaded Praça do Comércio beside the Tagus with the busy central square of Rossio. The streets were flanked by uniform, Neo-Classical buildings and named according to the shopkeepers and craftsmen who traded there.

The Baixa (lower town) is still the commercial hub of the capital, housing banks, offices and shops. At its centre, Rossio is a popular meeting point with cafés, theatres and restaurants. The geometric layout of the area has been retained, but most of the buildings constructed since the mid-18th century have not adhered to Pombaline formality. The streets are crowded by day, particularly the lively Rua Augusta, but after dark the quarter is almost deserted.

SIGHTS AT A GLANCE

Museums and Galleries
Museu da Sociedade de Geografia **4**

Churches
Nossa Senhora da Conceição Velha **9**

Parks and Gardens
Jardim Botânico **1**

Lifts
Elevador de Santa Justa **7**

Historic Streets and Squares
Avenida da Liberdade **2**
Praça do Comércio **10**
Praça da Figueira **6**
Praça dos Restauradores **3**
Rossio **5**
Rua Augusta **8**

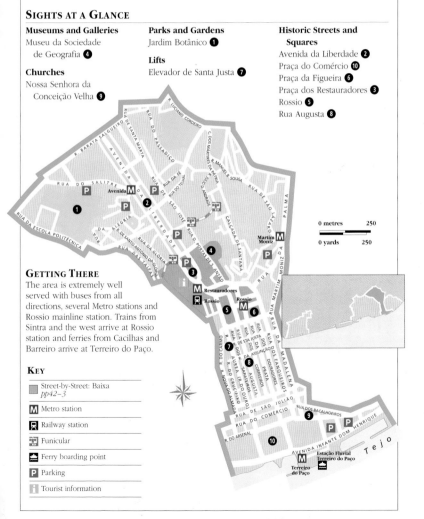

GETTING THERE
The area is extremely well served with buses from all directions, several Metro stations and Rossio mainline station. Trains from Sintra and the west arrive at Rossio station and ferries from Cacilhas and Barreiro arrive at Terreiro do Paço.

KEY

▨	Street-by-Street: Baixa *pp42–3*
Ⓜ	Metro station
▣	Railway station
▩	Funicular
⬛	Ferry boarding point
P	Parking
ⓘ	Tourist information

◁ **The triumphal arch in Praça do Comércio leading into Rua Augusta and the Baixa**

Street-by-Street: Baixa

THIS IS THE BUSIEST PART of the city, especially the central squares of Rossio and Praça da Figueira. Totally rebuilt after the earthquake of 1755 (*see pp20–21*), the area was one of Europe's first examples of town planning. Today, the large Neo-Classical buildings on the wide streets and squares house business offices. The atmosphere and surroundings are best absorbed from one of the busy pavement cafés. Rua das Portas de Santo Antão, a pedestrianized street where restaurants display tanks of live lobsters, is more relaxing for a stroll.

Tiled panel on façade of the Tabacaria Monaco

Palácio Foz, once a magnificent 18th-century palace built by the Italian architect Francesco Fabri, now houses a tourist office.

The Elevador da Glória is a bright yellow funicular that rattles up the hill to the Bairro Alto as far as the Miradouro de São Pedro de Alcântara (*see p54*).

Praça dos Restauradores
This large tree-lined square, named after the men who gave their lives during the War of Restoration, is a busy through road with café terraces on the patterned pavements ❸

Restauradores

Rossio station, designed by José Luís Monteiro, is an eye-catching late 19th-century Neo-Manueline building with two Moorish-style horseshoe arches.

KEY

--- Suggested route

STAR SIGHT

★ Rossio

Museu da Sociedade de Geografia
This collection from Portugal's former colonies is currently closed for refurbishment ❹

LOCATOR MAP
See Lisbon Street Finder map 7

Rua das Portas de Santo Antão recalls a 15th-century gate that once stood here. The lively street is now full of excellent seafood restaurants.

The Casa do Alentejo, restored in 1919, has a tranquil interior with a Neo-Moorish patio and fountain. It is a restaurant *(see p129)* and a meeting place for local Alentejans.

Church of São Domingos

Teatro Nacional Dona Maria II *(see p45)*

Praça da Figueira
Designed as the city's main marketplace in Pombal's reconstruction of the area, this square is now presided over by a 20th-century statue of João I ❻

★ Rossio
This attractively paved square is a social focal point with cafés, pastelarias and the National Theatre on the north side ❺

Café Nicola

Tabacaria Monaco

Rossio

Pastelaria Suiça

0 metres 50
0 yards 50

Bridge and pond shaded by trees in the Jardim Botânico

Jardim Botânico ❶

Rua da Escola Politécnica 58. **Map** 4 F1.
📞 21-392 18 00. 🚌 15, 58, 100.
Ⓜ *Avenida*. **Gardens** ⬤ 9am–6pm
*(Apr–Sep: 8pm) Mon–Fri, 10am–6pm
(Apr–Sep: 8pm) Sat & Sun.* ⬤ 1 Jan,
25 Dec. 🌐 ♿ **Museu de História
Natural** ⬤ *for exhibitions only.* 🌐
Museu da Ciência 📞 21-392 18
08. ⬤ 10am–1pm, 2–5pm Mon–
Fri, 3–6pm Sat. ⬤ *public hols.* 🌐

T HE COMPLEX, owned by the
university, comprises two
museums and four hectares
(10 acres) of gardens. The
botanical gardens, which slope
down from the upper level by
the main entrance towards Rua
da Alegria, have a distinct air
of neglect. However, it is worth
paying the entrance fee to
wander among the exotic trees
and dense shady paths of the
gardens as they descend to the
second entrance. A magnificent
avenue of lofty palms connects
the two different levels.

The **Museu de História
Natural** (Natural History
Museum) opens only for temporary exhibitions and these
are well advertised throughout
the city. The **Museu da
Ciência** (Science Museum),
whose exhibits demonstrate
basic scientific principles, is
popular with school children.

Avenida da Liberdade ❷

Map 7 A2. 🚌 2, 9, 36 & many other
routes. Ⓜ *Restauradores, Avenida.*

F OLLOWING THE earthquake
of 1755 *(see pp20–21)*, the
Marquês de Pombal created
the Passeio Público (public
promenade) in the area now
occupied by the lower part of
Avenida da Liberdade and
Praça dos Restauradores.

Despite its name,
enjoyment of the
park was restricted to
Lisbon's high society
and walls and gates
ensured the exclu-
sion of the lower
classes. In 1821,
when the Liberals
came to power, the
barriers were pulled
down and the
Avenida and square
became open to all.

The boulevard
you see today was
built in 1879–82 in
the style of the
Champs-Elysées
in Paris. The wide
tree-lined avenue
became a focus for
pageants, festivities
and demonstrations.
A war memorial
stands as a tribute to
those who died in
World War I. The
avenue still retains
a certain elegance
with fountains and
café tables shaded by trees,
however, it no longer makes
for a peaceful stroll. The once
majestic thoroughfare, 90 m
(295 ft) wide and decorated
with abstract pavement patterns, is now divided by seven
lanes of traffic linking Praça
dos Restauradores and Praça
Marquês de Pombal to the
north. Some of the original
mansions have been preserved,
including the Neo-Classical
Tivoli cinema at No. 188, with
an original 1920s kiosk outside,
and Casa Lambertini with its
colourful mosaic decoration at
No. 166. However, many of
the Art Nouveau façades have
unfortunately given way to
newer ones occupied by
offices, hotels or shopping
complexes.

**Detail from the memorial to the dead of
World War I in Avenida da Liberdade**

**19th-century monument in honour of the
Restoration in Praça dos Restauradores**

Praça dos Restauradores ❸

Map 7 A2. 🚌 2, 9, 36, 46 & many
other routes. Ⓜ *Restauradores.*

T HE SQUARE, distinguished by
its soaring obelisk, erected
in 1886, commemorates
Portugal's liberation from
the Spanish yoke in 1640. The
bronze figures on the pedestal
depict Victory, holding a palm
and a crown, and Freedom.
The names and dates that are
inscribed on the sides of the
obelisk are those of the battles
of the War of Restoration.

On the west side the Palácio
Foz, now housing a tourist
office, was built by Francesco
Savario Fabri in 1755–
77 for the Marquês
de Castelo-Melhor.
It was renamed
after the Marquês
de Foz, who lived
here in the 19th century.
The smart Avenida Palace
Hotel *(see p115)* stands on
the southwest side of the
square. This building was
designed by José Lúis
Monteiro (1849–1942),
who also built Rossio
railway station *(see p42)*.

Museu da Sociedade de Geografia ❹

Rua das Portas de Santo Antão 100. **Map** 7 A2. **C** 21-342 54 01. **🚌** 9, 80, 90. **M** Restauradores. **◐** until 2004. **📷** compulsory.

LOCATED in the Geographical Society building, the museum houses an idiosyncratic ethnographical collection brought back from Portugal's former colonies. On display are circumcision masks from Guinea Bissau, musical instruments and snake spears. From Angola there are neckrests to sustain coiffures and the original *padrão* – the stone pillar erected by the Portuguese in 1482 to mark their sovereignty over the colony. Most of the exhibits are arranged along the splendid Sala Portugal, a large hall used also for conferences.

Rossio ❺

Map 6 B3. **🚌** 2, 36, 44, 45 & many other routes. **M** Rossio.

FORMALLY CALLED Praça de Dom Pedro IV, this large square has been the nerve centre of Lisbon for six centuries. During its history it has been the stage of bullfights, festivals, military parades and also the burning of heretics during the Inquisition *(see p14)*. Today there is little more than an occasional political rally

Teatro Nacional Dona Maria II in Rossio illuminated by night

and the sober Pombaline buildings, disfigured on the upper level by old neon advertisements, are occupied at street level by souvenir shops, jewellers and cafés. Centre stage stands a statue of Dom Pedro IV, the first emperor of independent Brazil. At the foot of the statue, the four female figures are allegories of Justice, Wisdom, Strength and Moderation – qualities dubiously attributed to Dom Pedro.

In the mid-19th century the square was paved with wave-patterned mosaics which gave it the nickname of "Rolling Motion Square". The hand-cut grey and white stone cubes were the first such designs to decorate the city's pavements. Today, only a small central section of the design survives.

On the north side of the square is the Teatro Nacional Dona Maria II, named after Dom Pedro's daughter. The Neo-Classical structure was built in the 1840s by the Italian architect Fortunato Lodi. The interior was destroyed by fire in 1964 and reconstructed in the 1970s. On top of the pediment is Gil Vicente (1465–1536), the founder of Portuguese theatre.

Café Nicola on the west side of the square was a favourite meeting place among writers, including the poet Manuel du Bocage (1765–1805), who was notorious for his satires.

Praça da Figueira ❻

Map 6 B3. **🚌** 14, 43, 59, 60 & many other routes. **🚋** 15. **M** Rossio.

BEFORE THE 1755 earthquake *(see pp20–21)* the square next to Rossio was the site of the Hospital de Todos-os-Santos (All Saints). In Pombal's new design for the Baixa, the square took on the role of the city's central marketplace. In 1885 a covered market was introduced, but this was pulled down in the 1950s. Today, the four-storey buildings are given over to hotels, shops and cafés and the square is no longer a marketplace. Perhaps its most eye-catching feature is the multitude of pigeons that perch on the pedestal supporting Leopoldo de Almeida's bronze equestrian statue of João I, erected in 1971.

Bronze statue of King João I in Praça da Figueira

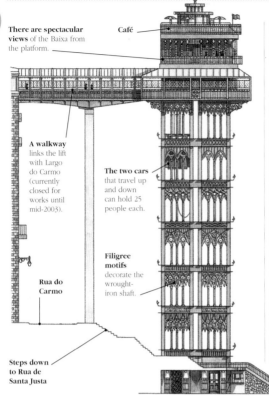

There are spectacular **views** of the Baixa from the platform.

Café

A walkway links the lift with Largo do Carmo (currently closed for works until mid-2003).

The two cars that travel up and down can hold 25 people each.

Filigree motifs decorate the wrought-iron shaft.

Rua do Carmo

Steps down to Rua de Santa Justa

Elevador de Santa Justa ❼

Rua de Santa Justa & Largo do Carmo.
Map 7 B3. ☎ 21-342 79 44.
🕐 8:30am–9:30pm Mon–Sat,
9am–9:30pm Sun.

ALSO KNOWN as the Elevador do Carmo, this Neo-Gothic lift, was built at the turn of the century by the French architect Raoul Mesnier du Ponsard, an apprentice of Alexandre Gustave Eiffel. Made of iron, and embellished with filigree, it is one of the more eccentric features of the Baixa. The ticket office is located behind the tower on the steps up to Rua do Carmo.

Passengers can travel up and down inside the tower in one of two smart wood-panelled cabins with brass fittings, but the walkway linking them to the Largo do Carmo in the Bairro Alto, 32 m (105 ft) above is currently closed for works.

The very top of the tower, reached via a tight spiral stairway, is given over to café tables. This high vantage point commands splendid views of Rossio, the grid pattern of the Baixa, the castle on the opposite hill, the river and the nearby ruins of the Carmo church. The fire that gutted the Chiado district in 1988 *(see p52)* was extinguished very close to the lift.

Café on the top platform of the Elevador de Santa Justa

Rua Augusta ❽

Map 7 B4. Ⓜ Rossio. 🚊 2, 14, 36, 40 & many other routes.

A LIVELY PEDESTRIANIZED street decorated with mosaic pavements and lined with boutiques and open-air cafés, Rua Augusta is the main tourist thoroughfare and the smartest in the Baixa. Street performers provide entertainment, while vendors sell lottery tickets, books and souvenirs. The eye is drawn to the triumphal Arco da Rua Augusta framing the equestrian statue of José I in Praça do Comércio. Designed by the architect Santos de Carvalho to commemorate the city's recovery from the earthquake *(see pp20–21)*, the arch was completed only in 1873.

The other main thoroughfares of the Baixa are Rua da Prata (silversmiths' street) and Rua do Ouro or Rua Aurea (goldsmiths' street). Cutting across these main streets full of shops and banks are smaller streets that give glimpses up to the Bairro Alto to the west and the Castelo de São Jorge *(see pp38–9)* to the east. Many of the streets retain shops that gave them their name: there are jewellers in Rua da Prata and Rua do Ouro, shoemakers in Rua dos Sapateiros and banks in Rua do Comércio.

The most incongruous sight in the heart of the Baixa is a small section of the Roman baths, located within the Banco Comercial Português in Rua dos Correeiros. The ruins and mosaics can be seen from the street window at the rear side of the bank; alternatively you can book ahead to visit the "museum" on 21-321 10 00.

Shoppers and strollers in the pedestrianized Rua Augusta

Nossa Senhora da Conceição Velha ❾

Rua da Alfândega. **Map** 7 C4.
☎ 21-887 02 02. 🚌 9, 46, 90.
🚋 18. ◯ 8am–6pm Mon–Fri, Sun
(services only). ● Aug. 🕆 📷 ♿

T HE ELABORATE Manueline
doorway of the church is
the only feature that survived
from the original 16th-century
Nossa Senhora da Misericórdia,
which stood here until the
1755 earthquake. The portal is
decorated with a profusion of
Manueline detail
including angels,
beasts, flowers,
armillary spheres and
the cross of the Order
of Christ. In the
tympanum, the Virgin
Mary spreads her
protective mantle over
various contemporary
figures. These include
Pope Leo X, Manuel I
and his sister, Queen
Leonor, widow of João
II. It was Leonor who
founded the original
Misericórdia (alms-
house) on the site of
a former synagogue.

**Detail from portal
of Conceição Velha**

Enjoyment of the
portal is hampered by the
constant stream of traffic
along Rua da Alfândega and
the cars parked right in front
of the church. The interior
has an unusual stucco ceiling;
in the second chapel on the
right is a statue of Our Lady
of Restelo. This came from the
Belém chapel where navigators prayed before embarking
on their historic voyages east.

Praça do Comércio ❿

Map 7 C5. 🚌 2, 14, 40, 46 & many
other routes. 🚋 15, 18.

M ORE COMMONLY known by
the locals as *Terreiro do
Paço* (Palace Square), this huge
open space was the site of the
royal palace for 400 years.
Manuel I transferred the royal
residence from Castelo de São
Jorge to this more convenient
location by the river in 1511.
The first palace, along with its
library and 70,000 books, was
destroyed in the earthquake
of 1755. In the rebuilding of
the city, the square became the
pièce de résistance of Pombal's
Baixa design. The new palace
occupied spacious arcaded
buildings that extended around
three sides of the square. After
the revolution of 1910 (*see
p15*) these were converted
into government administrative
offices and painted Republican
pink. However, they have since
been repainted royal yellow.

The south side, graced by
two square towers, looks
across the wide expanse of
the Tagus. This has
always been the
finest gateway to
Lisbon, where royalty
and ambassadors
would alight and take
the marble steps up
from the river. You
can still experience
the dramatic ap-
proach by taking a
ferry across from
Cacilhas on the
southern bank.
However, today the
spectacle is spoilt
by the busy Avenida
Infante Dom Hen-
rique, which runs
along the waterfront.

In the centre of Praça do
Comércio is the equestrian
statue of King José I erected
in 1775 by Machado de Castro,
the leading Portuguese sculptor
of the 18th century. The bronze
horse, depicted trampling on
serpents, earned the square
its third name of "Black Horse
Square", used by English travellers and merchants. Over
the years, however, the horse
has acquired a green patina.

**Shaded arcades along the north
side of Praça do Comércio**

The impressive triumphal arch
on the north side of the square
leads into Rua Augusta and is
the gateway to the Baixa.
Opened in January 2001, in
the northwest of the square,
the Lisboa Welcome Centre
has a tourist information service, gallery, restaurants and
shops. In the opposite corner,
stands Lisbon's oldest café, the
Martinho da Arcada, formerly
a haunt of the city's literati.

On 1 February 1908, King
Carlos and his son, Luís Felipe,
were assassinated as they were
passing through the square.
In 1974 the square saw the
first uprising of the Armed
Forces Movement which over-
threw the Caetano regime in
a bloodless revolution (*see
p15*). For many years the area
was requisitioned as a car
park, but today it has been
reclaimed for the use of
open-air cafés and stalls.

Statue of King José I in Praça do Comércio

Bairro Alto and Estrela

Laid out in a grid pattern in the late 16th century, the hilltop Bairro Alto is one of the most picturesque districts of the city. First settled by rich citizens who moved out of the disreputable Alfama, by the 19th century it had become a run-down area frequented by prostitutes. Today, it retains a traditional way of life, with small workshops and family-run *tascas* (cheap restaurants).

Tile panel in Largo Rafael Bordalo Pinheiro, Bairro Alto

Very different in character to the heart of the Bairro Alto is the elegant commercial district known as the Chiado, where affluent Lisboetas do their shopping. To the northwest, the Estrela quarter is centred on the huge domed basilica and popular gardens. The mid-18th century district of Lapa, to the southwest, is home to foreign embassies and large, smart residences.

Sights at a Glance

Museums and Galleries
Museu do Chiado ❺
Museu Nacional de Arte Antiga *pp56–9* ⓫
Museu da Marioneta ❻

Churches
Basílica da Estrela ⓭
Igreja do Carmo ❷
São Roque ❶

Historic Buildings and Districts
Chiado ❸
Palácio de São Bento ❿
Solar do Vinho do Porto ❼
Teatro Nacional de São Carlos ❹

Gardens and Belvederes
Jardim da Estrela ⓬
Miradouro de São Pedro de Alcântara ❽
Praça do Príncipe Real ❾

Getting There

This area is reached via the Elevador da Glória from Praça dos Restauradores, the Elevador de Santa Justa from the Baixa, or by a steep, but pleasant walk. There is also a metro station on Largo do Chiado. Tram 28 passes Bairro Alto on its way between Graça and Estrela.

Key

Street-by-Street: Bairro Alto and Chiado *pp50–51*
Metro station
Railway station
Funicular
Ferry boarding point
Parking
Railway line

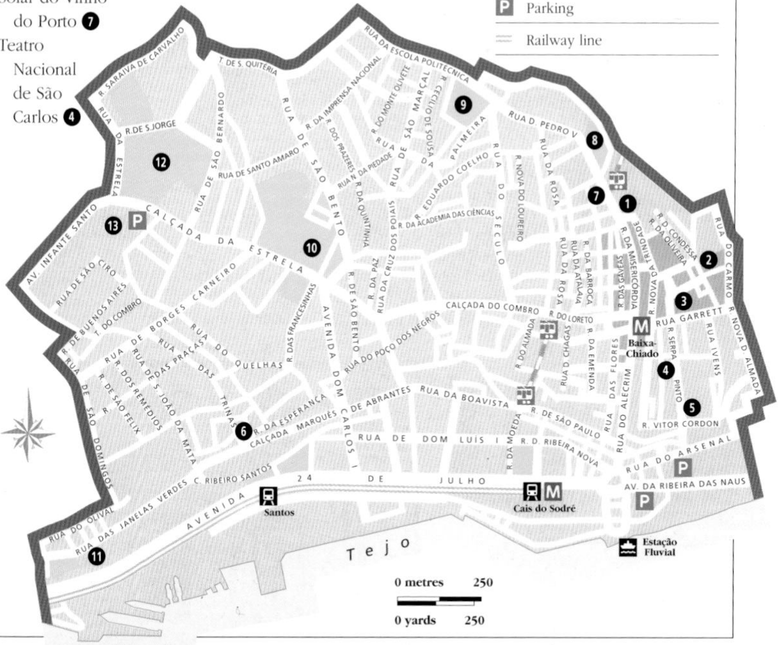

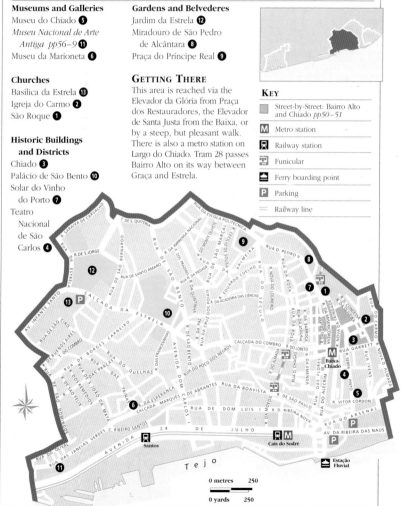

◁ **Art Nouveau decoration in the Chiado's Café Brasileira, once popular with writers and intellectuals**

Street-by-Street: Bairro Alto and Chiado

T HE BAIRRO ALTO (high quarter) is a
fascinating area of cobbled streets
adjacent to the Carmo and Chiado areas,
with peeling houses and tiny grocery
shops. In recent years the traditionally
bohemian Bairro Alto has lost its notoriety for
prostitution and gambling to become more of a
residential district. However, the area's many

**Baroque cherub,
Igreja do Carmo**

bars and *casas de fado* (see pp142–3) mean it
remains fashionable and very busy at night.
In contrast, the Chiado is an area of elegant
shops and old-style cafés that extends down from
Praça Luís de Camões towards Rua do Carmo
and the Baixa. Major renovation work has
taken place since a fire in 1988 (see p52)
destroyed many of the buildings.

Rua do Norte
marks the
start of the
traditional
Bairro
Alto.

RUA DO NORTE

RUA DAS GÁVEAS

**Praça Luís
de Camões**

Once a haunt of writers and
intellectuals, Chiado is now
an elegant shopping district.
The 1920s Brasileira café, on
Largo do Chiado, is adorned
with gilded mirrors.

L DO CHIADO

RUA DO ALECRIM

**Largo do
Chiado** is flanked
by the churches
of Loreto and Nossa
Senhora da Encarnação.

Ⓜ Baixa/Chiado

RUA GARRE

**The statue of Eça de
Queirós** (1845–1900), by
Teixeira Lopes, was erected
in 1903. The great novelist
takes inspiration from a
scantily veiled muse.

Baixa/Chiado

Rua Garrett
is the main shopping
street of the Chiado.

| 0 metres | 50 |
| 0 yards | 50 |

KEY

– – – Suggested route

Chiado

Tavares, at No. 37
Rua da Misericórdia,
first opened as a
café in 1784. Today
it is an elegant res-
taurant (see p129)
decorated at the turn
of the century with
mirrors and elabo-
rate stucco designs

Elevador da Glória

The Museu de Arte Sacra
has an interesting exhibition
of religious artefacts and
explains the history of the
treasures in the church of
São Roque next door.

LOCATOR MAP
See Lisbon Street Finder map 7

**Cervejaria
Trindade**
is a popular
beer hall and
restaurant de-
corated with
azulejo panels.

★ São Roque
*Opulent mosaics
and semiprecious
stones adorn the
Baroque Capela
de São João in-
side the 16th-
century church
of São Roque* ❶

**Teatro da
Trindade**

The tile decoration on
the façade of this house,
erected in 1864 on Largo
Rafael Bordalo Pinheiro,
features allegorical figures
of Science, Agriculture
Industry and Commerce.

★ Igreja do Carmo
*The graceful skeletal arches of this
Carmelite church, once the largest
in Lisbon, stand as a reminder of
the earthquake of 1755. The chancel,
and main body of the church
house an archaeological museum* ❷

Elevador de Santa Justa is
currently closed for works
until mid-2003.

The shops in Rua do Carmo have
been restored and renewed after the
devastating fire in 1988 *(see p52).*

STAR SIGHTS
★ São Roque
★ Igreja do Carmo

Ruins of the 14th-century Igreja do Carmo seen from the Baixa

São Roque ❶

Largo Trindade Coelho. **Map** 7 A3.
☎ 21-323 53 83. **🚌** 58, 100 &
Glória lift. **☉** 8:30 am–5pm Mon–
Fri, 9:30am–5pm Sat & Sun, 9:30am–
1pm saint's days. **🏛** Museu de
Arte Sacra ☎ 21-323 53 81.
☉ 10am–5pm Tue–Sun. **⬤** public
hols. 🎫 📷

S ÃO ROQUE'S plain façade
belies a remarkably
rich interior. The
church was founded
at the end of the 16th
century by the Jesuit
Order, then at the
peak of its power.
In 1742 the Chapel
of St John the
Baptist (last on the
left) was commis-
sioned by the
prodigal João V from   **Tile detail in the**
the Italian architects   **Chapel of St Roch**
Luigi Vanvitelli and
Nicola Salvi. Constructed in
Rome and embellished with
lapis lazuli, agate, alabaster,
amethyst, precious marbles,
gold, silver and mosaics, the
chapel was given the Pope's
blessing in the church of
Sant'Antonio dei Portoghesi in
Rome, dismantled and sent to
Lisbon in three ships.

Among the many tiles in the
church, the oldest and most
interesting are those in the
third chapel on the right, dating
from the mid-16th century
and dedicated to São Roque
(St Roch), protector against
the plague. Other features of
the church are the scenes of
the Apocalypse painted on the
ceiling and the sacristy, with its
coffered ceiling, as well as
painted panels of the life of St
Francis Xavier, the 16th-century

missionary. Treasures from the
Chapel of St John, including
the silver and lapis lazuli altar
front, are in the adjoining
Museu de Arte Sacra.

Igreja do Carmo ❷

Largo do Carmo. **Map** 7 B3. **☎** 21-
347 86 29. **🚊** 28. **Ⓜ** Baixa-Chiado.
☉ May–Sep: 10am–6pm Tue–Sun;
Oct–Apr: 10am–5pm Tue–Sun.
⬤ 1 Jan, Easter, 1 May, 25
Dec. 🎫

T HE GOTHIC RUINS
of this Carmelite
church, built on a
slope overlooking the
Baixa, are evocative
reminders of the dev-
astation left by the
earthquake of 1755. As
the congregation were
attending mass the
shockwaves caused
the church to collapse,
depositing tons of masonry
on to the people below.

Founded in the late 14th
century by Nuno Álvares
Pereira, the commander who
became a member of the
Carmelite Order, the church
was at one time the biggest
in Lisbon.

Nowadays the main body
of the church and the chancel,
whose roof withstood the
earthquake, house an
archaeological museum
with a small, heterogeneous
collection of sarcophagi,
statuary, ceramics and mosaics.
Among the more ancient
finds from Europe are a
remnant from a Visigothic
pillar and a Roman tomb
carved with reliefs depicting
the Muses. There are also
finds from Mexico and South
America, including ancient
mummies.

Outside the ruins, in the
Largo do Carmo, stands the
Chafariz do Carmo, an 18th-
century fountain designed by
Ângelo Belasco, elaborately
decorated with four dolphins.

Chiado ❸

Map 7 A4. **🚌** 58. **🚊** 28. **Ⓜ** Chiado.

H YPOTHESES abound for the
origin of the word Chiado,
in use since 1567. One of the
most interesting recalls the
creak (chiar) of the wheels of
the carts as they negotiated
the area's steep slopes. A second
theory refers to the nickname
given to the 16th-century poet
António Ribeiro, "O Chiado".
An area traditionally known

THE CHIADO FIRE

On 25 August 1988 a disastrous fire began in a store in
Rua do Carmo, the street that
links the Baixa with the Bairro
Alto. Fire engines were unable
to enter this pedestrianized
street and the fire spread into
Rua Garrett. Along with shops
and offices, many important
18th-century buildings were
destroyed, the worst damage
being in Rua do Carmo. The
renovation project, which is
now complete, has preserved
many original façades, and
was headed by Portuguese
architect, Álvaro Siza Vieira.

**Firemen attending the raging
fire in Rua do Carmo**

Stalls and circle of the 18th-century Teatro Nacional de São Carlos

for its intellectual associations, various statues of literary figures can be found here. Fernando Pessoa, Portugal's most famous 20th-century poet, is seated at a table outside the Café Brasileira. Established in the 1920s, this was a favourite rendezvous of intellectuals.

The name Chiado is often used to mean just Rua Garrett, the main shopping street of the area, named after the author and poet João Almeida Garrett (1799–1854). This elegant street, which descends from Largo do Chiado towards the Baixa, is known for its clothes shops, cafés and bookshops. Devastated by fire in 1988, the former elegance of this quarter has been recently restored.

On Largo do Chiado stand two Baroque churches: the Italian church, Igreja do Loreto, on the north side and opposite, Nossa Senhora da Encarnação, whose exterior walls are partly decorated with *azulejos*.

Teatro Nacional de São Carlos ❹

Rua Serpa Pinto 9. **Map** 7 A4. ☎ 21-325 30 45. ▦ 58, 100. ◫ 28. Ⓜ Baixa-Chiado. ◯ for performances.

REPLACING a former opera house which was ruined by the earthquake of 1755, the Teatro de São Carlos was built in 1792–5 by José da Costa e Silva. Designed on the lines of La Scala in Milan and the San Carlo in Naples, the building has a beautifully proportioned façade and an enchanting Rococo interior. Views of the exterior, however, are spoiled by the car park, invariably crammed, which occupies the square in front. The opera season lasts from September to June, but concerts and ballets are also staged here at other times of the year.

Museu do Chiado ❺

Rua Serpa Pinto 4–6. **Map** 7 A5. ☎ 21-343 21 48. ▦ 58, 100. ◫ 28. Ⓜ Baixa-Chiado. ◯ 10am–6pm Wed–Sun, 2–6pm Tue. ● 1 Jan, Easter, 1 May, 25 Dec. ▨

THE NATIONAL MUSEUM of Contemporary Art, whose collection of 1850–1950 paintings could no longer be described as contemporary, changed its name in 1994 and moved to a stylishly restored warehouse. The paintings and sculpture are arranged over three floors in 12 rooms. Each room has a different theme illustrating the development from

Romanticism to Modernism. The majority are works by Portuguese, often showing the marked influence from other European countries. This is particularly noticeable in the 19th-century landscape painters who had contact with artists from the French Barbizon School. The few international works of art on display include a collection of drawings by Rodin (1840–1917) and some French sculpture from the late 19th century. There are also temporary exhibitions which are held for "very new artists, preferably inspired by the permanent collection".

Grotesque puppet in Museu da Marioneta

Museu da Marioneta ❻

Convento das Bernardas, Rua da Esperança 146. **Map** 4 D3. ☎ 21-394 28 10. ▦ 6, 13, 27, 49, 60. Ⓜ Cais do Sodré. ◯ 10am–1pm, 2–6pm Wed–Sun. ▨

THIS SMALL, ECCENTRIC puppet museum moved to this elegantly refurbished convent building in 2001. The collection includes characters dating from 17th-and 18th-century theatre and opera, among them knights, jesters, princesses, devils and satirical figures. The puppets are finely crafted but a substantial proportion of them possess gruesome, contorted features, which are unlikely to appeal to small children. The museum explains the history of the art form and runs videos of puppet shows. It is worth calling ahead to see if a live performance is being held on the small stage set.

Art Nouveau façade of the popular Café Brasileira in the Chiado

The wide selection of port at the Solar do Vinho do Porto

Solar do Vinho do Porto ❼

Rua de São Pedro de Alcântara 45. **Map** 4 F2. ☎ 21-347 57 07. ▥ 58. ⛟ 28, Elevador da Glória. ◷ 2pm–midnight Mon–Sat. ● public hols.

THE PORTUGUESE WORD *solar* means mansion or manor house and the Solar do Vinho do Porto occupies the ground floor of an 18th-century mansion. The building was once owned by the German architect, Johann Friedrich Ludwig (Ludovice), who built the monastery at Mafra *(see p92)*. Up to 6,000 varieties of port are stored here, including some rare vintages that date back as far as 1937. Visitors are permitted to try a selection of these rich fortified wines in the bar. They range from the younger red-coloured ruby port, through the lighter tawny, to the aristocratic vintages from the great shippers of Oporto. Although rather expensive, these ports can be tasted at the bar or in the comfort of armchairs in the club-like sitting room.

Miradouro de São Pedro de Alcântara ❽

Rua de São Pedro de Alcântara. **Map** 7 A2. ▥ 58. ⛟ 28, Elevador da Glória.

THE BELVEDERE *(miradouro)* commands a sweeping view of eastern Lisbon, seen across the Baixa. A tiled map, conveniently placed against the balustrade, helps you locate the landmarks in the city below. The panorama extends from the battlements of the Castelo de São Jorge *(see pp38–9)*, clearly seen surrounded by trees on the hill to the southeast, to the 18th-century church of Penha da França in the northwest. The large monastery complex of the Igreja da Graça *(see p37)* is also visible on the hill, and in the distance São Vicente de Fora *(see p35)* is recognizable by the symmetrical towers that flank its white façade.

Benches and ample shade from the trees make this terrace a pleasant stop after the steep walk up Calçada da Glória from the Baixa. Alternatively, the yellow funicular, Elevador da Glória, will drop you off nearby.

The memorial in the garden, erected in 1904, depicts Eduardo Coelho (1835–89), founder of the newspaper *Diário de Notícias*, and below him a ragged paper boy running with copies of the famous daily. This area was once the centre of the newspaper industry, however the modern printing presses have now moved to more spacious premises west of the city.

The view is most attractive at sunset and by night when the castle is floodlit and the terrace becomes a popular meeting point for young Lisboetas.

Praça do Príncipe Real ❾

Map 4 F1. ▥ 58, 100.

Playing cards in Praça do Príncipe Real

LAID OUT IN 1860 as a prime residential quarter, the square still retains an air of affluence. Smartly painted mansions surround a particularly pleasant park with an open-air café, statuary and some splendid robinia, magnolia and Judas trees. The branches of a huge cedar tree have been trained on a trellis, creating a wide shady spot for the locals who play cards beneath it. On the large square, at No. 26, the eye-catching pink and white Neo-Moorish building with domes and pinnacles is part of Lisbon university.

View across the city to Castelo de São Jorge from Miradouro de São Pedro de Alcântara

Attractive wrought-iron music pavilion in Jardim da Estrela

Palácio de São Bento ❿

Largo das Cortes, Rua de São Bento.
Map 4 E2. **C** *21-391 90 00.* 6, 49, 100. 28. ⬤ *by appt only.*

ALSO KNOWN as the Palácio da Assembleia Nacional, this enormous white Neo-Classical building is the seat of the Portuguese Parliament. It started life at the end of the 16th century as the Benedictine monastery of São Bento. After the dissolution of the religious orders in 1834, the building became the seat of Parliament, known as the Palácio das Cortes. The interior is suitably grandiose with marble pillars and Neo-Classical statues.

Museu Nacional de Arte Antiga ⓫

See pp56–9.

Jardim da Estrela ⓬

Praça da Estrela. **Map** 4 D2. 9, 20, 38. 25, 28. ⬤ *7am–midnight daily.*

LAID OUT IN the middle of the 19th century, opposite the Basílica da Estrela, the popular gardens are a focal part of the Estrela quarter. Local families congregate here at weekends to feed the ducks and carp in the lake, sit at the waterside café or wander among the flower beds, plants and trees. The formal gardens are planted with herbaceous borders and shrubs surrounding plane trees and elms. The central feature of the park is a green wrought-iron bandstand, decorated with elegant filigree, where musicians strike up in the summer months. This was built in 1884 and originally stood on the Passeio Público, before the creation of Avenida da Liberdade *(see p44).*

The English Cemetery to the north of the gardens is best known as the burial place of Henry Fielding (1707–54), the English novelist and playwright who died in Lisbon at the age of 47. The *Journal of a Voyage to Lisbon,* published posthumously in 1775, recounts his last voyage to Portugal made in a fruitless attempt to recover his failing health.

Basílica da Estrela ⓭

Praça da Estrela. **Map** 4 D2.
C *21-396 09 15.* 9, 20, 22, 38. 25, 28. ⬤ *8am–1pm, 3–8pm daily.*

The tomb of the pious Maria I in the Basílica da Estrela

IN THE SECOND half of the 18th century Maria I *(see p105),* daughter of José I, vowed she would build a church if she bore a son and heir to the throne. Her wish was granted and construction of the basilica began in 1779. Her son José, however, died of smallpox two years before the completion of the church in 1790. The huge domed basilica, set on a hill in the west of the city, is one of Lisbon's great landmarks. A simpler version of the basilica at Mafra *(see p92),* this church was built by architects from the Mafra School in late Baroque and Neo-Classical style. The façade is flanked by twin belltowers and decorated with an array of statues of saints and allegorical figures.

The spacious, somewhat awe-inspiring interior, where light streams down from the pierced dome, is clad in grey, pink and yellow marble. The elaborate Empire-style tomb of Queen Maria I, who died in Brazil, lies in the right transept. Locked in a room nearby is Machado de Castro's extraordinary Nativity scene, composed of over 500 cork and terracotta figures. (To see it, ask the sacristan.)

Neo-Classical façade and stairway of Palácio de São Bento

Museu Nacional de Arte Antiga ⓫

Portugal's national art collection is housed in a 17th-century palace that was built for the counts of Alvor. In 1770 it was acquired by the Marquês de Pombal and remained in the possession of his family for over a century. Inaugurated in 1884, the museum is known to locals as the Casa das Janelas Verdes, referring to the former green windows of the palace. In 1940 a modern annexe (including the main façade) was added. This was built on the site of the St Albert Carmelite monastery, which was destroyed in the 1755 earthquake (*see pp20–21*). The only surviving feature was the chapel, now integrated into the museum.

15th-century wood carving of St George

★ St Jerome
This masterly portrayal of old age by Albrecht Dürer expresses one of the central dilemmas of Renaissance humanism: the ephemeral nature of man (1521).

GALLERY GUIDE

The ground floor contains 14th–19th-century European paintings, as well as some decorative arts and furniture. Oriental and African art, Chinese and Portuguese ceramics and silver, gold and jewellery are on display on the first floor. The top floor is dedicated to Portuguese art and sculpture.

Stairs down to

St Augustine by Piero della Francesca

The Temptations of St Antony by Hieronymus Bosch

The Virgin and Child and Saints
Hans Holbein the Elder's balanced composition of a Sacra Conversazione (1519) is set among majestic Renaissance architecture with saints in detailed contemporary costumes sewing or reading.

Ecce Homo
Painted in the late 15th century by an artist of the Portuguese school, the unusual depiction of the accused Jesus, with the shroud lowered over his eyes, retains an air of dignified calm, despite the crown of thorns, the rope and the specks of blood.

KEY TO FLOORPLAN

- ☐ European art
- ☐ Portuguese painting and sculpture
- ☐ Portuguese and Chinese ceramics
- ☐ Oriental and African art
- ☐ Silver, gold and jewellery
- ☐ Decorative arts
- ☐ Chapel of St Albert
- ▨ Textiles and furniture
- ☐ Non-exhibition space

STAR EXHIBITS

- ★ **St Jerome by Dürer**
- ★ **Namban Screens**
- ★ **Adoration of St Vincent by Gonçalves**

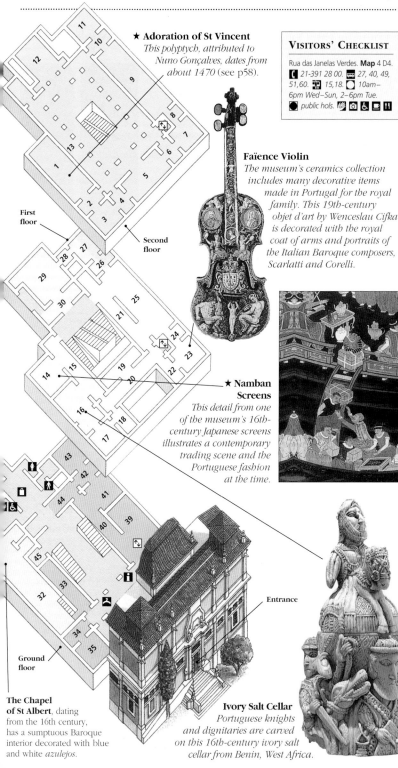

★ Adoration of St Vincent
This polyptych, attributed to Nuno Gonçalves, dates from about 1470 (see p58).

VISITORS' CHECKLIST

Rua das Janelas Verdes. **Map** 4 D4.
📞 21-391 28 00. 🚌 27, 40, 49, 51, 60. 🚋 15, 18. ⏰ 10am–6pm Wed–Sun, 2–6pm Tue. ⬤ public hols. 🚫 📷 ⬤ 🚻

Faïence Violin
The museum's ceramics collection includes many decorative items made in Portugal for the royal family. This 19th-century objet d'art by Wenceslau Cifka is decorated with the royal coat of arms and portraits of the Italian Baroque composers, Scarlatti and Corelli.

First floor

Second floor

★ Namban Screens
This detail from one of the museum's 16th-century Japanese screens illustrates a contemporary trading scene and the Portuguese fashion at the time.

Entrance

Ground floor

The Chapel of St Albert, dating from the 16th century, has a sumptuous Baroque interior decorated with blue and white *azulejos*.

Ivory Salt Cellar
Portuguese knights and dignitaries are carved on this 16th-century ivory salt cellar from Benin, West Africa.

Exploring the Collections of the Museu Nacional de Arte Antiga

THE MUSEUM has the largest collection of paintings in Portugal and is particularly strong on early religious works by Portuguese artists. The majority of exhibits came from convents and monasteries following the suppression of religious orders in 1834. There are also extensive displays of sculpture, silverware, porcelain and applied arts giving an overview of Portuguese art from the Middle Ages to the 19th century, complemented by many fine European and Oriental pieces. The theme of the discoveries is ever-present, illustrating Portugal's links with Brazil, Africa, India, China and Japan.

Cistercian monks from Alcobaça in central Portugal

Friar

Fisherman

EUROPEAN ART

PAINTINGS by European artists, dating from the 14th to the 19th century, are arranged chronologically on the ground floor. Unlike the Portuguese art, most of the works were donated from private collections, contributing to the great diversity of works on display. The first rooms, dedicated to the 14th and 15th centuries, trace the transition from medieval Gothic taste to the aesthetic of the Renaissance.

The painters best represented in the European Art section are 16th-century German and Flemish artists. Notable works are *St Jerome* by Albrecht Dürer (1471–1528), *Salomé* by Lucas Cranach the Elder (1472–1553), *Virgin and Child* by Hans Memling (c.1430–94) and *The Temptations of St Antony* by the great Flemish master of fantasy, Hieronymus Bosch (1450–1516). Of the small number of Italian works, the finest are *St Augustine* by

the Renaissance painter, Piero della Francesca (c.1420–92) and a graceful early altar panel representing the Resurrection by Raphael (1483–1520).

Some Portuguese painters, including Josefa de Óbidos (1631–84) and Gregório Lopes (1490–1550), are also displayed in the galleries of European art.

PORTUGUESE PAINTING AND SCULPTURE

MANY OF THE EARLIEST works of art are by the Portuguese primitive painters who were influenced by the realistic detail of Flemish artists. There had always been strong trading links between Portugal and Flanders and in the 15th and 16th centuries several painters of Flemish origin, for example Frey Carlos of Évora, set up workshops in Portugal.

Pride of place, however, goes to the São Vicente de Fora polyptych, the most important painting of 15th-century Portuguese art and one that has

become a symbol of national pride in the Age of Discovery. Painted in about 1467–70, and generally believed to be by Nuno Gonçalves, the altarpiece portrays the *Adoration of St Vincent*, patron saint of Portugal, surrounded by dignitaries, knights and monks as well as fishermen and beggars. The accurate portrayal of contemporary figures makes the painting an invaluable historical and social document.

Later works include a 16th-century portrait of the young Dom Sebastião (1557–78) by Cristóvão de Morais and paintings by Neo-Classical artist Domingos António de Sequeira.

The museum's sculpture collection has many Gothic polychrome stone and wood statues of Christ, the Virgin and saints. There are also statues from the 17th century and an 18th-century nativity scene by Machado de Castro in the Chapel of St Albert.

PORTUGUESE AND CHINESE CERAMICS

THE EXTENSIVE collection of ceramics enables visitors to trace the evolution of Chinese porcelain and Portuguese faïence and to see the influence of oriental designs on

Central panel of *The Temptations of St Antony* by Hieronymus Bosch

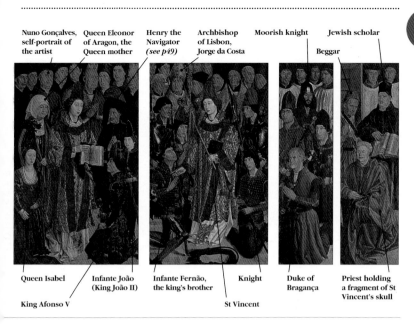

Nuno Gonçalves, self-portrait of the artist
Queen Eleonor of Aragon, the Queen mother
Henry the Navigator *(see p49)*
Archbishop of Lisbon, Jorge da Costa
Moorish knight
Jewish scholar
Beggar

Queen Isabel
Infante João (King João II)
King Afonso V
Infante Fernão, the king's brother
St Vincent
Knight
Duke of Bragança
Priest holding a fragment of St Vincent's skull

Portuguese pieces, and vice versa. From the 16th century Portuguese ceramics show a marked influence of Ming, and conversely the Chinese pieces bear Portuguese motifs such as coats of arms. By the mid-18th century individual potters had begun to develop an increasingly personalized, European style, with popular, rustic designs. The collection also includes ceramics from Italy, Spain and the Netherlands.

Chinese porcelain vase, 16th century

ORIENTAL AND AFRICAN ART

THE COLLECTION of ivories and furniture, with their European motifs, further illustrates the reciprocal influences of Portugal and her colonies. The 16th-century predilection for the exotic gave rise to a huge demand for items such as carved ivory hunting horns from Africa. The fascinating 16th-century Japanese Namban screens show the Portuguese trading in Japan. *Namban-jin* (barbarians from the south) is the name the Japanese gave to the Portuguese.

SILVER, GOLD AND JEWELLERY

AMONG THE MUSEUM'S fine collection of ecclesiastical treasures are King Sancho I's gold cross (1214) and the Belém monstrance (1506). Also on display is the 16th-century Madre de Deus reliquary which allegedly holds a thorn from the crown of Christ. Highlight of the foreign collection is a sumptuous set of rare 18th-century silver tableware. Commissioned by José I from the Paris workshop of Thomas Germain, the 1,200 pieces include intricately-decorated tureens, sauce boats and salt cellars. The rich collection of jewels came from the convents, originally donated by members of the nobility and wealthy bourgeoisie on entering the religious orders.

APPLIED ARTS

FURNITURE, tapestries and textiles, liturgical vestments and bishops' mitres are among the wide range of objects on display. The furniture collection has many examples, both from the Middle Ages and the Rennaissance, and from the reigns of King João V, King José and Queen Maria I. Of the foreign furniture, French pieces from the 18th century are the most prominent.

The textiles include 17th-century bedspreads, tapestries, many of Flemish origin, such as the *Baptism of Christ* (16th century), embroidered rugs and Arraiolos carpets.

Gold Madre de Deus reliquary inlaid with precious stones (c.1502)

BELÉM

AT THE MOUTH of the River Tagus, where the caravels set sail on their voyages of discovery, Belém is inextricably linked with Portugal's golden age of discovery. When Manuel I came to power in 1495 he reaped the profits of those heady days of expansion, building grandiose monuments and churches that mirrored the spirit of the time. Two of the finest examples of the exuberant and exotic Manueline style of architecture are the Mosteiro dos Jerónimos and the Torre de Belém. Today Belém is a

Generosity, statue at entrance to Palácio da Ajuda

spacious, relatively green suburb with many museums, parks and gardens, as well as an attractive riverside setting with cafés and a promenade. On sunny days there is a distinct seaside feel to the river embankment.

Before the Tagus receded, the monks in the monastery used to look out onto the river and watch the boats set forth. In contrast today several lanes of traffic along the busy Avenida da Índia cut central Belém off from the picturesque waterfront, and silver and yellow trains rattle regularly past.

SIGHTS AT A GLANCE

Museums and Galleries
Museu de Arte Popular ⑩
Museu de Marinha ⑦
Museu Nacional de Arqueologia ⑤
Museu Nacional dos Coches ②
Planetário Calouste Gulbenkian ⑥

Parks and Gardens
Jardim Agrícola Tropical ③
Jardim Botânico da Ajuda ⑭

Churches and Monasteries
Ermida de São Jerónimo ⑫
Igreja da Memória ⑬
Mosteiro dos Jerónimos pp66–7 ④

Historic Buildings
Palácio de Belém ①
Palácio Nacional da Ajuda ⑮
Torre de Belém p70 ⑪

Monuments
Monument to the Discoveries ⑨

Cultural Centres
Centro Cultural de Belém ⑧

KEY

▨ Street-by-Street: Belém *pp62–3*

🚉 Railway station

⛴ Ferry boarding point

🅿 Parking

= Railway line

GETTING THERE

The best way to reach Belém is to take tram 15 from Praça do Comércio along the busy waterfront. Buses 14, 27, 28, 43, 49, 51 and 112 also go to Belém. Slow trains from Cais do Sodré to Oeiras stop at Belém.

0 metres   500
0 yards   500

◁ **Nave of Santa Maria de Belém, the church of the Jerónimos monastery**

Street-by-Street: Belém

Stone caravel, Jerónimos monastery

PORTUGAL'S FORMER maritime glory, expressed in the imposing, exuberant buildings such as the Jerónimos monastery, is evident all around Belém. In Salazar's *(see p15)* attempted revival of awareness of Portugal's Golden Age, the area along the waterfront, which had silted up since the days of the caravels, was restructured to celebrate the former greatness of the nation. Praça do Império was laid out for the Exhibition of the Portuguese World in 1940, and Praça Afonso de Albuquerque was dedicated to Portugal's first viceroy of India. The royal Palácio de Belém, restored with gardens and a riding school by João V in the 18th century, briefly housed the royal family after the 1755 earthquake.

★ **Mosteiro dos Jerónimos**
Vaulted arcades and richly carved columns adorned with foliage, exotic animals, and navigational instruments decorate the Manueline cloister of the Jerónimos monastery ❹

LARGO

DOS

JERÓNIMOS

PRAÇA DO IMPÉRIO

Museu Nacional de Arqueologia
Archaeological finds ranging from an Iron Age gold bracelet to Moorish artifacts are among the interesting exhibits on display ❺

Torre de Belém
(see p70)

STAR SIGHTS

★ **Mosteiro dos Jerónimos**

★ **Museu Nacional dos Coches**

KEY

— — — Suggested route

Praça do Império, an impressive square that opens out in front of the monastery, is lit up on special occasions with a colorful light display in the central fountain.

Rua Vieira Portuense runs along a small park. Its colorful 16th- and 17th-century houses contrast with the typically imposing buildings in Belém.

Jardim Agrícola Tropical

Exotic plants and trees gathered from Portugal's former colonies fill these peaceful gardens, which were once part of the Palácio de Belém ❸

LOCATOR MAP
See Lisbon Street Finder maps 1 & 2

Antiga Confeitaria de Belém, a 19th-century café, sells *pastéis de Belém*, rich custard in a flaky pastry cup.

Central Lisbon

RUA DE BELÉM

TRAVESSA DOS FERREIROS

MARTA PINTO

RUA VIEIRA PORTUENSE

Palácio de Belém

Also known as the Palácio Cor de Rosa (pink palace) because of its faded pink façade, the 16th-century former royal palace is the official residence of the President of the Republic of Portugal ❶

| 0 meters | 50 |
| 0 yards | 50 |

★ Museu Nacional dos Coches

This 18th-century coach used by the ambassador to Pope Clement XI is part of the collection in the old riding school of the Palácio de Belém ❷

Praça Afonso de Albuquerque is named after the first Portuguese viceroy of India. A Neo-Manueline column in the center bears his statue, with scenes of his life carved on the base.

Palácio de Belém ●

Praça Afonso de Albuquerque.
Map 1 C4. 🔶 21-361 46 00. 🚍 14,
27, 28, 43, 49, 51. 🚋 15. 🚉
Belém. ◯ 9am–1pm, 3rd Sun of
month. 📷

BUILT BY the Conde de
Aveiras in 1559 before the
Tagus had receded, this summer palace once had gardens
bordering the river. In the
18th century it was bought by
João V, who had acquired vast
wealth through gold from
Brazil. He radically altered the
palace, added a riding school
and rendered the interior
suitably lavish for his many
amorous liaisons.

When the great earthquake
struck in 1755 (see pp20–21),
the king, José I, and his family
were staying here and thus
survived the devastation of
central Lisbon. Fearing another
earth tremor, the royal family
temporarily set up camp in
tents in the palace grounds
and the palace interior was
used as a hospital. Today
the elegant pink building, is
the residence of the President
of Portugal.

Pink façade of the Palácio de Belém, home of the President of Portugal

Museu Nacional dos Coches ●

Praça Afonso de Albuquerque. **Map** 2
D4. 🔶 21-361 08 50. 🚍 14, 27, 28,
43, 49, 51. 🚋 15. 🚉 Belém. ◯
10am– 5:30pm Tue–Sun. ● 1 Jan,
Easter, 1 May, 25 Dec. 📷 📷
♿ ground floor only.

THE MUSEUM'S collection of
coaches is arguably the
finest in Europe. Occupying
the east wing of the Palácio
de Belém, this was formerly
the riding school built by the
Italian architect Giacomo
Azzolini in

1726. Seated in the upper
gallery, the royal family used to
watch their beautiful Lusitanian
horses performing in the arena.
In 1905 the riding school was
turned into a museum by King
Carlos's wife, Dona Amélia,
whose riding cloak is on show.

Made in Portugal, Italy,
France, Austria and Spain, the
coaches span three centuries
and range from the plain to
the preposterous. The main
gallery, in Louis XVI style
with splendid painted ceiling,
is the setting for two straight,
regimented rows of coaches
created for Portuguese royalty.
The collection starts with
the comparatively plain 17th-
century red leather and
wood coach of Philip II
of Spain. The coaches be-
come more sumptuous, the
interiors are lined with red
velvet and gold, the
exteriors are carved and
decorated with allegories
and royal coats of arms. The
rows end with three huge
Baroque coaches made in
Rome for the Portuguese
ambassador to the Vatican,
Dom Rodrigo Almeida e
Menezes, the Marquês de
Abrantes. The epitome of
pomp and extravagance,
but not necessarily of
comfort, these 5-tonne
carriages are embellished
with a plush interior and
life-size gilded statues.
The neighbouring gallery
has further examples of
royal carriages, including
two-wheeled cabriolets,
landaus and pony-drawn
chaises used by young
members of the royal
family. There is also a 19th-
century Lisbon cab, painted
black and green, the colours of

**Rear view of a coach built in 1716 for the Marquês de
Abrantes, the Portuguese ambassador to Pope Clement XI**

taxis right up to the 1990s. The 18th-century Eyeglass Chaise, whose black leather hood is pierced by sinister eye-like windows, was made during the era of Pombal (see p15) when lavish decoration was discouraged. The upper gallery has a collection of harnesses, court costumes and portraits of members of the royal family.

Jardim Agrícola Tropical ❸

Largo dos Jerónimos. **Map** 1 C4. 21-362 02 10. 27, 28, 43, 51, 112. 15. 10am–5pm Tue–Fri, 11am– 6pm Sat & Sun. public hols. Tue–Fri only. **Museu Tropical** by appt only.

A LSO KNOWN AS the Jardim do Ultramar, this peaceful park with ponds, waterfowl and peacocks, attracts surprisingly few visitors. Designed at the beginning of the 20th century as the research centre of the Institute for Tropical Sciences, it is more of an arboretum than a flower garden. The emphasis is on rare and endangered tropical and subtropical trees and plants. Among the most striking are dragon trees, native to the Canary Islands and Madeira, monkey puzzle trees from South America and a handsome avenue of lofty Washington palms. The oriental garden with its streams, bridges and hibiscus is heralded by a large Chinese-style gateway which represented Macau in the Exhibition of the Portuguese World in 1940 (see p62).

The research buildings and **Museu Tropical** are housed in the Palácio dos Condes da Calheta, whose interior walls are covered with *azulejos* spanning three centuries. The museum has 50,000 dried plant specimens and 2,414 samples of wood.

Mosteiro dos Jerónimos ❹

See pp66–7.

Washington palms in the Jardim Agrícola Tropical

Museu Nacional de Arqueologia ❺

Praça do Império. **Map** 1 B4. 21-362 00 00. 28, 43, 49, 51, 112. 15. 10am–6pm Wed–Sun, 2pm–6pm Tue. 1 Jan, Easter, 1 May, 25 Dec.

T HE LONG west wing of the Mosteiro dos Jerónimos (see pp66–7), formerly the monks' dormitory, has been a museum since 1893. Reconstructed in the middle of the 19th century, the building is a poor imitation of the Manueline original. The museum houses Portugal's main archaeological research centre and the exhibits, from sites all over the country, include a gold Iron Age bracelet, Visigothic jewellery found in the Alentejo in southern Portugal, Roman ornaments and early 8th-century Moorish artefacts. The main Greco-Roman and Egyptian section is strong on funerary art, featuring figurines, tombstones, masks, terracotta amulets and funeral cones inscribed with hieroglyphics alluding to the solar system. The dimly-lit Room of Treasures has a fine collection of coins, necklaces, bracelets and other jewellery dating from 1800–500 BC. Along with other parts of the museum, this

Visigothic gold buckle, Museu de Arqueologia

room is being refurbished to allow more of the permanent collection to be shown. The new space is scheduled to open by the end of 2002.

Planetário Calouste Gulbenkian ❻

Praça do Império. **Map** 1 B4. 21-362 00 02. 27, 28, 29, 43, 49, 51, 112. 15. for shows: 4pm & 5pm Sat & Sun (also school hols: 11am, 3pm & 4:15pm Wed & Thu). Special shows for children 11am Sun. public hols.

F INANCED BY the Gulbenkian Foundation (see p79) and built in 1965, this modern building sits incongruously beside the Jerónimos monastery. Inside, the Planetarium reveals the mysteries of the cosmos. There are shows in Portuguese, English and French explaining the movement of the stars and our solar system, as well as presentations on more specialist themes, such as the constellations or the Star of Bethlehem (Belém).

The dome of the Planetário Calouste Gulbenkian

Mosteiro dos Jerónimos ➍

Armillary sphere in the cloister

A MONUMENT TO THE WEALTH of the Age of Discovery *(see pp18–19)*, this monastery is the culmination of Manueline architecture in this period. Commissioned by Manuel I in around 1501, after Vasco de Gama's return from his historic voyage, it was financed largely by "pepper money," a tax levied on spices, precious stones and gold. Various masterbuilders worked on the building, the most notable of whom was Diogo Boitac, replaced by João de Castilho in 1517. The monastery was cared for by the Order of St Jerome (Hieronymites) until 1834, when all religious orders were disbanded.

Tomb of Vasco da Gama
The 19th-century tomb of the explorer (see p68) is carved with ropes, armillary spheres and other seafaring symbols.

The fountain is in the shape of a lion, the heraldic animal of St Jerome.

Refectory
The walls of the refectory are tiled with 18th-century azulejos. The panel at the northern end depicts the Feeding of the Five Thousand.

The modern wing, built in 1850 in Neo-Manueline style, houses the Museu Nacional de Arqueologia *(see p65)*.

The west portal was designed by the French sculptor Nicolau Chanterène.

Entrance to church and cloister

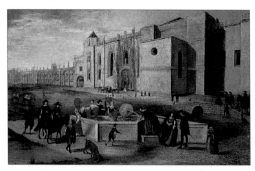

Gallery

View of the Monastery
This 17th-century scene by Felipe Lobo shows women at a fountain in front of the Mosteiro dos Jerónimos.

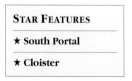

STAR FEATURES
★ **South Portal**
★ **Cloister**

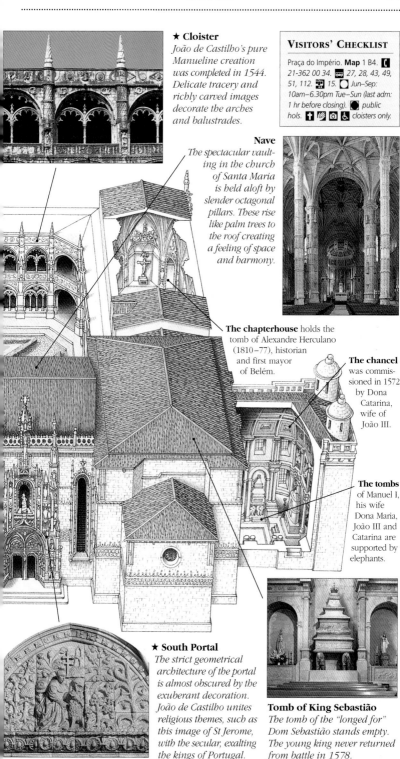

★ Cloister
*João de Castilho's pure
Manueline creation
was completed in 1544.
Delicate tracery and
richly carved images
decorate the arches
and balustrades.*

Nave
*The spectacular vault-
ing in the church
of Santa Maria
is held aloft by
slender octagonal
pillars. These rise
like palm trees to
the roof creating
a feeling of space
and harmony.*

The chapterhouse holds the
tomb of Alexandre Herculano
(1810–77), historian
and first mayor
of Belém.

The chancel
was commis-
sioned in 1572
by Dona
Catarina,
wife of
João III.

The tombs
of Manuel I,
his wife
Dona Maria,
João III and
Catarina are
supported by
elephants.

★ South Portal
*The strict geometrical
architecture of the portal
is almost obscured by the
exuberant decoration.
João de Castilho unites
religious themes, such as
this image of St Jerome,
with the secular, exalting
the kings of Portugal.*

Tomb of King Sebastião
*The tomb of the "longed for"
Dom Sebastião stands empty.
The young king never returned
from battle in 1578.*

Façade of the Museu de Marinha

Museu de Marinha ❼

Praça do Império. **Map** 1 B4. ☎ 21-362 00 19. ➤ 27, 28, 43, 49, 51, 112. ➤ 15. ⭘ 10am–6pm (Oct–Jun: 5pm) Tue–Sun. ⬤ public hols. ▨ ⊙ ♿

T HE MARITIME MUSEUM was inaugurated in 1962 in the west wing of the Jerónimos monastery (see p66–7). It was here, in the chapel built by Henry the Navigator (see p19), that mariners took mass before embarking on their historic voyages. A hall devoted to the Discoveries illustrates the rapid progress in shipbuilding from the mid-15th century, capitalizing on the experience of the long-distance explorers. Small replicas show the transition from the bark to the lateen-rigged caravel, through the faster square-rigged caravel, to the Portuguese *nau*. Also relating to the Discoveries are navigational instruments, astrolabes and replicas of 16th-century maps showing the world as it was known then. The stone pillars, carved with the Cross of the Knights of Christ, are replicas of the types of *padrão* set up as monuments to Portuguese sovereignty on the lands discovered. Beyond the Hall of Discoveries a series of rooms displaying models of modern Portuguese ships leads on to the Royal Quarters where you can see the exquisitely furnished wood-panelled cabin of King Carlos and Queen Amélia from the royal yacht *Amélia*, built in Scotland in 1900.

The modern, incongruous pavilion opposite houses original royal barges, the most extravagant of which is the royal brig built in 1780 for Maria I. The collection ends with a display of seaplanes, including the *Santa Clara* which made the first crossing of the South Atlantic in 1922.

VASCO DA GAMA (c.1460–1524)

In 1498 Vasco da Gama sailed around the Cape of Good Hope and opened the sea route to India (see pp18–9). Although the Hindu ruler of Calicut, who received him wearing diamond and ruby rings, was not impressed by his humble offerings of cloth and wash basins, da Gama returned to Portugal with a cargo of spices. In 1502 he sailed again to India, establishing Portuguese trade routes in the Indian Ocean. João III nominated him Viceroy of India in 1524, but he died of a fever soon after.

16th-century painting of Vasco da Gama in Goa

Centro Cultural de Belém ❽

Praça do Império. **Map** 1 B5. ☎ 21-361 24 00. ➤ 27, 28, 43, 49, 51, 112. ➤ 15. **Exhibition Centre** ⭘ 11am–8pm. ▨ ♿

T HE CONSTRUCTION of a stark modern building directly between the Jéronimos monastery and the Tagus was clearly controversial. Built in 1990 as the headquarters of the Portuguese presidency of the European Community, it opened as a cultural and conference centre in 1993. It stresses music, performing arts and photography, with a large **Exhibition Centre** used for temporary displays and a permanent design museum.

Both the café and restaurant overlook minimalist gardens and the river. At weekends, the centre's atmosphere can be enlivened by street performers, actors and rollerbladers.

The modern complex of the Centro Cultural de Belém

Monument to the Discoveries ❾

Padrão dos Descobrimentos, Avenida de Brasília. **Map** 1 C5. ☎ 21-303 19 50. ➤ 27, 28, 43, 49, 51, 112. ➤ 15. ⭘ 9am–5pm (Jul–Aug: 7pm) Tue–Sun. ⬤ public hols. ▨ for lift. ⊙

S TANDING PROMINENTLY on the Belém waterfront, this massive angular monument, the Padrão dos Descobrimentos, was built in 1960 to mark the 500th anniversary of the death of Henry the Navigator (see p19). The 52-m (170-ft) high monument, commissioned by the Salazar regime, commemorates the mariners, royal patrons and all those who participated in the rapid development of the Portuguese Age

The huge pavement compass in front of the Monument to the Discoveries

Museu de Arte Popular ⓾

Avenida de Brasília. **Map** 1 B5.
📞 21-301 12 82. 🚌 27, 28, 43, 49, 51, 112. 🚋 15. ☐ 10am–12:30pm, 2–5pm Tue–Sun. ⬤ 1 Jan, Easter, 1 May, 25 Dec. 📷

THE DRAB BUILDING on the waterfront, between the Monument to the Discoveries and the Torre de Belém (see p70), houses the museum of Portuguese folk art and traditional handicrafts, opened in 1948. While·the rooms housing the permanent collections are closed for alterations until 2003, a temporary exhibition space is open. The exhibits, which are arranged by province, include local pottery, agricultural tools, costumes, musical instruments, jewellery and brightly coloured saddles. The display gives a vivid indication of the diversity between the regions of Portugal. Each area has its speciality such as the colourful ox yokes and ceramic cocks from the Minho and basketware from Trás-os-Montes, both in northern Portugal, and cowbells and terracotta casseroles from the Alentejo. If you are planning to travel around Portugal the museum offers an excellent preview to the handicrafts of the various provinces.

Traditional costume from Trás-os-Montes

of Discovery. The monument is designed in the shape of a caravel, with Portugal's coat of arms on the sides and the sword of the Royal House of Avis rising above the entrance. Henry the Navigator stands at the prow with a caravel in hand. In two sloping lines either side of the monument are stone statues of Portuguese heroes linked with the Age of Discovery. On the western face these include Dom Manuel I holding an armillary sphere, the poet Camões with a copy of Os Lusíadas, the painter Nuno Gonçalves with a paint pallet as well as famous navigators, cartographers and kings.

On the monument's north side, the huge mariner's compass cut into the paving stone was a present from the Republic of South Africa

in 1960. The central map, dotted with galleons and mermaids, shows the routes of the discoverers in the 15th and 16th centuries. Inside the monument a lift whisks you up to the sixth floor where steps then lead to the top for a splendid panorama of the river and Belém. The basement level is used for temporary exhibitions, but not necessarily related to the Discoveries.

The rather ostentatious Padrão is not to everyone's taste but the setting is undeniably splendid and the caravel design is imaginative. The monument looks particularly dramatic when viewed from the west in the light of the late afternoon sun.

EASTERN FACE OF THE MONUMENT TO THE DISCOVERIES

Afonso V (1432–81), patron of the first explorers

Pedro Álvares Cabral (1467–1520), discoverer of Brazil

Henry the Navigator (1394–1460)

Vasco da Gama (1460–1524)

Fernão Magalhães (Magellan), who crossed the Pacific in 1520–21

Padrão erected by Diogo Cão in the Congo in 1482

Torre de Belém ⓫

Arms of Manuel I

COMMISSIONED BY Manuel I, the tower was built as a fortress in the middle of the Tagus in 1515–21. The starting point for the navigators who set out to discover the trade routes, this Manueline gem became a symbol of Portugal's great era of expansion. The real beauty of the tower lies in the decoration of the exterior. Adorned with rope carved in stone, it has openwork balconies, Moorish-style watchtowers and distinctive battlements in the shape of shields. The Gothic interior below the terrace, which served as a storeroom for arms and a prison, is very austere but the private quarters in the tower are worth visiting for the loggia and the panorama.

VISITORS' CHECKLIST

Avenida da India. **Map** 1 A5.
📞 21-301 93 46. 🚌 27, 28, 29, 43, 49, 51, 112. 🚋 15. 🚉 Belém. ⏰ 10am–5pm Tue–Sun, (6pm Jun–Sep). ⬤ public hols.
📷 ♿ ground floor only.

Renaissance Loggia
The elegant arcaded loggia, inspired by Italian architecture, gives a light touch to the defensive battlements of the tower.

Armillary spheres and nautical rope are symbols of Portugal's seafaring prowess.

Royal coat of arms of Manuel I

Chapel

Battlements are decorated with the cross of the Order of Christ.

Governor's room

Virgin and Child
A statue of Our Lady of Safe Homecoming faces the sea, a symbol of protection for sailors on their voyages of discovery.

Gangway to shore

Entrance

Sentry posts

The vaulted dungeon was used as a prison until the 19th century.

The Torre de Belém in 1811
This painting of a British ship navigating the Tagus, by JT Serres, shows the tower further from the shore than it is today. Land on the north bank was reclaimed in the 19th century, making the river narrower.

**The simple Manueline chapel,
Ermida de São Jerónimo**

Ermida de São Jerónimo ⑫

Rua Pero de Covilhã. **Map** 1 A3.
📞 21-301 86 48. 🚌 28, 43, 49, 51.
🕐 by appt only.

ALSO KNOWN AS the Capela de
São Jerónimo, this elegant
little chapel was constructed in
1514 when Diogo Boitac was
working on the Jerónimos
monastery (see pp66–7).
Although a far simpler
building, it is also Manueline
in style and may have been
built to a design by Boitac.
The only decorative elements
on the monolithic chapel are
the four pinnacles, corner
gargoyles and Manueline
portal. Perched on a quiet hill
above Belém, the chapel has
fine views down to the River
Tagus and a path from the
terrace winds down the hill
towards the Torre de Belém.

Igreja da Memória ⑬

Calçada do Galvão, Ajuda. **Map** 1 C3.
📞 21-363 52 95. 🚌 14, 27, 28, 32.
🚋 18. 🕐 4–6pm Mon–Sat. 🚹 ♿

BUILT IN 1760, the church was
founded by King José I in
gratitude for his escape from
an assassination plot on this
site in 1758. The king was returning from a secret liaison
with a lady of the noble Távora
family when his carriage was
attacked and a bullet hit him in
the arm. Pombal (see p15),
whose power had now be-
come absolute, used this as an
excuse to get rid of his en-
emies in the Távora family,

accusing them of conspiracy.
In 1759 they were savagely
tortured and executed. Their
deaths are commemorated
by a pillar in Beco do Chão
Salgado, off Rua de Belém.
  The Neo-Classical domed
church has a marble-clad interior and a small chapel, on
the right, containing the tomb
of Pombal. He died at the age
of 83, a year after he had
been banished from Lisbon.

Jardim Botânico da Ajuda ⑭

Calçada da Ajuda. **Map** 1 C2. 📞 21-
362 25 03. 🚌 14, 27, 28, 32. 🚋 18.
🕐 9am–5pm Thu–Tue. ● public
hols. 🎟 (free 9am–2pm Sun). ♿

LAID OUT on two levels by
Pombal (see p15) in
1768, these Italian-
style gardens provide
a pleasant respite
from the noisy
suburbs of Belém.
The entrance
(wrought-iron
gates in a pink
wall) is easy to
miss. The park
comprises
tropical trees
and box-hedge
gardens sur-
rounding neat
flower beds.

**19th-century throne from the
Palácio Nacional da Ajuda**

Notable features are the 400-
year-old dragon tree, native of
Madeira, and the flamboyant
18th-century fountain decorated with writhing serpents,
winged fish, sea horses and
mythical creatures. A majestic
terrace looks out over the
lower level of the gardens.

Palácio Nacional da Ajuda ⑮

Calçada da Ajuda. **Map** 2 D2. 📞 21-
363 70 95. 🚌 14, 27, 28, 32, 42,
60. 🚋 18. 🕐 10am–5pm Thu–Tue.
● public hols. 🎟 ♿ 🚻

THE ROYAL PALACE, destroyed
by fire in 1795, was re-
placed in the early 19th century
by the Neo-Classical building
you see today. This was left
incomplete when the royal
family was forced into exile
in Brazil during 1807.
  The palace only became a
permanent residence of the
royal family when Luís I became king in 1861 and married
an Italian Princess, Maria Pia
di Savoia. No expense was
spared in furnishing the apartments. The ostentatious
rooms are decorated
with silk wallpaper,
Sèvres porcelain and
crystal chandeliers.
  A prime example of
regal excess is the
extraordinary Saxe
Room, a wedding
present to Maria Pia
from the King of
Saxony, in which
every piece of
furniture is deco-
rated with Meissen
porcelain. On the
first floor the huge
Banqueting Hall, with crystal
chandeliers, silk-covered chairs
and an allegory of the birth of
João VI on the frescoed ceiling,
is truly impressive. At the other
end of the palace, Luís I's
Neo-Gothic painting studio is
a more intimate display of
intricately carved furniture.

Manicured formal gardens of the Jardim Botânico da Ajuda

FURTHER AFIELD

THE MAJORITY of the outlying sights, which include some of Lisbon's finest museums, are easily accessible by bus or metro from the city centre. A ten-minute walk north from the gardens of the Parque Eduardo VII brings you to Portugal's great cultural complex, the Calouste Gulbenkian Foundation, set in a pleasant park. Few tourists go further north than the Gulbenkian, but the Museu da Cidade on Campo Grande is worth a detour for its fascinating overview of Lisbon's history.

Azulejo panel from Palácio Fronteira

The charming Palácio Fronteira, decorated with splendid tiles, is one of the many villas built for the aristocracy that now overlook the city suburbs. Those interested in tiles will also enjoy the Museu Nacional do Azulejo in the cloisters of the Madre de Deus convent. Visitors with a spare half day can cross the Tagus to the Cristo Rei monument. Northeast of Lisbon is the vast oceanarium, Oceanário de Lisboa, in the Parque das Nações, which includes other family-oriented attrations, hotels and shops.

SIGHTS AT A GLANCE

Museums and Galleries
Centro de Arte Moderna **7**
Museu da Água **9**
Museu Calouste Gulbenkian pp76–9 **6**
Museu da Cidade **13**
Museu Nacional do Azulejo pp82–3 **10**

Modern Architecture
Amoreiras Shopping Centre **3**
Cristo Rei **1**
Parque das Nações **11**
Ponte 25 de Abril **2**

Historic Architecture
Aqueduto das Águas Livres **15**
Campo Pequeno **8**
Palácio Fronteira **16**
Praça Marquês de Pombal **4**

Parks and Gardens
Parque Eduardo VII **5**
Parque do Monteiro-Mor **17**

Zoos
Jardim Zoológico **14**
Oceanário de Lisboa **12**

KEY

▨	Main sightseeing areas
✈	Airport
⛴	Ferry boarding point
═	Motorway
═	Major road
═	Minor road

0 kilometres   4

0 miles   2

SIGHTS BEYOND THE CITY CENTRE

Map showing the Lisbon area with numbered sights, including locations: Vila Franca de Xira, Pontinha, Amadora, Olivais, Campo Grande, Benfica, Xabregas, Estefânia, Carnaxide, Cascais, PARQUE FLORESTAL DE MONSANTO, Graça, Alcântara, Montijo, Tejo, Barreiro, Cacilhas, Almada, Porto Brandão, Setúbal, Seixal. Roads labelled A9, IC17, IC19, IC16, IC15–A5, N117, N6, IP1–A1 (E1), IP1–A2 (E1), N10.

◁ **Nymph fountain among tropical vegetation inside the Estufa Fria, Parque Eduardo VII**

Cristo Rei ❶

Santuário Nacional do Cristo Rei, Alto
do Pragal, Almada. 【 21-275 10 00.
🚢 from Praça do Comércio & Cais do
Sodré to Cacilhas then 🚌 101. **Lift** 🔵
for works, reopening mid-2003. 🗓

M ODELLED ON the more
famous Cristo Redentor
in Rio de Janeiro, this giant-
sized statue stands with arms
outstretched on the south
bank of the Tagus. The 28 m
(92 ft) tall figure of Christ,
mounted on a huge pedestal,
was built by Francisco Franco
in 1949–59 at the instigation
of Prime Minister Salazar.
   You can see the monument
from various viewpoints in
the city, but it is fun to take a
ferry to the Outra Banda (the
other bank), then a bus or
taxi to the monument. (Rush
hour is best avoided.) A lift,
plus some steps, takes you up
82 m (269 ft) to the top of the
pedestal, affording fine views
of the city and river.

Ponte 25 de Abril ❷

Map 3 A5. 🚌 52, 53.

O RIGINALLY CALLED the Ponte
Salazar after the dictator
who had it built in 1966,
Lisbon's suspension bridge
was renamed (like many other

**The towering monument of Cristo
Rei overlooking the Tagus**

monuments) to commemorate
the revolution of 25 April 1974
which restored democracy to
Portugal (see p15).
   Inspired by San Francisco's
Golden Gate Bridge in the
United States, this steel construction stretches for 1 km
(half a mile). The lower tier

was modified in 1999 to
accommodate a much-needed
railway across the Tagus.
   The bridge's notorious
traffic congestion has been
partly resolved by the
opening of the 11-km (7-mile)
Vasco da Gama bridge.
Spanning the river from
Montijo to Sacavém, north of
the Parque das Nações, this
bridge was completed in
1998.

Amoreiras
Shopping Centre ❸

Avenida Engenheiro Duarte Pacheco.
Map 5 A5. 【 21-381 02 00. 🚌
11, 18, 23, 48, 51, 53, 58, 74, 83.
⭕ 10am–11pm daily. ⬤ 25 Dec. ♿

I N THE 18TH CENTURY, the
Marquês de Pombal (see
p15) planted mulberry trees
(amoreiras) on the western
edge of the city to create food
for silk worms. Hence the
name of the futuristic shopping
centre that was built here in
1985. This massive complex,
with pink and blue towers,
houses 370 shops, ten cinemas,
and numerous cafés. Once an
incongruous feature of Lisbon,
it still draws the crowds,
particularly the young, and
has been joined by other
new buildings and shopping
centres in the area.

Ponte 25 de Abril linking central Lisbon with the Outra Banda, the south bank of the Tagus

Tropical plants in the Estufa Quente glasshouse, Parque Eduardo VII

Praça Marquês de Pombal ❹

Map 5 C5. Ⓜ *Marquês de Pombal.* 🚌 *1, 2, 12, 20, 38 & many other routes.*

A T THE TOP of the Avenida da Liberdade *(see p44)*, traffic thunders round the "Rotunda" (roundabout), as the praça is also known. At the centre rises the lofty monument to Pombal, unveiled in 1934. The despotic statesman, who virtually ruled Portugal from 1750–77, stands on the top of the column, his hand on a lion (symbol of power) and his eyes directed down to the Baixa, whose creation he masterminded *(see p15)*.

Detail representing agricultural toil on the base of the monument in Praça Marquês de Pombal

Allegorical images depicting Pombal's political, educational and agricultural reforms decorate the base of the monument. Standing figures represent Coimbra University where he introduced a new Faculty of Science. Although greatly feared, this dynamic politician propelled the country into the Age of Enlightenment. Broken blocks of stone at the foot of the monument and tidal waves flooding the city are an allegory of the destruction caused by the 1755 earthquake.

An underpass, which is not always open, leads to the centre of the square where the sculptures on the pedestal and the inscriptions relating to Pombal's achievements can be seen. Nearby, the well-tended Parque Eduardo VII extends northwards behind the square. The paving stones around the Rotunda are decorated with a mosaic of Lisbon's coat of arms. Similar patterns in small black and white cobbles decorate many of the city's streets and squares.

Parque Eduardo VII ❺

Praça Marquês de Pombal. **Map** 5 B4. 🛈 *21-388 22 78.* Ⓜ *Marquês de Pombal.* 🚌 *2, 12, 22, 38.* **Estufa Fria** 🛈 *21-388 22 78.* 🕐 *Apr–Sep: 9am–6pm daily; Oct–Mar: 9am–5pm daily (last admission 30 mins before closing).* ● *public hols.* 📷

T HE LARGEST PARK in central Lisbon was named in honour of King Edward VII of England who came to Lisbon in 1902 to reaffirm the Anglo-Portuguese alliance. The wide grassy slope, that extends for 25 hectares (62 acres), was laid out as Parque da Liberdade, a continuation of Avenida da Liberdade *(see p44)*, in the late 19th century. Neatly clipped box hedges, flanked by mosaic patterned walkways, stretches uphill from the Praça Marquês de Pombal to a belvedere at the top. From here there are fine views of the city and the distant hills on the far side of the Tagus. On clear days it is possible to see as far as the Serra da Arrábida *(see p107)*.

Located at the northwest corner, the most inspiring feature of this rather monotonous park is the jungle-like **Estufa Fria**, or greenhouse, where exotic plants, streams and waterfalls provide an oasis from the city streets.

There are in fact two greenhouses: in the Estufa Fria (cold greenhouse), palms push through the slatted bamboo roof and paths wind through a forest of ferns, fuchsias, flowering shrubs and banana trees; the warmer Estufa Quente, or hot-house, is a glassed-over garden with lush plants, water-lily ponds and cacti, as well as tropical birds in cages.

Near the estufas a pond with carp and a galleon-shaped play area are popular with children. On the east side the **Pavilhão Carlos Lopes**, named after the 1984 Olympic marathon winner, is now used for concerts and conferences. The façade is decorated with tiled scenes by *azulejo* artist, Jorge Colaço, mainly of Portuguese battles.

Museu Calouste Gulbenkian ⑥

Thanks to a wealthy Armenian oil magnate, Calouste Gulbenkian (*see p79*), with wide-ranging tastes and an eye for a masterpiece, the museum has one of the finest collections of art in Europe. Inaugurated in 1969, the purpose-built museum was created as part of the charitable institution bequeathed to Portugal by the multimillionaire. The design of the building, set in a spacious park allowing natural light to fill some of the rooms, was devised to create the best layout for the founder's varied collection.

Mustard Barrel
This 18th-century silver mustard barrel was made in France by Antoine Sébastien Durand.

Lalique Corsage Ornament
The sinuous curves of the gold and enamel snakes are typical of René Lalique's Art Nouveau jewellery.

★ Diana
This fine marble statue (1780) by the French sculptor Jean-Antoine Houdon, was once owned by Catherine the Great of Russia but was considered too obscene to exhibit. The graceful Diana, goddess of the hunt, stands with a bow and arrow in hand.

Entrance

Stairs to

★ St Catherine
This serene bust of St Catherine was painted by the Flemish artist Rogier Van der Weyden (1400–64). The thin strip of landscape on the left of the wooden panel brings light and depth to the still portrait.

STAR EXHIBITS

★ **Portrait of an Old Man by Rembrandt**

★ **Diana by Houdon**

★ **St Catherine by Van der Weyden**

★ Portrait of an Old Man
Rembrandt was a master of light and shade. In this expressive portrait, dated 1645, the fragile countenance of the old man is contrasted with the strong and dramatic lighting.

VISITORS' CHECKLIST

Avenida de Berna 45. **Map** 5 B2.
21-782 30 00.
Ⓜ Praça de Espanha or São Sebastião. 🚌 16, 18, 26, 31, 46, 56. ⏰ 10am–6pm Wed–Sun, 2–6pm Tue.
⚫ Mon & public hols. ♿ ♿
📷 🍴 ⓦ www.gulbenkian.pt

Renaissance art

Vase of a Hundred Birds
The enamel decoration that adorns this Chinese porcelain vase is known as Famille Verte. *This type of elaborate design is characteristic of the Ch'ing dynasty during the reign of the Emperor K'ang Hsi (1662–1722).*

GALLERY GUIDE
The galleries are laid out both chronologically and geographically, the first section (rooms 1–6) dedicated to Classical and Oriental art, the second section (rooms 7–17) housing the European collection of paintings, sculpture, furniture, silverware and jewellery.

Armenian art

Egyptian Bronze Cat
This bronze of a cat feeding her kittens dates from the Saite Period (8th century BC). Other stunning Egyptian pieces include a gilded mask of a mummy.

Persian faïence

Turkish Faïence Plate
The factories at Iznik in Turkey produced some of the most beautiful jugs, plates and vases of the Islamic world, including this 17th-century deep plate decorated with stylized animal forms.

KEY TO FLOORPLAN

☐ Egyptian, Classical and Mesopotamian art

☐ Oriental Islamic art

☐ Far Eastern art

☐ European art (14th–17th centuries)

☐ French 18th-century decorative arts

☐ European art (18th–19th centuries)

☐ Lalique collection

☐ Non-exhibition space

Exploring the Gulbenkian Collection

Housing Calouste Gulbenkian's unique collection of art, the museum ranks with the Museu de Arte Antiga (*see pp56–9*) as the finest in Lisbon. The exhibits, which span over 4,000 years from ancient Egyptian statuettes, through translucent Islamic glassware, to Art Nouveau brooches, are displayed in spacious and well-lit galleries, many overlooking the gardens or courtyards. The museum is quite small, however each individual work of art, from the magnificent pieces that make up the rich display of Oriental and Islamic art, to the selection of European paintings and furniture, is worthy of attention.

Late 16th-century Persian faïence tile from the School of Isfahan

Egyptian, Classical and Mesopotamian Art

Priceless treasures chart the evolution of Egyptian art from the Old Kingdom (c.2700 BC) to the Roman Period (1st century BC). The exhibits range from an alabaster bowl of the 3rd Dynasty to a surprisingly modern-looking blue terracotta torso of a statuette of *Venus Anadyomene* from the Roman period.

Outstanding pieces in the Classical art section are a magnificent red-figure Greek vase and 11 Roman medallions, found in Egypt. These are believed to have been struck to commemorate the athletic games held in Macedonia in AD 242 in honour of Alexander the Great. In the Mesopotamian art section the large Assyrian

5th-century BC Greek vase

alabaster bas-relief represents the winged genius of Spring, carrying a container of sacred water (9th century BC).

Oriental Islamic Art

Being armenian, Calouste Gulbenkian had a keen interest in art from the Near and Middle East. The Oriental Islamic gallery has a fine collection of Persian and Turkish carpets, textiles, costumes and ceramics. In the section overlooking the courtyard, the Syrian mosque lamps and bottles commissioned by princes and sultans, are beautifully decorated with coloured enamel on glass. The Armenian section has some exquisite illustrated manuscripts from the 16th to 18th centuries, produced by Armenian refugees in Istanbul, Persia and the Crimea.

Far Eastern Art

Calouste gulbenkian acquired a large collection of Chinese porcelain between 1910 and 1930. One of the rarest pieces is the small blue-glazed bowl from the Yüan Dynasty (1279–1368), on the right as you go into the gallery. The majority of exhibits, however, are the later, more exuberantly decorated *famille verte* porcelain and the K'ang Hsi biscuitware of the 17th and 18th centuries. Further exhibits from the Far East are translucent Chinese jades and other semi-precious stones, Japanese prints, brocaded silk hangings and bound books, and lacquerwork.

European Art (14th–17th Centuries)

Illuminated manuscripts, rare printed books and medieval ivories introduce the section on Western art. The delicately sculpted 14th-century ivory diptychs and triptychs, made in France, show scenes from the lives of Christ and the Virgin.

The collection of early European paintings starts with panels of *St Joseph* and *St Catherine* by Rogier van der Weyden, leading painter of the mid-15th century in Flanders. Italian Renaissance painting is represented by Cima da Conegliano's *Sacra Conversazione* from the late 15th century and Domenico Ghirlandaio's *Portrait of a Young Woman* (1485).

The collection progresses to Flemish and Dutch works of the 17th century, including two works by Rembrandt: *Portrait of an Old Man* (1645),

French ivory triptych of
Scenes from the Life of the Virgin **(14th century)**

a masterpiece of psychological penetration, and *Alexander the Great* (1660), said to have been modelled on Rembrandt's son, Titus, and previously thought to have portrayed the Greek goddess Pallas Athena. Rubens is represented by three paintings, the most remarkable of which is the *Portrait of Hélène Fourment* (1630), the artist's second wife.

The gallery beyond the Dutch and Flemish paintings has tapestries and textiles from Italy and Flanders, Italian ceramics, rare 15th-century medallions and sculpture.

View of the Molo with the Ducal Palace (1790) by Francesco Guardi

FRENCH 18TH-CENTURY DECORATIVE ARTS

SOME REMARKABLY elaborate Louis XV and Louis XVI pieces, many commissioned by royalty, feature in the collection of French 18th-century furniture. The exhibits, many of them embellished with laquer panels, ebony and bronze, are grouped together according to historical style with Beauvais and "chinoiserie" Aubusson tapestries decorating the walls.

The French silverware from the same period, much of which once adorned the dining tables of Russian palaces, includes lavishly decorated soup tureens, salt-cellars and platters.

Louis XV chest of drawers inlaid with ebony and bronze

EUROPEAN ART (18TH–19TH CENTURIES)

THE ART of the 18th century is dominated by French painters, including Watteau (1684–1721), Fragonard (1732–1806) and Boucher (1703–70). The most celebrated piece of sculpture is a statue of *Diana* by Jean-Antoine Houdon. Commissioned in 1780 by the Duke of Saxe-Gotha for his

gardens, it became one of the principal exhibits in the Hermitage in Russia during the 19th and early 20th centuries.

One whole room is devoted to views of Venice by the 18th-century Venetian painter Francesco Guardi, and a small collection of British art includes works by leading 18th-century portraitists, such as Gainsborough's *Portrait of Mrs Lowndes-Stone* (c.1775) and Romney's *Portrait of Mrs Constable* (1787). There are also two stormy seascapes by JMW Turner (1775–1851). French 19th-century landscape painting is well represented here, reflecting Gulbenkian's preference for naturalism, with works by the Barbizon school, the Realists and the Impressionists. The best-known paintings in the section, however, are probably Manet's *Boy with Cherries*, painted in about 1858 at the beginning of the artist's career, and *Boy Blowing*

Bubbles, painted about 1867. Renoir's *Portrait of Madame Claude Monet* was painted in about 1872 when the artist was staying with Monet at his country home in Argenteuil, in the outskirts of Paris.

LALIQUE COLLECTION

THE TOUR of the museum ends with an entire room filled with the flamboyant creations of French Art Nouveau jeweller, René Lalique (1860–1945). Gulbenkian was a close friend of Lalique's and he acquired many of the pieces of jewellery, glassware and ivory on display here directly from the artist. Inlaid with semi-precious stones and covered with enamel or gold leaf, the brooches, necklaces, vases and combs are decorated with the dragonfly, peacock or sensual female nude motifs characteristic of Art Nouveau.

CALOUSTE GULBENKIAN

Born in Scutari (Turkey) in 1869, Gulbenkian started his art collection at the age of 14 when he bought some ancient coins in a bazaar. In 1928 he was granted a 5 per cent stake in four major oil companies, including BP and Shell, in thanks for his part in the transfer of the assets of the Turkish Petroleum Company to those four companies. He thereby earned himself the nickname of "Mr Five Percent". With the wealth he accumulated, Gulbenkian was able to indulge his passion for fine works of art. During World War II, he went to live in neutral Portugal and, on his death in 1955, bequeathed his estate to the Portuguese in the form of a charitable trust. The Foundation supports many cultural activities and has its own orchestra, libraries, ballet company and concert halls.

Henry Moore sculpture in garden of the Centro de Arte Moderna

Centro de Arte Moderna ⓻

Rua Dr Nicolau de Bettencourt.
Map 5 B3. 📞 *21-782 30 00.*
Ⓜ *São Sebastião.* 🚌 *16, 26, 31, 46, 56.* 🕐 *10am–6pm Wed–Sun, 2–6pm Tue.* ● *public hols.* 📷 ♿
🌐 *www.gulbenkian.pt*

T HE MODERN ART MUSEUM lies across the gardens from the Calouste Gulbenkian museum and is part of the same cultural foundation *(see p59).*
The permanent collection features paintings and sculpture by Portuguese artists from the turn of the 20th century to the present day. The most

famous painting is the striking portrait of poet Fernando Pessoa in the Café Irmãos Unidos (1964) by José de Almada Negreiros (1893–1970), a main exponent of Portuguese Modernism. Also of interest are paintings by Eduardo Viana (1881–1967), Amadeo de Sousa Cardoso (1887–1910), as well as contemporary artists such as Paula Rego, Rui Sanches, Graça Morais and Teresa Magalhães.
The museum is light and spacious with pleasant gardens and a cafeteria which attracts very long queues at weekends.

Campo Pequeno ⓼

Map 5 C1. Ⓜ *Campo Pequeno.*
🚌 *22, 45.* **Bullring** 📞 *21-793 24 42.*
🕐 *Easter–Oct: for bullfights.* 📷 ♿

T HIS SQUARE is dominated by the red-brick Neo-Moorish bullring built in the late 19th century. Closed until mid-2003, the building is undergoing major works to build an underground car park and leisure centre. Much of the bullring's distinctive architecture, such as keyhole-shaped windows and double cupolas will be

retained. Call the tourist office or the number listed above for information on this and other bull fight venues.

Renovated 19th-century steam pump in the Museu da Água

Museu da Água ⓽

Rua do Alviela 12. 📞 *21-810 02 15.*
🚌 *35, 104, 105, 107.* 🕐 *10am–6pm Mon–Sat.* ● *public hols.*
📷 📷

D EDICATED TO the history of Lisbon's water supply, this small but informative museum was imaginatively created around the city's first steam pumping station. It commemorates Manuel da Maia, the 18th-century engineer who masterminded the Águas Livres aqueduct *(see p84).* The excellent layout of the museum earned it the Council of Europe Museum Prize in 1990.
Pride of place goes to four lovingly preserved steam engines, one of which still functions (by electricity) and can be switched on for visitors. The development of technology relating to the city's water supply is documented in photographs. Particularly interesting are the sections on the Águas Livres aqueduct and the Alfama's 17th-century Chafariz d'El Rei, one of Lisbon's first fountains. Locals used to queue at one of six founts, depending on their social status.

Museu Nacional do Azulejo ⓾

See pp82–3.

Neo-Moorish façade of the bullring in Campo Pequeno

The impressive Oriente Station, located next to Parque das Nações

Parque das Nações 🕚

Avenida Dom João. **(** 21-891 93 33. **M** Oriente. **█** 5, 10, 19, 21, 28, 44, 50, 68, 82. **▤** Gare de Oriente. **○** 10am–8pm daily. ♿ ⅲ 🏺 **Pavilhão do Conhecimento (** 21-891 71 00. **○** 10am–6pm Mon–Fri, 11am–7pm Sat & Sun. 🎨 **Pavilhão da Realidade Virtual (** 21-891 70 02. **○** noon–5:30pm Tue–Sun. 🎨

ORIGINALLY THE SITE of Expo '98, Parque das Nações has become a new focus for Lisbon. With its startling contemporary architecture, family-oriented attractions and modern living spaces, the park has renewed the eastern waterfront, an industrial wasteland as recently as 1990. Even from a distance, the soaring geometry of the platform canopies over Santiago Calatrava's Oriente Station set the architectural tone for the development. The impressive **Portugal Pavilion**, designed by the Portuguese architect Álvaro Siza Vieira has an enormous reinforced-concrete roof suspended almost miraculously, like a sailcloth, above its forecourt.

Families with children of any age will enjoy the **Pavilhão do Conhecimento** (Knowledge Pavilion), a modern museum of science and technology that houses several interactive exhibitions. The **Pavilhão da Realidade Virtual** (Virtual Reality Pavilion) appeals to older children and adults by showcasing the latest multi-sensory entertainment technology. Views can be had from the cable car that lifts visitors from one end of the park to the other or the **Torre Vasco da Gama**, Lisbon's tallest building. The promenade along the river, with its view of the Tagus at its widest and the Vasco da Gama bridge, is not to be missed.

Oceanário de Lisboa 🕛

Esplanada D. Carlos 1, Parque das Nações. **(** 21-891 70 02. **M** Oriente. **█** 5, 10, 19, 21, 28, 44, 50, 68, 82. **▤** Gare de Oriente. **○** Apr–Oct: 10am–8pm daily; Nov–Mar: 10am–7pm daily. 🎨 ♿

CENTREPIECE OF Expo 98 and now the main attraction at Parque das Nações, the somewhat aircraft carrier-like oceanarium was designed by American architect Peter Chermayeff, and is perched on the end of a pier, surrounded by water. It is the second-largest aquarium in the world, and holds an impressive array of species – birds and some mammals as well as fish and other underwater dwellers.

18th-century Indian toy, Museu da Cidade

Four separate sea- and landscapes represent the habitats of the Atlantic, Pacific, Indian and Antarctic oceans, with suitable fauna and flora. The main attraction for most visitors, though, is the vast central tank with a dazzling variety of fish, large and small, swimming round and round. Hammerhead sharks co-exist peaceably with bream, barracudas with rays.

The softly-lit waters can be viewed through any number of glass panes, on two levels.

Museu da Cidade 🕙

Campo Grande 245. **(** 21-759 16 17. **M** Campo Grande. **█** 1, 3, 33, 36, 47, 50, 101. **○** 10am–1pm, 2–6pm Tue–Sun. **●** public hols. 🎨 ♿

PALÁCIO PIMENTA was allegedly commissioned by João V *(see p17)* for his mistress Madre Paula, a nun from the nearby convent at Odivelas. When the mansion was built, in the middle of the 18th century, it occupied a peaceful site outside the capital. Nowadays it has to contend with the teeming traffic of Campo Grande. The house itself, however, retains its period charm and the city museum is one of the most interesting in Lisbon.

The displays follow the development of the city, from prehistoric times, through the Romans, Visigoths and Moors, traced by means of tiles, drawings, paintings, models and historical documents. Some of the most fascinating exhibits are those depicting the city before the earthquake of 1755, including a highly detailed model made in the 1950s and an impressive 17th-century oil painting by Dirk Stoop (1610–86) of *Terreiro do Paço*, as Praça do Comércio was known then *(see p47)*. One room is devoted to the Águas Livres aqueduct *(see p84)* with detailed architectural plans for its construction as well as prints and watercolours of the completed aqueduct.

The earthquake theme is resumed with pictures of the city amid the devastation and various plans for its reconstruction. The museum brings you into the 20th century with a large colour poster celebrating the Revolution of 1910 and the proclamation of the new republic *(see p15)*.

Museu Nacional do Azulejo ⑩

Pelican on the Manueline portal

Dona Leonor, widow of King João II, founded the Convento da Madre de Deus in 1509. Originally built in Manueline style, the church was restored under João III using simple Renaissance designs. The striking Baroque decoration was added by João V. The convent cloisters provide a stunning setting for the National Tile Museum. Decorative panels, individual tiles and photographs trace the evolution of tile-making from its introduction by the Moors, through Spanish influence and the development of Portugal's own style up to the present day.

Panorama of Lisbon
A striking 18th-century panel, along one wall of the cloister, depicts Lisbon before the 1755 earthquake (see pp20–21). This detail shows the royal palace on Terreiro do Paço.

Hunting Scene
Artisans rather than artists began to decorate tiles in the 17th century. This detail shows a naive representation of a hunt.

KEY TO FLOORPLAN

- ☐ Moorish tiles
- ☐ 16th-century tiles
- ☐ 17th-century tiles
- ☐ 18th-century tiles
- ☐ 19th-century tiles
- ☐ 20th-century tiles
- ☐ Temporary exhibition space
- ☐ Non-exhibition space

STAR FEATURES

- ★ **Madre de Deus**
- ★ **Manueline Cloister**
- ★ **Nossa Senhora da Vida**

Level 2

Level 1

★ **Nossa Senhora da Vida**
This detail showing St John is part of a fine 16th-century maiolica altarpiece. The central panel of the huge work de-picts The Adoration of the Shepherds.

Tiles from the 17th century with oriental influences are displayed here.

Café Tiles
The walls of the restaurant are lined with 20th-century tiles showing hanging game, including wild boar and pheasant.

Level 3

VISITORS' CHECKLIST

Rua da Madre de Deus 4. 21-814 77 47. 18, 42, 104, 105. 2–6pm Tue, 10am–6pm Wed–Sun (last adm: 30 mins before closing). 1 Jan, Easter, 1 May, 25 Dec.

Moorish Tiles
Decorated with a stylized animal motif, this 15th-century tile is typical of Moorish azulejo *patterns.*

Entrance

The Renaissance cloister
is the work of Diogo de Torralva (1500–66).

★ Madre de Deus
Completed in the mid-16th century, it was not until two centuries later, under João V, that the church of Madre de Deus acquired its ornate decoration. The sumptuous Rococo altarpiece was added after the earthquake of 1755.

GALLERY GUIDE
The rooms around the central cloister are arranged chronologically with the oldest tiles on the ground floor. Access to the Madre de Deus is via level 2 of the museum. The front entrance of the church is used only during religious services.

The carved Manueline portal was recreated from a 16th-century painting.

★ Manueline Cloister
An important surviving feature of the original convent is the graceful Manueline cloister. Fine geometrical patterned tiles were added to the cloister walls in the 17th century.

Jardim Zoológico ⑬

Estrada de Benfica 158–60. ☏ 21-723 29 10. Ⓜ Jardim Zoológico.
▦ 16, 31, 55, 58 and other routes.
◯ 10am–6pm (Apr–Sep: 8pm)
daily. 🖼️ 📷

THE GARDENS of the Jardim Zoológico are as much a feature as the actual zoo. Opened in 1905, the zoo has recently been revamped and the majority of its aviaries and cages now provide more comfortable conditions for the specimens. The most bizarre feature is the dogs' cemetery, complete with tombstones and flowers. Current attractions of the zoo include a cable car which tours the park, a reptile house and dolphin shows. The area is divided into four zones and the admission charge is based on how many you visit.

Dolphins performing in the aquarium of the Jardim Zoológico

Aqueduto das Águas Livres ⑭

Best seen from Calçada da Quintinha.
◯ for guided tours by appt (Apr–Oct only), phone Museu da Água. ☏ 21-813 55 22. **Mãe d'Água das Amoreiras,** Praça das Amoreiras.
☏ 21-325 16 46. ◯ 10am–6pm Mon–Sat.

CONSIDERED THE most beautiful sight in Lisbon at the turn of the century, the Aqueduto das Águas Livres looms over the Alcântara valley to the northwest of the city. The construction of an aqueduct gave João V (see p17) an ideal opportunity to indulge his passion for grandiose build-

ing schemes, as the only area of Lisbon with fresh drinking water was the Alfama. A tax on meat, wine, olive oil and other comestibles funded the project, and although not complete until the 19th century, it was already supplying the city with water by 1748. The main pipeline measures 19 km (12 miles), but the total length, including all the secondary channels, is 58 km (36 miles). The most visible part of this imposing structure are the 35 arches that cross the Alcântara valley, the tallest of which rise to a spectacular 65 m (213 ft) above the ground.

The public walkway along the aqueduct, once a pleasant promenade, has been closed since 1853. This is partly due to Diogo Alves, the infamous robber who threw his victims over the edge. Today, it is possible to take a lively, informative guided tour over the

Alcântara arches. There are also occasional tours of the Mãe d'Água reservoir and trips to the Mãe d'Água springs, the source of the water supply. These tours can be irregular, so it is best to contact the Museu da Água (see p80) for details of the trips on offer.

At the end of the aqueduct, the **Mãe d'Água das Amoreiras** is a castle-like building which once served as a reservoir for the water supplied from the aqueduct. The original design of 1745 was by the Hungarian architect, Carlos Mardel, who worked under Pombal (see pp20–21) in the rebuilding of the Baixa. Completed in 1834, it became a popular meeting place and acquired a reputation as the rendezvous for kings and their mistresses. Today the space is used for art exhibitions, fashion shows and other events. There are great views from the roof.

Imposing arches of the Aqueduto das Águas Livres spanning the Alcântara valley

Palácio Fronteira ⑮

Largo São Domingos de Benfica 1.
C *21-778 20 23.* **M** *Jardim
Zoológico.* **▬** *72.* **R** *Benfica.*
◯ *Mon–Sat:* **✗** *Jun–Sep: 10:30, 11,
& 11:30am & noon; Oct–May: 11am
& noon.* ◯ *public hols.* ▨

THIS DELIGHTFUL country
manor house was built as
a hunting pavilion for João de
Mascarenhas, the first Marquês
de Fronteira, in 1640. Although
skyscrapers are visible in the
distance, it still occupies a
quiet spot, by the Parque
Florestal de Monsanto. Both
house and garden have *azulejo*
decoration whose subjects
include battle scenes and
trumpet-blowing monkeys.

Although the palace is still
occupied by the 12th Marquis,
some of the living rooms and
the library, as well
as the formal gar-
dens, are included
in the tour. The
Battles Room has
lively tiled panels
depicting scenes
of the War of
Restoration
(1640–1668), with
a detail of João de
Fronteira fighting
a Spanish general.
It was his loyalty
to Pedro II during
this war that earned him the
title of Marquis. Interesting
comparisons can be made between these naive 17th-century
Portuguese tiles and the Delft
ones from the same period in
the dining room, depicting
naturalistic scenes. The dining
room is also decorated with
frescoed panels and portraits
of Portuguese nobility by artists
such as Domingos António de
Sequeira (1768–1837).

The late 16th-century chapel
is the oldest part of the house.
The façade is adorned with
stones, shells, broken glass and
bits of china. These fragments
of crockery are believed to
have been used at the feast
inaugurating the palace and
then smashed to ensure no one
else could sup off the same set.
Visits to the **garden** start at the
chapel terrace, where tiled
niches are decorated with
figures personifying the arts
and mythological creatures.

**Bust of João I in gardens
of Palácio Fronteira**

Tiled terrace leading to the chapel of the Palácio Fronteira

In the formal Italian garden the
immaculate box hedges are
cut into shapes to represent
the seasons of the year. To
one end, tiled
scenes of dashing
knights on horse-
back, representing
ancestors of the
Fronteira family,
are reflected in the
waters of a large
tank. On either
side of the water,
a grand staircase
leads to a terrace
above. Here,
decorative niches
contain the busts
of Portuguese kings and colourful majolica reliefs adorn
the arcades. More blue and
white tiled scenes, realistic and
allegorical, decorate the wall
at the far end of the garden.

**Entrance to the theatre museum
in Parque do Monteiro-Mor**

Parque do Monteiro-Mor ⑯

Largo Júlio Castilho. **C** *21-759 03 18.*
▬ *1, 3, 4, 7, 36, 101, 108.* Park ◯
10am–6pm Tue–Sun. ◯ *1 Jan,
Easter, 1 May, 25 Dec.* **Museu
Nacional do Traje** ◯ *10am–6pm
Tue–Sun.* **Museu Nacional do Teatro.**
C *21-756 74 10.* ◯ *10am–6pm
Wed–Sun, 2–6pm Tue.* ▨ *combined
ticket for park & museums.* ◉ &

MONTEIRO-MOR PARK was
sold to the state in 1975
and the 18th-century palace
buildings were converted to
museums. Relatively few
visitors come here because
of the distance from the city
centre, but the gardens are
attractive and rather more
romantic than the manicured
box-hedge gardens so typical
of Lisbon. Much of the land
is wooded, though the area
around the museums has
gardens with flowering shrubs,
duck ponds and tropical trees.

The rather old-fashioned
Museu Nacional do Traje
(costume museum) has a
varied collection of costumes
worn by musicians, politicians,
poets, aristocrats and soldiers.

The **Museu Nacional do
Teatro** has two buildings, one
devoted to temporary exhibitions, the other containing a
very small permanent collection. Photographs, posters
and cartoons feature famous
20th-century Portuguese actors
and one section is devoted to
Amália Rodrigues, the famous
fado singer *(see pp142–3).*

THE LISBON COAST

PALÁCIO DE MAFRA • ERICEIRA
COLARES 92-93

SERRA DE SINTRA TOUR
MONSERRATE 94-95

SINTRA 96-101

CASCAIS • ESTORIL • ALCOCHETE
COSTA DA CAPARICA • CABO ESPICHEL 102-103

PALÁCIO DE QUELUZ 104-105

SESIMBRA • PALMELA
SERRA DA ARRÁBIDA 106-107

SETÚBAL • PENÍNSULA DE TRÓIA
ALCÁCER DO SAL 108-109

THE LISBON COAST

···

WITHIN AN HOUR'S DRIVE *northwest of Lisbon you can reach the rocky Atlantic coast, the wooded slopes of Sintra or countryside dotted with villas and royal palaces. South of Lisbon you can enjoy the sandy beaches and fishing towns along the coast or explore the lagoons of the Tagus and Sado river estuaries.*

Traders and invaders, from the Phoenicians to the Spanish, have left their mark in this region, in particular the Moors whose forts and castles, rebuilt many times over the centuries, can be found all along this coast. After Lisbon became the capital in 1256, Portuguese kings and nobles built summer palaces and villas in the countryside west of the city, particularly on the cool, green heights of the Serra de Sintra.

Across the Tagus, the less fashionable southern shore (Outra Banda) could be reached only by ferry, until the suspension bridge was built in 1966. Now, the long sandy beaches of the Costa da Caparica, the coast around the fishing town of Sesimbra and even the remote Tróia peninsula have become popular resorts during the summer months. Fortunately, large stretches of coast and unspoilt countryside are being protected as conservation areas and nature reserves.

Despite the region's rapid urbanization, small fishing and farming communities still flourish. Lively fish markets offer a huge variety of fresh fish and seafood; Palmela and the Sado region are noted for their wine; sheep still roam the unspoilt Serra da Arrábida, providing milk for Azeitão cheese; and rice is the main crop in the Sado estuary. Traditional industries also survive, such as salt panning near Alcochete and marble quarries at Pero Pinheiro.

Though the sea is cold and often rough, especially on west-facing coasts, the beaches are among the cleanest in Europe. As well as surfing, fishing and scuba diving, the region provides splendid golf courses, horse riding facilities and a motor-racing track. Arts and entertainment range from music and cinema festivals to bullfights and country fairs where regional crafts, such as hand-painted pottery, lace and baskets, are on display.

Tiled façades of houses in Alcochete, an attractive town on the Tagus estuary

◁ **Brightly painted fishing boats moored in the harbour at Sesimbra**

Exploring the Lisbon Coast

NORTH OF THE TAGUS, the beautiful hilltown of Sintra is dotted with historic palaces and surrounded by wooded hills, at times enveloped in an eerie sea mist. On the coast, cosmopolitan Cascais and the traditional fishing town of Ericeira are both excellent bases from which to explore the rocky coastline and surrounding countryside. South of the Tagus, the Serra da Arrábida and the rugged coast around Cabo Espichel can be visited from the small port of Sesimbra. Inland, the nature reserves of the Tagus and Sado estuaries offer a quiet retreat.

SIGHTS AT A GLANCE

Alcácer do Sal **18**
Alcochete **10**
Cabo Espichel **12**
Cascais **7**
Colares **3**
Costa da Caparica **11**
Ericeira **2**
Estoril **8**
LISBON pp26–85
Monserrate **5**
Palácio de Mafra **1**
*Palácio de Queluz
    pp104–5* **9**
Palmela **14**
Península de Tróia **17**
Serra da Arrábida **15**
Sesimbra **13**
Setúbal **16**
Sintra pp96–101 **6**

Tours
Serra de Sintra **4**

0 kilometres   10

0 miles   5

Torres Vedras

VILA FRANCA DO ROSÁRIO

ERICEIRA **2**

1 *PALÁCIO DE MAFRA*

MONSERRATE **5**

COLARES **3**   **6** *SINTRA*

CABO DA ROCA

SERRA DE SINTRA **4**

LOURES

PALÁCIO DE QUELUZ **9**

LISBO

8 *ESTORIL*

CASCAIS **7**

COSTA DA CAPARICA **11**

Lagoa de Albufeira

CABO ESPICHEL **12**

KEY

▬▬	Motorway
▬▬	Major road
—	Minor road
▬▬	Scenic route
～	River
- -	Ferry route
⁂	Viewpoint

Cabo da Roca on the western edge of Serra de Sintra

**Convento da Arrábida in the hills
of the Serra da Arrábida**

GETTING AROUND

Motorways give quick access from
Lisbon to Sintra, Estoril, Palmela and
Setúbal. Main roads are generally
well signposted and surfaced, though
traffic congestion can be a problem,
particularly at weekends and holidays.
Watch out for potholes on smaller
roads. Fast, frequent trains run west
from Lisbon's Cais do Sodré station to
Estoril and Cascais, and from Rossio
station to Queluz and Sintra. For trains
south to Setúbal, Alcácer do Sal and
beyond, take a ferry to Barreiro on
the southern bank of the Tagus. There
are good bus services to all parts of
the region, most of which leave from
Lisbon's Praça de Espanha.

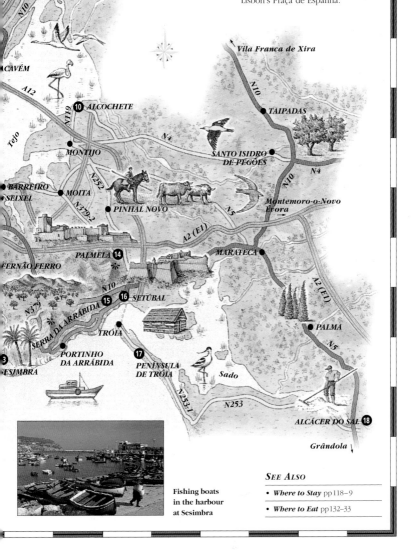

Vila Franca de Xira

Santarém

CAVÉM

A12

Tejo

N119

⑩ ALCOCHETE

TAIPADAS

N4

MONTIJO

SANTO ISIDRO
DE PEGÕES

N10

N4

BARREIRO
SEIXAL

N252

MOITA

PINHAL NOVO

A5

Montemoro-o-Novo
Évora

A2 (E1)

MARATECA

PALMELA ⑭

FERNÃO FERRO

N10

⑮ ⑯ SETÚBAL

A2 (E1)

N379

SERRA DA ARRÁBIDA

TRÓIA

PALMA

N5

SESIMBRA

PORTINHO
DA ARRÁBIDA

⑰
PENÍNSULA
DE TRÓIA

Sado

N253-1

N253

ALCÁCER DO SAL ⑱

Grândola

**Fishing boats
in the harbour
at Sesimbra**

SEE ALSO

• **Where to Stay** pp118–9

• **Where to Eat** pp132–33

The stunning library in the Palácio de Mafra, paved with chequered marble

Palácio de Mafra ❶

Terreiro de Dom João V, Mafra.
☎ 261-81 75 50. 🚌 from Lisbon.
🕐 10am–4:30pm Wed–Mon.
⬤ 1 Jan, Easter, 1 May, 25 Dec.
✝ 📷 free Sun am. 🎫 compulsory.

T HIS MASSIVE BAROQUE palace and monastery dwarfs the small town of Mafra. It was built during the reign of João V, Portugal's most extravagant monarch and began with a vow by the young king to build a new monastery and basilica, supposedly in return for an heir (but more likely, to atone for his well-known sexual excesses). Work began in 1717 on a modest project to house 13 Franciscan friars but, as the wealth began to pour into the royal coffers from Brazil, the king and his Italian-trained architect, Johann Friedrich Ludwig (1670–1752), made ever more extravagant plans. No expense was spared:

52,000 men were employed and the finished project eventually housed not 13, but 330 friars, a royal palace and one of the finest libraries in Europe, decorated with precious marble, exotic wood and countless works of art. The magnificent basilica was consecrated on the king's 41st birthday, 22 October 1730, with festivities lasting for eight days.

The palace was never a favourite with the members of the royal family, except for those who enjoyed hunting deer and wild boar in the adjoining *tapada* (hunting reserve). Most of the finest furniture and art works were taken to Brazil when the royal family escaped the French invasion in 1807. The monastery was abandoned in 1834 following the dissolution of all religious orders, and the palace itself was finally abandoned in 1910, when the last Portuguese king, Manuel II, escaped from here to the Royal Yacht anchored off Ericeira.

Allow at least an hour for the lengthy tour which starts in the rooms of the monastery, through the pharmacy, with

fine old medicine jars and some alarming medical instruments, to the hospital, where 16 patients in private cubicles could see and hear mass in the adjoining chapel without leaving their beds.

Upstairs, the sumptuous palace state rooms extend across the whole of the monumental west façade, with the King's apartments at one end and the Queen's apartments at the other, a staggering 232 m (760 ft) apart. Halfway between the two, the long, imposing façade is relieved by the twin towers of the domed basilica. The interior of the church is decorated in contrasting colours of marble and furnished with six early 19th-century organs. Fine Baroque sculptures, executed by members of the Mafra School of Sculpture, adorn the atrium of the basilica. Begun by José I in 1754, many renowned Portuguese and foreign artists trained in the school under the directorship of the Italian sculptor Alessandro Giusti (1715–99). Further on, the Sala da Caça has a grotesque collection of hunting trophies and boars' heads.

Mafra's greatest treasure, however, is its magnificent library, which has a patterned marble floor, Rococo-style wooden bookcases, and a collection of over 40,000 books in gold embossed leather bindings, which includes a prized first edition of *Os Lusíadas* (1572) by the celebrated Portuguese poet, Luís de Camões (1524–80).

Statue of St Bruno in the atrium of Mafra's basilica

ENVIRONS: Once a week, on Thursday mornings, the small country town of **Malveira**, 10 km (6 miles) east of Mafra, has the region's biggest market, selling clothes and household goods as well as food.

At the village of **Sobreiro**, 6 km (4 miles) west of Mafra, Zé Franco's model village is complete with houses, farms, a waterfall and working windmill, all in minute detail.

The king's bedroom in the Royal Palace

Tractor pulling a fishing boat out of the sea at Ericeira

Ericeira ❷

🏃 4,500. 🚌 🛈 Rua Mendes Leal (261-863 122). 🎪 Apr–Oct daily.

Ericeira is an old fishing village which keeps its traditions despite an ever-increasing influx of summer visitors, from Lisbon and abroad, who enjoy the bracing climate, clean, sandy beaches and fresh seafood. In July and August, when the population leaps to 30,000, pavement cafés, restaurants and bars around the tree-lined Praça da República are buzzing late into the night. Red flags warn when swimming is dangerous: alternative attractions include a crazy golf course in Santa Marta park and an interesting local history museum, the **Museu da Ericeira**, exhibiting model boats and traditional regional fishing equipment.

The unspoilt old town, a maze of whitewashed houses and narrow, cobbled streets, is perched high above the ocean. From Largo das Ribas, at the top of a 30-m (100-ft) stone-faced cliff, there is a bird's-eye view over the busy fishing harbour below, where tractors have replaced the oxen that once hauled the boats out of reach of the tide. On 16 August, the annual fishermen's festival is celebrated with a candlelit procession to the harbour at the foot of the cliffs for the blessing of the boats.

On 5 October 1910, Manuel II, the last king of Portugal (see p17), finally sailed into exile from Ericeira as the Republic was declared in Lisbon; a tiled panel in the fishermen's chapel of Santo António above the harbour records the event. The banished king settled in Twickenham, southwest London, where he died in 1932.

🏛 Museu da Ericeira

Largo da Misericórdia. 📞 261-864 079. ⏱ Jun–Sep: Tue–Sun; Oct–May: Mon–Sat (pm only). 🔴 public hols. 🎫

Colares ❸

🏃 6,500. 🚌 🛈 Praça da República 23, Sintra, 21-923 11 57.

On the lower slopes of the Serra de Sintra, this lovely village faces towards the sea over a green valley, the Várzea de Colares. A leafy avenue winds its way up to the village, lined with pine and chestnut trees. Small quantities of famous Colares wine are still made, but current vintages lack the character and ageing potential of classic Colares and growers face a financial struggle to survive. Their hardy old vines grow in a sandy soil, with their roots set deep below in clay; these were among the few vines in Europe to survive the disastrous phylloxera epidemic brought from America in the late 19th century with the first viticultural exchanges. The insect, which destroyed vineyards all over Europe by eating the tender roots, could not penetrate the dense sandy soil of the Atlantic coast. Wine can be sampled at the Adega Regional de Colares on Alameda de Coronel Linhares de Lima.

Environs: There are several popular beach resorts west of Colares. From the village of Banzão you can ride 3 km (2 miles) to **Praia das Maçãs** on the old tramway, which opened in 1910 and still runs from 1 July to 30 September. Just north of Praia das Maçãs is the picturesque village of **Azenhas do Mar**, clinging to the cliffs; to the south is the larger resort of **Praia Grande**. Both have natural pools in the rocks, which are filled by sea-water at high tide and are now closed to swimmers. The unspoilt **Praia da Adraga**, 1 km (half a mile) further south, has a delightful beach café and restaurant. In the evenings and off-season, fishermen catch bass, bream and flat fish that swim in on the high tide.

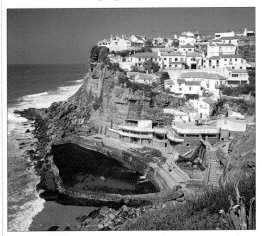

Natural rock pool at Azenhas do Mar, near Colares

Serra de Sintra Tour ❹

Atlantic coastline seen from Peninha

THIS ROUND TRIP from Sintra follows a dramatic route over the top of the wooded Serra. The first part is a challenging drive with hazardous hairpin bends on steep, narrow roads that are at times poorly surfaced. It passes through dense forest and a surreal landscape of giant moss-covered boulders, with breathtaking views over the Atlantic coast, the Tagus estuary and beyond.

Tiled angels, Peninha chapel

After dropping down to the rugged, windswept coast, the route returns along small country roads passing through hill villages and large estates on the cool, green northern slopes of the Serra de Sintra.

Colares ⑥
The village of Colares rests on the lower slopes of the wooded Serra, surrounded by gardens and vineyards *(see p93).*

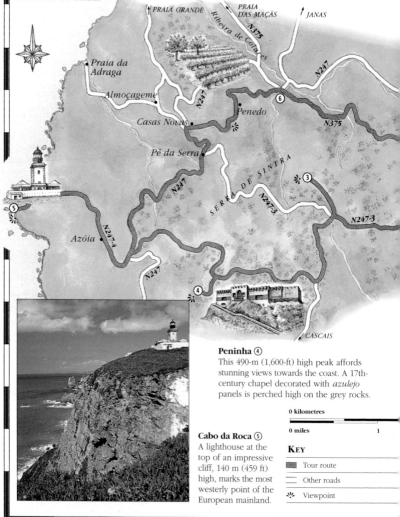

Peninha ④
This 490-m (1,600-ft) high peak affords stunning views towards the coast. A 17th-century chapel decorated with *azulejo* panels is perched high on the grey rocks.

Cabo da Roca ⑤
A lighthouse at the top of an impressive cliff, 140 m (459 ft) high, marks the most westerly point of the European mainland.

0 kilometres

0 miles   1

KEY
▓▓ Tour route
══ Other roads
🔆 Viewpoint

Seteais ⑧

The elegant, pink palace, now a luxury hotel and restaurant *(see p113 & p119)*, was built in the 18th century for the Dutch Consul, Daniel Gildemeester.

Monserrate ⑦

The cool, overgrown forest park and elaborate 19th-century palace epitomize the romanticism of Sintra.

Sintra ①

From the centre of the old town the road winds steeply upwards past magnificent *quintas* (country estates) hidden among the trees.

Palácio da Pena

Parque da Pena ②

This huge, exotic park can be explored on foot *(see p97)*. It is also possible to drive as far as Cruz Alta, the highest point of the Serra de Sintra.

Convento dos Capuchos ③

Two huge boulders guard the entrance to this remote Franciscan monastery, founded in 1560, where the monks lived in tiny rock-hewn cells lined with cork. There are stunning views of the coast from the hill above this austere, rocky hideaway.

Palace of Monserrate

Monserrate ❺

Estrada de Monserrate. ☎ 21-923 73 00. 🚌 to Sintra then taxi. ⏲ Apr–Oct: 9am–7pm daily; Nov–Mar: 9am–6pm daily. 🎫 🅦 www.parquesdesintra.pt

THE WILD, ROMANTIC garden of this once magnificent estate is a jungle of exotic trees and flowering shrubs. Among the sub-tropical foliage and valley of tree ferns, the visitor will come across a waterfall, a small lake and a chapel, built as a ruin, tangled in the roots of a giant *Ficus* tree. Its history dates back to the Moors, but it takes its name from a small 16th-century chapel dedicated to Our Lady of Montserrat in Catalonia, Spain. The gardens were landscaped in the late 18th century by a wealthy young Englishman, the eccentric aesthete William Beckford. They were later immortalized by Lord Byron in *Childe Harold's Pilgrimage* (1812).

In 1856, the abandoned estate was bought by another Englishman, Sir Francis Cook, who built a fantastic Moorish-style palace (which now stands eerily empty) and transformed the gardens with a large sweeping lawn, camellias and sub-tropical trees from all over the world. These include the giant *Metrosideros* (Australian Christmas tree, covered in a blaze of red flowers in July), the native *Arbutus* (known as the strawberry tree because of its juicy red berries), from which the *medronho* firewater drink is distilled, and cork oak, with small ferns growing on its bark.

The Friends of Monserrate is an organization that has been set up to help restore the sadly neglected house and gardens to their former glory.

Sintra ❻

Sintra's stunning setting on the north slopes of the granite Serra, among wooded ravines and fresh water springs, made it a favourite summer retreat for the kings of Portugal. The tall conical chimneys of the Palácio Nacional de Sintra (see pp98–9) and the fabulous Palácio da Pena (see pp100–101), eerily impressive on its peak when the Serra is blanketed in mist, are unmistakable landmarks.

Today, the town (recognized as a UNESCO World Heritage site in 1995) draws thousands of visitors all through the year. Even so, there are many quiet walks in the wooded hills around the town, especially beautiful in the long, cool evenings of the summer months.

Fonte Mourisca on Volta do Duche

Exploring Sintra

Present-day Sintra is in three parts, Sintra Vila, Estefânia and São Pedro, joined by a confusing maze of winding roads scattered over the surrounding hills. In the pretty cobbled streets of the old town, Sintra Vila, which is centred on the **Palácio Nacional de Sintra**, are the museums and beautifully tiled **post office**. The curving **Volta do Duche** leads from the old town, past the lush **Parque da Liberdade**, north to the Estefânia district and the striking Neo-Gothic **Câmara Municipal** (Town Hall). To the south and east, the hilly village of São Pedro spreads over the slopes of the Serra. The fortnightly Sunday **market** here extends across the broad market square and along Rua 1º de Dezembro.

Exploring Sintra on foot involves a lot of walking and climbing up and down its steep hills. For a more leisurely tour, take one of the horse and carriage rides around the town. The **Miradouro da Vigia** in São Pedro offers impressive views, as does the cosy **Casa de Sapa** café, where you can sample *queijadas*, the local sweet speciality (see p135).

The many fountains dotted around the town are used by locals for their fresh spring drinking water. Two of the most striking are the tiled **Fonte Mourisca** (Arab Fountain), named for its Neo-Moorish decoration, and Fonte da Sabuga, where the water spouts from a pair of breasts.

🏛 Museu do Brinquedo

Rua Visconde de Monserrate. 📞 21-924 21 71. ◯ Tue–Sun. ▨ ♿

This small museum has a fine international collection of toys, ranging from model planes, cars and trains, including 1930s Hornby sets, to battalions of toy soldiers, dolls and dolls' houses, tin toys and curious clockwork models of cars and soldiers. The museum is fun for a rainy day, particularly for nostalgic adults.

Toy Alfa Romeo, Museu do Brinquedo

🏛 Museu de Arte Moderna

Avenida Heliodoro Salgado. 📞 21-924 81 70. ◯ Tue–Sun. ▨ ♿ 🚻 ▣

The Berardo Collection, accumulated by entrepreneur Joe Berardo, is regarded as one of the world's best private collections of 20th-century art and includes such big names as René Magritte, Jackson Pollock, Francis Bacon and Andy Warhol. Located at the north end of Sintra, it is a pedagogic exposé of movements and styles, particularly those of the post-war era.

🏯 Quinta da Regaleira

Rua Barbosa du Bocage. 📞 21-910 66 50. ◯ daily. 🗓 mandatory; call to book. ▨ 🚻 ▣

Built during the 1890s, this neo-Manueline palace and extensive gardens are a feast of historical and religious references, occult symbols and mystery. The obsession of the eccentric millionaire António Augusto Carvalho Monteiro, they are an absolute must for anyone interested in freemasonry, alchemy and other esoterica.

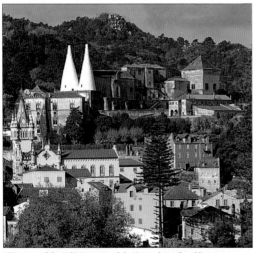

Chimneys of the Palácio Nacional de Sintra above the old town

♠ Castelo dos Mouros

Estrada da Pena. (21-923 73 00.
○ daily. ● 1 Jan, 25 Dec.
Standing above the old town,
like a sentinel, the ramparts
of the 8th-century Moorish
castle, conquered by Afonso
Henriques in 1147, snake
over the top of the Serra. On
a fine day, there are breathtaking views from the castle
walls over the old town to
Palácio da Pena, on a neighbouring peak, and far along

the coast. Hidden inside the
walls are a ruined chapel and
an ancient Moorish cistern. For
walkers, a steep footpath
threads up through wooded
slopes from the 12th-century
church of **Santa Maria**. Follow
the signs to a dark green swing
gate where the footpath begins.
The monogram "DFII" carved
on the gateway is a reminder
that the castle walls were
restored by Fernando II (see
p101) in the 19th century.

♣ Parque da Pena

Estrada da Pena. (21-923 73 00.
○ daily. ● 1 Jan, 25 Dec. ♿
A huge park surrounds the
Palácio da Pena where foot-
paths wind among a lush
vegetation of exotic trees and
shrubs. Hidden among the
foliage are gazebos, follies
and fountains, and a Romantic
chalet built by Fernando II for
his mistress in 1869. Cruz Alta,
the highest point of the Serra
at 530 m (1,740 ft), commands
spectacular views of the Serra
and surrounding plain. On a
nearby crag stands the statue
of Baron Von Eschwege, architect of the palace and park.

Battlements of the Castelo dos Mouros perched on the slopes of the Serra

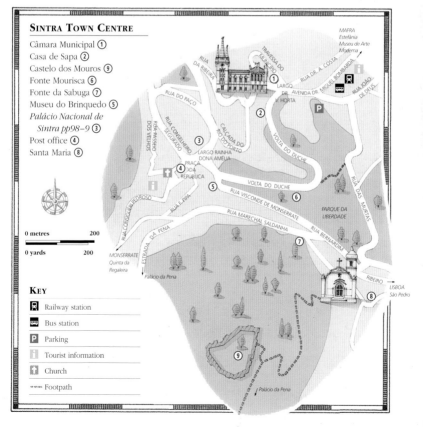

SINTRA TOWN CENTRE

Câmara Municipal ①
Casa de Sapa ②
Castelo dos Mouros ⑨
Fonte Mourisca ⑥
Fonte da Sabuga ⑦
Museu do Brinquedo ⑤
*Palácio Nacional de
   Sintra pp98–9* ③
Post office ④
Santa Maria ⑧

0 metres   200
0 yards   200

MONSERRATE
Quinta da
Regaleira

KEY

🚉 Railway station
🚌 Bus station
P Parking
🛈 Tourist information
✝ Church
▪▪▪ Footpath

Palácio Nacional de Sintra

Swan panel, Sala dos Cisnes

AT THE HEART of the old town of Sintra (Sintra Vila), a pair of strange conical chimneys rises high above the Royal Palace. The main part of the palace, including the central block with its plain Gothic façade and the large kitchens beneath the chimneys, was built by João I in the late 14th century, on a site once occupied by the Moorish rulers. The Paço Real, as it is also known, became the favourite summer retreat for the court, and continued as a residence for Portuguese royalty until the 1880s. Additions to the building by the wealthy Manuel I, in the early 16th century, echo the Moorish style. Gradual rebuilding of the palace has resulted in a fascinating amalgamation of various different styles.

★ Sala das Pegas
It is said that King João I had the ceiling panels painted as a rebuke to the court women for indulging in idle gossip like chattering magpies (pegas).

The Torre da Meca has dovecotes below the cornice decorated with armillary spheres and nautical rope.

The Sala das Galés (galleons) houses temporary exhibitions.

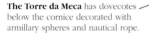

★ Sala dos Brasões
The domed ceiling of this majestic room is decorated with stags holding the coats of arms (brasões) of 74 noble Portuguese families. The lower walls are lined with 18th-century Delft-like tiled panels.

Jardim da Preta, a walled garden

Sala de Dom Sebastião, the audience chamber

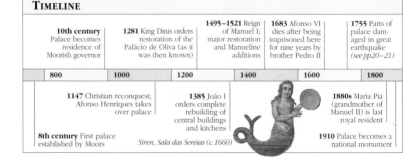

TIMELINE

	1281 King Dinis orders restoration of the Palácio de Oliva (as it was then known)	**1495–1521** Reign of Manuel I; major restoration and Manueline additions	**1683** Afonso VI dies after being imprisoned here for nine years by brother Pedro II		**1755** Parts of palace damaged in great earthquake (see pp20–21)
10th century Palace becomes residence of Moorish governor					

800	1000	1200	1400	1600	1800

1147 Christian reconquest; Afonso Henriques takes over palace	**1385** João I orders complete rebuilding of central buildings and kitchens		**1880s** Maria Pia (grandmother of Manuel II) is last royal resident
8th century First palace established by Moors	*Siren, Sala das Sereias (c.1660)*		**1910** Palace becomes a national monument

★ Sala dos Cisnes
The magnificent ceiling of the former banqueting hall, painted in the 17th century, is divided into octagonal panels decorated with swans (cisnes).

The Sala dos Árabes is decorated with fine *azulejos*.

Sala das Sereias
Intricate Arabesque designs on 16th-century tiles frame the door of the Room of the Sirens.

VISITORS' CHECKLIST

Largo Rainha Dona Amélia.
🕿 21-910 68 40. ⏱ 10am–5:30pm Thu–Tue (last adm: 30 mins before closing). ● 1 Jan, Easter, 1 May, 29 Jun, 25 Dec.
🎫 💺 (free 10am–1pm Sun).

The kitchens, beneath the huge conical chimneys, have spits and utensils once used for preparing royal banquets.

Entrance

Sala dos Archeiros, the entrance hall

Manuel I added the *ajimece* windows, a distinctive Moorish design with a slender column dividing two arches.

Chapel
Symmetrical Moorish patterns decorate the original 14th-century chestnut and oak ceiling and the mosaic floor of the private chapel.

STAR FEATURES

★ **Sala dos Brasões**

★ **Sala dos Cisnes**

★ **Sala das Pegas**

Sintra: Palácio da Pena

Triton Arch

ON THE HIGHEST PEAKS of the Serra de Sintra stands the spectacular palace of Pena, an eclectic medley of architectural styles built in the 19th century for the husband of the young Queen Maria II, Ferdinand Saxe-Coburg-Gotha. It stands over the ruins of a Hieronymite monastery founded here in the 15th century on the site of the chapel of Nossa Senhora da Pena. Ferdinand appointed a German architect, Baron Von Eschwege, to build his summer palace filled with oddities from all over the world and surrounded by a park. With the declaration of the Republic in 1910, the palace became a museum, preserved as it was when the royal family lived here. Allow at least an hour and a half to visit this enchanting place.

Entrance Arch
A studded archway with crenellated turrets greets the visitor at the entrance to the palace. The palace buildings are painted the original daffodil yellow and strawberry pink.

Manuel II's Bedroom
The oval-shaped room is decorated with bright red walls and stuccoed ceiling. A portrait of Manuel II, the last king of Portugal, hangs above the fireplace.

In the kitchen the copper pots and utensils still hang around the iron stove. The dinner service bears the coat of arms of Ferdinand II.

★ Ballroom
The spacious ball-room is sumptuously furnished with German stained-glass windows, precious Oriental porcelain and four lifesize turbaned torch-bearers holding giant candelabra.

★ Arab Room
Marvellous trompe-l'oeil frescoes cover the walls and ceiling of the Arab Room, one of the loveliest in the palace. The Orient was a great inspiration to Romanticism.

VISITORS' CHECKLIST

Estrada da Pena, 5 km (3 mile) S of Sintra. **(** 21-910 53 40. **🚌** from Avenida Dr Miguel Bombarda, Sintra. **◯** 10am–5pm Tue–Sun (6pm in summer, last adm: 30 mins before closing). **●** 1 Jan, Easter, 1 May, 29 Jun, 25 Dec. **📷** (except 10am–1pm Sun).

★ Chapel Altarpiece
The impressive 16th-century alabaster and marble retable was sculpted by Nicolau Chanterène. Each niche portrays a scene of the life of Christ, from the manger to the Ascension.

The Triton Arch is encrusted with Neo-Manueline decoration and is guarded by a fierce sea monster.

The cloister, decorated with colourful patterned tiles, is part of the original monastery buildings.

Entrance

FERDINAND: KING CONSORT

Ferdinand was known in Portugal as Dom Fernando II, the "artist" king. Like his cousin Prince Albert, who married the English Queen Victoria, he loved art, nature and the new inventions of the time. He was himself a watercolour painter. Ferdinand enthusiastically adopted his new country and devoted his life to patronizing the arts. In 1869, 16 years after the death of Maria II, Ferdinand married his mistress, the opera singer Countess Edla. His lifelong dream of building the extravagant palace at Pena was completed in 1885, the year he died.

STAR FEATURES

★ Arab Room

★ Ballroom

★ Chapel Altarpiece

Outdoor café in the popular holiday resort of Cascais

Cascais ❼

🏃 30,000. 🚉 🚌 🛈 Rua Visconde da Luz 14 (21-486 82 04). 🚢 1st and 3rd Sun of the month.

Having been a holiday resort for well over a century, Cascais possesses a certain illustriousness that younger resorts lack. Its history is most clearly visible in the villas along the coast, built as summer residences by wealthy *Lisboetas* during the late 19th century, after King Luís I had moved his summer activities to the 17th-century fortress here. The military importance of Cascais, now waned, is much older as it sits on the north bank of the mouth of the Tagus.

The sandy, sheltered bay around which the modern suburb has sprawled was a fishing harbour in prehistoric times. Fishing still goes on, and was recently given a municipal boost with the

decision to build a new quay for the landing and initial auctioning of the fishermen's catch. But Cascais today is first of all a favoured suburb of Lisbon, a place of apartments with a sea view and pine-studded plots by golf courses. It may sometimes seem more defined by its ceaseless construction boom than by any historic or even touristic qualities, but the beautiful, windswept coastline beyond the town has been left relatively undeveloped.

The Museu do Conde de Castro Guimarães is perhaps the best place to get a taste of Cascais as it was just over a century ago. A castle-like villa on a small creek by a headland, its grounds are today part of a park. The house and its contents were bequeathed to the municipality.

Across the road from the museum is the new marina, one of the most emblematic new developments in Cascais. With its small shopping centre, restaurants and cafés it is becoming a weekend magnet for today's car-borne Cascais residents and tourists.

🏛 Museu do Conde de Castro Guimarães

Avenida Rei Humberto de Itália. 📞 21-482 54 07. **Museum** ⏲ 10am–5pm Tue–Sun. 📷 **Library** Casa da Horta de Santa Clara. ⏲ 10am–7pm Mon–Sat. ⬤ public hols.

ENVIRONS: At **Boca do Inferno** (Mouth of Hell), about 3 km (2 miles) west on the coast road, the sea rushes into clefts and caves in the rocks making an ominous booming sound and sending up spectacular spray in rough weather. The place is almost obscured by a roadside market and cafés but a small platform gives a good view of the rocky arch with the sea roaring in below.

The magnificent sandy beach of **Guincho**, 10 km (6 miles) further west, is backed by sand dunes with clumps of umbrella pines, and a new cycle path. A small fort (now a luxury hotel) stands perched on the rocks above the sea. Atlantic breakers rolling in make this a paradise for experienced windsurfers and surfers, though beware of the strong currents.

Spectacular view of the weatherbeaten coastline at Boca do Inferno, near Cascais

Estoril ❽

🏃 40,000. 🚉 🚌 🛈 Arcadas do Parque (21-466 38 13).

Despite once being the haunt of exiled royalty and obscure nobility fleeing European republicanism, the lovely resort town of Estoril does not rest on its historical laurels. Estoril is a tourist and business resort, and a place for comfortable retirement. As such, it relies equally on its historical reputation and on the natural attractiveness it has always possessed. There are also a number of good golf courses.

What separates Estoril from Cascais, besides a pleasant beach promenade of 3 km (2 miles) and a mansion covered ridge known as Monte Estoril, is its sense of place. The heart of Estoril is immediately accessible from the train station. To the west of the station lies a relaxed Riviera-

Sandy beach and promenade along the bay of Estoril

like beach. To its east is a palm-lined park flanked by grand buildings, stretches up past fountains to what is said to be Europe's biggest casino. Dwarfing the casino is the Estoril Congress Centre, a vast multipurpose edifice that speaks confidently of Estoril's latest role.

Palácio de Queluz ❾

See pp104–5.

Alcochete ❿

🏠 *13,000.* 🚌 ℹ️ *Largo da Misericórdia (21-234 26 31).*

THIS DELIGHTFUL old town overlooks the wide Tagus estuary from the southern shore. Salt has long been one of the main industries here, and saltpans can still be seen to the north and south of the town, while in the town centre a large statue of a muscular salt worker has the inscription: "Do Sal a Revolta e a Esperança" (From Salt to Rebellion and Hope). On the outskirts of town, is a statue of Manuel I *(see p16),* who was born here on 1 June 1469 and granted the town a Royal Charter in 1515.

Statue of a salt worker in Alcochete (1985)

ENVIRONS: The **Reserva Natural do Estuário do Tejo** covers a vast area of estuary water, salt marshes and small islands around Alcochete and is a very important breeding ground for water birds. Particularly interesting are the flocks of flamingos that gather here during the autumn and spring migration, en route from colonies such as the Camargue in France and Fuente de Piedra in Spain. Ask at the tourist office about boat trips to see the wildlife of the estuary, which includes wild bulls and horses.

🦋 **Reserva Natural do Estuário do Tejo**
Avenida dos Combatentes da Grande Guerra 1. 🅒 *21-234 17 42.*

Pilgrims' lodgings, Cabo Espichel

Costa da Caparica ⓫

🏠 *40,000.* 🚍 *to Cacilhas or Trafaria then bus.* 🚉 *to Pragal then bus.* ℹ️ *Av. da República 18 (21-290 00 71).*

LONG SANDY beaches, backed by sand dunes, have made this a popular holiday resort for Lisboetas who come here to swim, sunbathe and enjoy the seafood restaurants and beach cafés. A railway, with open carriages, runs for 10 km (6 miles) along the coast during the summer months. The first beaches reached from the town are popular with families with children, while the furthest beaches suit those seeking quiet isolation. Further south, sheltered by pine forests, **Lagoa do Albufeira** is a peaceful windsurfing centre and camp site.

Cabo Espichel ⓬

🚍 *from Sesimbra.*

SHEER CLIFFS DROP straight into the sea at this windswept promontory where the land ends dramatically. The Romans named it Promontorium Barbaricum, alluding to its dangerous location, and a lighthouse warns sailors of the treacherous rocks below. Stunning views of the ocean and the coast can be enjoyed from this bleak outcrop of land but beware of the strong gusts of wind on the cliff edge.

In this desolate setting stands the impressive **Santuário de Nossa Senhora do Cabo**, a late 17th-century church with its back to the sea. On either side of the church a long line of pilgrims' lodgings facing inwards form an open courtyard. Baroque paintings, ex votos and a frescoed ceiling decorate the interior of the church. There are plans to fully restore the building and open it as a hotel. Nearby, a domed chapel has tiled blue and white *azulejo* panels depicting fishing scenes. The site became a popular place of pilgrimage in the 13th century when a local man had a vision of the Madonna rising from the sea on a mule. Legend has it that the tracks of the mule can be seen embedded in the rock. The large footprints, on Praia dos Lagosteiros below the church, are actually believed to be fossilized dinosaur tracks.

Spring flowers by the saltpans of the Tagus estuary near Alcochete

Palácio de Queluz 🄈

A sphinx in the gardens

IN 1747, PEDRO, younger son of João V,
commissioned Mateus Vicente to trans-
form his 17th-century hunting lodge into a
Rococo summer palace. The central section,
including a music room and chapel, was
built, but after Pedro's marriage in 1760 to
the future Maria I, the palace was again
extended. The French architect, Jean-
Baptiste Robillion, added the sumptuous
Robillion Pavilion and gardens, cleared
space for the Throne Room and redesigned the Music
Room. During Maria's reign, the royal family kept a
menagerie and went boating on the *azulejo*-lined canal.

Corridor of the Sleeves
Painted azulejo *panels (1784)
representing the continents and
the seasons, as well as hunting
scenes, line the walls of the bright
Corredor das Mangas (sleeves).*

Neptune's Fountain

★ **Sala dos Embaixadores**
*Built by Robillion, this stately
room was used for diplo-
matic audiences as
well as concerts.
The* trompe l'oeil
*ceiling shows the
royal family
attending a
concert.*

The Lion Staircase is an
impressive and graceful
link from the lower
gardens to the palace.

STAR FEATURES

★ **Throne Room**

★ **Sala dos
  Embaixadores**

★ **Palace Gardens**

To canal

Lion
Fountain

**The Robillion
Pavilion** displays the
flamboyance of the French
architect's Rococo style.

Don Quixote Chamber
*The royal bedroom, where Pedro IV
(see p17) was born and died, has a
domed ceiling and magnificent floor
decoration in exotic woods, giving the
square room a circular appearance.
Painted scenes by Manuel de Costa
(1784) tell the story of* Don Quixote.

Music Room

Operas and concerts were performed here by Maria I's orchestra, "the best in Europe" according to English traveller, William Beckford. A portrait of the queen hangs above the grand piano.

VISITORS' CHECKLIST

Largo do Palácio, Queluz.
📞 21-435 00 39. 🚉 Queluz-Belas or Queluz-Massama. 🚌 from Lisbon (Colégio Militar).
🕐 10am–5pm Wed–Mon.
⬤ 29 Nov, Easter, 1 May, 25 Dec, 1 Jan. 🎫 (free 10am–noon Sun) 🅿 🛗 🍴 Cozinha Velha (see p133).

Chapel

The royal family's living rooms and bedrooms opened out onto the Malta Gardens.

★ Throne Room

The elegant state room (1770) was the scene of splendid balls and banquets. The gilded statues of Atlas are by Silvestre Faria Lobo.

Entrance

Malta Gardens

The Hanging Gardens, designed by Robillion, were built over arches, raising the ground in front of the palace above the surrounding gardens.

MARIA I (1734–1816)

Maria, the eldest daughter of José I, lived at the palace in Queluz after her marriage to her uncle, Pedro, in 1760. Serious and devout, she conscientiously filled her role as queen, but suffered increasingly from bouts of melancholia. When her son José died from smallpox in 1788, she went hopelessly mad. Visitors to Queluz were dismayed by her agonizing shrieks as she suffered visions and hallucinations. After the French invasion of 1807, her younger son João (declared regent in 1792) took his mad mother to Brazil.

★ Palace Gardens

The formal gardens, adorned with statues, fountains and topiary, were often used for entertaining. Concerts performed in the Music Room would spill out into the Malta Gardens.

Sesimbra ⑬

🏃 *27,000.* 🚌 ℹ️ *Largo da Marinha 26–7 (21-223 57 43).* 🔼 *1st & 3rd Fri of month.*

A STEEP NARROW ROAD leads down to this busy fishing village in a sheltered south-facing bay. Protected from north winds by the slopes of the Serra da Arrábida, the town has become a popular holiday resort with Lisboetas. It was occupied by the Romans and later the Moors until King Sancho II *(see p16)* conquered its heavily defended forts in 1236. The old town is a maze of steep narrow streets, with the **Santiago Fort** (now a customs post) in the centre overlooking the sea. From the terrace, which is open to the public during the day, there are views over the town, the Atlantic and the wide sandy beach that stretches out on either side. Sesimbra is fast developing as a resort, with holiday flats mushrooming on the surrounding hillsides and plentiful pavement cafés and bars are always busy on sunny days, even in winter.

The fishing fleet of brightly painted boats is moored in the **Porto do Abrigo** to the west of the main town. The harbour is reached by taking Avenida dos Náufragos, a sweeping

Colourful fishing boats in the harbour at Sesimbra

promenade that follows the beach out of town. On the large trawlers *(traineiras)*, the catch is mainly sardines, sea bream, whiting and swordfish; on the smaller boats, octopus and squid. In the late after-noon, when the fishing boats return from a day at sea, a colourful, noisy fish auction takes place on the quayside. The day's catch can be tasted in the town's excellent fish restaurants along the shore.

High above the town is the **Moorish castle**, greatly restored in the 18th century when a church and small flower-filled cemetery were added inside the walls. There are wonderful views from the ramparts, especially at sunset.

Palmela ⑭

🏃 *14,000.* 🚌 🚉 ℹ️ *Castelo de Palmela (21-233 21 22).* 🔼 *every other Tue.*

T HE FORMIDABLE castle at Palmela stands over the small hilltown, high on a north-eastern spur of the wooded Serra da Arrábida. Its strategic position dominates the plain for miles around, especially when floodlit at night. Heavily defended by the Moors, it was finally conquered in the 12th century and given by Sancho I *(see p16)* to the Knights of the Order of Santiago. In 1423, João I transformed the castle into a monastery for the Order, which has now been restored and converted into a splendid *pousada (see p119)*, with a restaurant in the monks' refectory and a swimming pool for residents, hidden inside the castle walls. From the castle terraces, and espe-cially from the top of the 14th-century keep, there are fantastic views all around, over the Serra da Arrábida to the south and on a clear day across the Tagus to Lisbon. In the town square below, the church of **São Pedro** contains 18th-century tiles of scenes from the life of St Peter.

The annual wine festival, the Festa das Vindimas, is held on the first weekend of September in front of the 17th-century Paços do Concelho (town hall). Traditionally dressed villagers press the wine barefoot and on the final day of celebrations there is a spectacular firework display from the castle walls.

The castle at Palmela with views over the wooded Serra da Arrábida

Serra da Arrábida

🚌 Setúbal. ℹ️ *Parque Natural da Arrábida, Praça da República, Setúbal (265-54 11 40).*

THE PARQUE NATURAL da Arrábida covers the small range of limestone mountains which stretches east-west along the coast between Sesimbra and Setúbal. It was established to protect the wild, beautiful landscape and rich variety of birds and wildlife, including eagles, wildcats and badgers.

The name Arrábida is from Arabic meaning a place of prayer, and the wooded hill-sides are indeed a peaceful, secluded retreat. The sheltered, south-facing slopes are thickly covered with aromatic and evergreen shrubs and trees such as pine and cypress, more typical of the Mediterranean. Vineyards also thrive on the sheltered slopes and the town of **Vila Nogueira de Azeitão** is known for its wine, especially the Moscatel de Setúbal.

The **Estrada de Escarpa** (the N379-1) snakes across the top of the ridge and affords astounding views. A narrow road winds down to **Portinho da Arrábida**, a sheltered cove with a beach of fine white sand and crystal clear sea, popular with underwater fishermen. The sandy beaches of **Galapos** and **Figueirinha** are a little further east along the coast road towards Setúbal. Just east of Sesimbra, the Serra da Arrábida drops to the sea in the sheer 380-m (1,250-ft) cliffs of Risco, the highest in mainland Portugal.

Portinho da Arrábida on the dramatic coastline of the Serra da Arrábida

🔒 Convento da Arrábida

Serra da Arrábida. 📞 *21-218 05 20.* ⏰ *by appt only, via Fundação Oriente (phone 21-352 70 02).* ♿

Half-hidden among the trees on the southern slopes of the Serra, this large 16th-century building was once a Franciscan monastery. The five round towers were probably used for solitary meditation.

🏛 Museu Oceanográfico

Fortaleza de Santa Maria, Portinho da Arrábida. 📞 *265-54 11 40.* ⏰ *9am–noon, 2–5pm Tue–Fri.* ♿

This small fort, just above Portinho da Arrábida, was built by Pedro, the Prince Regent, in 1676 to protect local communities from attacks by Moorish pirates. It now houses a Sea Museum and Marine Biology Centre where visitors can see aquaria containing many local sea creatures, including sea urchins, octopus and starfish.

🍷 José Maria da Fonseca

Rua José Augusto Coelho 11, Vila Nogueira de Azeitão. 📞 *21-219 89 40.* 📠 *21-219 89 42.* ⏰ *9am–noon, 2:15–4:15pm Mon–Fri; 10am–12:15pm, 2:15–4:30pm Sat.* ⬤ *Dec 25–Jan 1.* ♿ 🔲 🔒

The Fonseca winery produces quality table wines and is famous for its fragrant dessert wine, Moscatel de Setúbal *(see p125)*. Tours of the winery explain the process of making moscatel and a visit to a series of old cellars containing huge oak and chestnut vats. Tours last about 45 minutes and include a wine tasting.

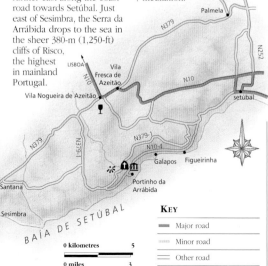

LISBOA

Palmela

N379

LISBOA

Vila Fresca de Azeitão

N10

N10

N252

Setúbal

Vila Nogueira de Azeitão

N379

N379-1

N10-4

Galapos   Figueirinha

Santana

Portinho da Arrábida

Sesimbra

BAÍA DE SETÚBAL

KEY

▬▬▬	Major road
▭▭▭	Minor road
══	Other road

0 kilometres   5

0 miles   3

Manueline interior of Igreja de Jesus, Setúbal

Setúbal ⓰

🏠 120,000. 🚆 🚌 ⛴
ℹ Casa do Corpo Santo, Praça do Quebedo (265-53 42 22).

Aᴸᴛʜᴏᴜɢʜ ᴛʜɪs is an important industrial town, and the third largest port in Portugal (after Lisbon and Oporto), Setúbal can be used to explore the area. To the south of the central gardens and fountains are the fishing harbour, marina and ferry port, and a lively covered market. North of the gardens is the old town, with attractive pedestrian streets and squares full of shops and cafés.

The 16th-century **cathedral**, dedicated to Santa Maria da Graça, has glorious tiled panels dating from the 18th century, and gilded altar decoration. Street names commemorate two famous Setúbal residents: Manuel Barbosa du Bocage (1765–1805), whose satirical poetry landed him in prison, and Luísa Todi (1753–1833), a celebrated opera singer.

In Roman times, fish-salting was the most important industry here. Rectangular tanks, carved from stone, can be seen under the glass floor of the Regional Tourist Office at No. 10 Travessa Frei Gaspar.

🏛 Igreja de Jesus
Praça Miguel Bombarda. ☎ 265-52 41 50. ◗ 9am–noon, 2–5pm Tue–Sun. ♿ **Museum** ☎ 265-52 47 72. ◗ Tue–Sat. ● public hols.
To the north of the old town, this striking Gothic church is one of Setúbal's architectural treasures. Designed by the

architect Diogo Boitac in 1494, the lofty interior is adorned with twisted columns, carved in three strands from pinkish Arrábida limestone, and rope-like stone ribs decorating the roof, recognized as the earliest examples of the distinctive and ornate Manueline style.

On Rua do Balneário, in the old monastic quarters, a **museum** houses 14 remark-able paintings of the life of Christ. Painted in glowing colours, the works are attrib-uted to the followers of Jorge Afonso (1520–30), influenced by the Flemish school.

🏛 Museu de Arqueologia e Etnografia
Avenida Luísa Todi 162. ☎ 265-23 93 65. ◗ Tue–Sat. ● public hols.
The archaeological museum displays a wealth of finds from digs around Setúbal, including Bronze Age pots, Roman coins and amphorae made to carry wine and *garum*, a sauce made from fish marinated in salt and herbs considered a great delicacy in Rome. The ethnography display shows local arts, crafts and industries, including the processing of salt and cork over the centuries.

♣ Castelo de São Filipe
Estrada de São Filipe.
☎ 265-52 38 44. ◗ daily.
The star-shaped fort was built in 1595 by Philip II of Spain during Portugal's period under Spanish rule to keep a wary eye on pirates, English invaders and the local population. A massive gateway and stone tunnel lead to the sheltered interior, which now houses a *pousada (see p119)* and an exquisite small chapel, tiled with scenes from the life of São Filipe by Policarpo de Oliveira Bernardes (1695–1778). A broad terrace offers marvellous views over the city and the Sado estuary.

Eɴᴠɪʀᴏɴs: Setúbal is an excellent starting point for a tour by car of the unspoilt **Reserva Natural do Estuário do Sado**, a vast stretch of mud flats, shallow

Fisherman's boat on the shallow mud flats of the Reserva Natural do Estuário do Sado

lagoons and salt marshes with patches of pine forest, which has been explored and inhabited since 3500 BC. Otters, water birds (including storks and herons), oysters and a great variety of fish are found in the reserve. The old tidal water mill at Mouriscas, 5 km (3 miles) to the east of Setúbal, uses the different levels of the tide to turn the grinding stones. Rice-growing and fishing are the main occupations today, and pine trees around the lagoon are tapped for resin.

⚑ Reserva Natural do Estuário do Sado
ℹ️ *Praça da República, Setúbal (265-54 11 40).*

Península de Tróia **⑰**

🚊 🚢 *Tróia.* ℹ️ *Complexo Turístico de Tróia (265-49 43 12).*

Thatched fisherman's cottage in the village of Carrasqueira

HIGH-RISE HOLIDAY apartments dominate the tip of the Tróia peninsula, easily accessible from Setúbal by ferry. The Atlantic coast, stretching south for 18 km (11 miles) of untouched sandy beach, lined with dunes and pine woods, is now the haunt of sun-seekers in the summer.

Near Tróia, in the sheltered lagoon, the Roman town of **Cetóbriga** was the site of a thriving fish-salting business; the stone tanks and ruined buildings are open to visit. To the south, smart new holiday villas and golf clubs are springing up along the lagoon.

Further on, **Carrasqueira** is an old fishing community where you can still see traditional reed houses, with walls and roofs made from thatch. The narrow fishing boats

View over Alcácer do Sal and the River Sado from the castle

moored along the mud flats are reached by walkways raised on stilts. From here to Alcácer do Sal, great stretches of pine forest line the road, and there are the first glimpses of the cork oak countryside typical of the Alentejo region.

⛪ Cetóbriga
N253-1. 📞 *265-49 43 18.* 🕐 *daily.*

Alcácer do Sal **⑱**

🚹 *15,000.* 🚌 🚆 ℹ️ *Rua da República 76. (265-61 00 70).* 🗓️ *1st Sat of month.*

BYPASSED by the main road, the ancient town of Alcácer do Sal (*al-kasr* from the Arabic for castle, and *do sal* from its trade in salt) sits peacefully on the north bank of the River Sado. The imposing castle was a hillfort as early as the 6th century BC.

The Phoenicians made an inland trading port here, and the castle later became a Roman stronghold. Rebuilt by the Moors, it was conquered by Afonso II in 1217. The buildings have now taken on a new life as a *pousada (see p118)*, with views over the rooftops and storks' nests on top of trees and buildings.

There are pleasant cafés along the riverside promenade and several historic churches. The small church of Espírito Santo now houses a **Museu Arqueológico** exhibiting local finds and the 18th-century **Santo António** holds a marble Chapel of the 11,000 Virgins. The bullring is a focus for summer events and hosts the agricultural fair in October.

🏛 Museu Arqueológico
Igreja do Espírito Santo, Praça Pedro Nunes. ℹ️ *265-61 00 70.* 🕐 *9am–12:30pm, 2–5:30pm daily.*

BIRDS OF THE TAGUS AND SADO ESTUARIES

Many waterbirds, including black-winged stilts, avocets, Kentish plovers and pratincoles are found close to areas of open water and mud flats as well as the dried out lagoons of the Tagus and Sado estuaries. Reed-beds also provide shelter for nesting and support good numbers of little bitterns, purple herons and marsh harriers. From September to March, the area around the Tagus estuary is extremely important for wildfowl and wintering waders.

Black-winged stilt, a wader that feeds in the estuaries

TRAVELLERS' NEEDS

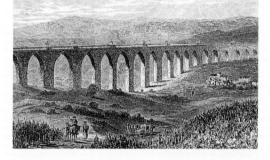

WHERE TO STAY 112-119
RESTAURANTS, CAFÉS AND BARS 120-135
SHOPS AND MARKETS 136-139
ENTERTAINMENT IN LISBON 140-143

WHERE TO STAY

ISBON AND ITS ENVIRONS offer a variety of accommodation, from restored palaces to family-run hostels. The hotels in Lisbon range from modern and luxurious or elegant and old-fashioned to cosy *pensões* and comfortable chain hotels. There are many hotels in and around the main sightseeing areas of the city.

The hotels in Estoril and Cascais along the Lisbon coast are mostly purpose-built and get busy in the summer. In the countryside

Porter services are available in Lisbon's top hotels

around Lisbon, hotels are fairly scarce, although Sintra offers a selection of places to stay and is a good base for exploring the area west of Lisbon. *Pousadas*, often historic buildings converted into hotels, are an alternative in the Lisbon Coast area. If you prefer self-catering, farmhouses, villas and apartments usually offer flexibility and good value. The hotels listed on pages 114–19 have been selected from every price category as offering the best value for money in each area.

Bedroom at the York House Hotel in Lisbon, a converted 16th-century convent *(see p116)*

CHOOSING A HOTEL

THE MAJORITY of the modern, luxury hotels in Lisbon are situated around Parque Eduardo VII, at the north end of Avenida de Liberdade.

Centrally located, the Baixa is an ideal district in which to stay, and has plenty of small *pensões* to offer. However, there is no shortage of hotels in other areas, although one problem which visitors may come across is a lack of midrange hotels.

Lapa and Rato, to the west of the city centre, offer a selection of older, more exclusive hotels. They are pleasant areas in which to stay and an alternative from the popular area around the Parque Eduardo VII.

TYPES OF HOTEL

HOTELS IN LISBON vary in quality, price and facilities. In addition to the conventional hotel there are other types of lodging, such as

albergarias (inns) that offer a pleasant stay at a lower price than a hotel of similar quality. *Pensões* or guesthouses are another alternative. They generally fall into the lowest price range and can be excellent value. At its simplest, accommodation in a *pensão* consists of a clean room with a shared bathroom. At the top end of the market, four-star *pensões* can rival the most luxurious hotels in terms of comfort. A *residencial* is like a *pensão* but often includes breakfast.

If you wish to stay outside Lisbon, then a *pousada*, a state-run country inn, is an ideal choice. These offer accommodation in scenic locations, and are often in converted country houses and palaces.

HOTEL CHAINS

AT THE TOP END of the market, two small hotel chains offer the most luxurious surroundings and facilities. The **Hotéis Alexandre de Almeida**, founded in 1917, is the older chain, and includes the gracious and appealing Metropole hotel *(see p115)*, which is located in the Baixa. The **Hotéis Tivoli** group has seven hotels in converted palaces, some of which are located in Lisbon and Sintra.

Lower down the scale, **Choice Hotels Portugal** operate two categories of modern hotel: Comfort Hotels and Quality Suites. The latter are usually rated at a higher level, but Comfort Hotels have better facilities for disabled travellers. The hotel group **Best Western** offers quality service and comfort in properties that each have their own style.

The impressive façade of the luxurious Lapa Palace *(see p116)*

◁ **Breakfasting beneath the wisteria at the Pousada da Palmela**

View from the Seteais Palace, Sintra, now a luxury hotel *(see p119)*

GRADINGS

MOST CATEGORIES of tourist accommodation are graded by the Portuguese Tourist Board with a star rating from one to five (five being the most luxurious). The stars indicate the size, degree of comfort and facilities offered, and bear no relation to the hotel's appeal or location. The establishment has to adhere to a set of criteria to achieve and maintain its star rating. However, the quality can vary from one type of lodging to another; for example, a three-star *pensão* can surpass a one- or two-star hotel in comfort.

PRICES

IN PORTUGAL, establishments are free to set their own prices, but tariffs must be clearly displayed at reception and in the rooms. The cost of the room usually includes all taxes and a continental breakfast. Other meals are charged as extras. It is sometimes possible to bargain for a better rate, especially in low season. As a rule, the cost of a single room is around 60 to 75 per cent of the cost of a double room. The coastal resort of Estoril can be expensive, but prices drop substantially out of season. *Pousadas* charge two rates for low (Nov–Mar except New year and carnival), and high (Apr–Oct) season.

BOOKING

YOU WILL NEED to book in advance for locations in Estoril and Cascais in high season, when much accommodation is taken by tour operators. Book ahead for central Lisbon, which can also get full. Most hoteliers speak English so it should not be a problem to book by fax or phone. Deposits are not usually required and major credit cards are accepted.

If you wish to stay in a *pousada*, these can be booked through the **Portuguese National Tourist Office** *(see p146)* or **Enatur**, who will also supply information. The **Direcção Geral do Turismo** (State Tourist Office) publishes two guides which are revised annually: *Guia do Alojamento Turístico*, (Guide to Tourist Accommodation) and *Turismo no Espaço Rural* (Guide to Tourism in the Country), both of which contain up-to-date listings of accommodation available in the area. However, these guides do not provide recommendations.

TRAVELLING WITH CHILDREN

THE PORTUGUESE adore children and will welcome them warmly into hotels and restaurants. Travellers who have children with them will find an immediate point of contact with their hosts.

DISABLED TRAVELLERS

THE PORTUGUESE National Tourist Office lists hotels with facilities for the disabled, and produces a general information leaflet. Some youth hostels and campsites provide special facilities and these are listed by the relevant organizations, and in a guide that is published by the **Secretariado Nacional de Reabilitação**.

DIRECTORY

HOTEL CHAINS

Best Western
US: 1800-528 1234.
UK: 0800-39 31 30.
Portugal: 800-839 361.
(All toll free.)

Choice Hotels Portugal
US: 1800-228 5150
or 1800-228 5151.
UK: 0800-44 44 44.
Portugal: 800-201 166.
(All toll free.)

Hotéis Alexandre de Almeida
Rua Dr Álvaro de Castro 73,
1600-058 Lisbon. 21-799 19
35. FAX 21-793 04 45.

Hotéis Tivoli
Avenida da Liberdade 185,
1250-050 Lisbon. 21-319 89
00. FAX 21-319 89 50.

BOOKING

Direcção Geral do Turismo
Avenida António Augusto
de Aguiar 86, 1050 Lisbon.
21-358 64 00; 800-296 296.
FAX 21-358 66 66.

Enatur
Lisbon: 21-844 20 00.
FAX 21-844 20 88.
UK: 020-74 02 81 82.

DISABLED TRAVELLERS

Secretariado Nacional de Reabilitação
Avenida Conde de Valbom 63,
1050 Lisbon. 21-793 65 17.
FAX 21-795 82 74.

Choosing a Hotel

THE HOTELS in this guide have been selected across a wide price range for their excellent facilities and locations. Many also have a recommended restaurant. The chart lists the hotels by areas within Lisbon. Hotels in the Lisbon Coast area are listed separately on pages 118–9. For restaurant listings see pp128–133.

	CREDIT CARDS	RESTAURANT	GARDEN	SWIMMING POOL	NUMBER OF ROOMS
LISBON					
BAIRRO ALTO: *Borges* €€ Rua Garrett 108-205, 1200. **Map** 7 A4. ☎ 21-346 19 51. ☏ 21-342 66 17. The Borges, one of the few places to stay in the smart Chiado area, successfully combines elegant furnishings with pleasant surroundings. ▣	AE DC MC V				100
BAIRRO ALTO: *Pensão Londres* €€ Rua Dom Pedro V 53, 2°, 1250-092. **Map** 4 F2. ☎ 21-346 22 03. ☏ 21-346 56 82. One of the better basic *pensões* in the area, avoiding the worst of the Bairro Alto's night-time noise. ▣	DC MC V				36
BAIXA: *Beira Minho* € Praça da Figueira 6, 2° E, 1150. **Map** 7 B3. ☎ 21-346 18 46. ☏ 21-886 78 11. The spectacular views up towards the Bairro Alto from this simple *pensão* make up for the lack of facilities. ▣					24
BAIXA: *Norte* € Rua dos Douradores 159, 1100-205. **Map** 7 B3. ☎ 21-887 89 41. ☏ 21-886 84 62. Centrally located near Praça da Figueira, this *pensão* has few facilities and no breakfast but the rooms are neat and comfortable. Good value. ▣ ▣	MC V				36
BAIXA: *Alegria* €€ Praça da Alegria 12, 1250-004. **Map** 4 F1. ☎ 21-322 06 70. ☏ 21-347 80 70. This basic, good-value *pensão* offers clean and homely rooms. It borders on the red-light district, although the police station is next door. ▣	AE DC MC V				36
BAIXA: *Coimbra e Madrid* €€ Praça da Figueira 3, 3°, 1100-240. **Map** 7 B3. ☎ 21-342 17 60. ☏ 21-342 32 64. A plain and simple *pensão* with rather sparse decoration. Some of the rooms, however, have magnificent views of the Castelo de São Jorge. ▣					32
BAIXA: *Duas Nações* €€ Rua da Vitória 41, 1100-618. **Map** 7 B4. ☎ 21-346 07 10. ☏ 21-347 02 06. The "Two Nations" is a friendly place to stay, right in the heart of the Baixa, but the rooms overlooking Rua Augusta can be noisy. ▣	AE DC MC V				69
BAIXA: *Florescente* €€ Rua das Portas de S. Antão 99, 1150-266. **Map** 7 A2. ☎ 21-342 66 09. ☏ 21-342 77 33. For a *pensão* the rooms of the Florescente are extremely well equipped. The street is known for its many fine restaurants. No breakfast. ▣ ▣ ▤	AE MC V				60
BAIXA: *Nova Goa* €€ Rua do Arco do Marquês de Alegrete 13, 1100-034. **Map** 7 C3. ☎ 21-888 11 37. ☏ 21-886 78 11. Just around the corner from Praça da Figueira, this *pensão* is like many in the vicinity: clean, comfortable and fairly basic. ▣ ▣	€€				42
BAIXA: *Restauradores* €€ Praça dos Restauradores 13, 4°, 1250-187. **Map** 7 A2. ☎ 21-347 56 60. A very small and fairly basic *pensão* on the fourth floor of a building with a great location in the busy centre of the city. No breakfast. ▣					30
BAIXA: *Suíço Atlântico* €€ Rua da Glória 3–19, 1250-114. **Map** 7 A2. ☎ 21-346 17 13. ☏ 21-346 90 13. In a small side street by the Elevador da Glória, this hotel has large old-fashioned rooms and public areas with stone arches and wooden beams. ▣	AE DC MC V				90
BAIXA: *Internacional* €€€ Rua da Betesga 3, 1100-090. **Map** 7 B3. ☎ 21-346 64 01. ☏ 21-347 86 35. This hotel features modern and spacious rooms. Residents can relax in the hotel's large, comfortable TV lounge and small bar. ▣ ▣ ▤	AE DC MC V				52

Price categories in Euros for a standard double room per night, including breakfast: € under 35, €€ 35–60, €€€ 60–100, €€€€ 100–150, €€€€€ over 150	RESTAURANT The hotel has one or more restaurants open for lunch and supper, sometimes reserved for residents. GARDEN A garden, courtyard or large terrace for the use of hotel guests. SWIMMING POOL The hotel has its own indoor or outdoor pool. CREDIT CARDS Major credit cards accepted: AE American Express, DC Diners Club, MC MasterCard and V Visa.	CREDIT CARDS	RESTAURANT	GARDEN	SWIMMING POOL	NUMBER OF ROOMS
BAIXA: *Portugal* €€€ Rua João das Regras 4, 1100-294. **Map** 7 C3. **(** 21-887 75 81. **FAX** 21-886 73 43. Though plain on the outside, this hotel situated off Praça Martim Moniz is surprisingly elegant with stylish old-fashioned decor.		AE DC MC V				60
BAIXA: *Roma* €€€ Travessa da Glória 22a, 1°, 1250-118. **Map** 7 A2. **(** 21-346 05 57. **FAX** 21-346 05 57. This simple *pensão* has a fine location just off Avenida da Liberdade, convenient for shops and sightseeing. There is a 24-hour bar service.		AE MC V				24
BAIXA: *Metrópole* @ sales@almeidahotels.com €€€€ Praça Dom Pedro IV 30, 1100-200. **Map** 7 B3. **(** 21-321 90 30. **FAX** 21-346 91 66. This turn-of-the-century building has been renovated in a style reminiscent of the 1920s. The result is a charming and elegant hotel. The famous Buçaco wines *(see p210)* can also be bought here.		AE DC MC V				36
BAIXA: *Orion Eden* @ lisbon@citadines.com €€€€ Praça dos Restauradores 24, 1250-187. **Map** 7 A2. **(** 21-321 66 00. **FAX** 21-321 66 66. The modern Orion Eden offers apartments and studios, all with a private kitchen. Three studios have been adapted for the disabled.		AE DC MC V			●	134
BAIXA: *Tivoli Lisboa* @ htlisboa@mail.telepac.pt €€€€€ Av. da Liberdade 185, 1269-050. **Map** 4 F1. **(** 21-319 89 00. **FAX** 21-319 89 50. This large and elegant hotel has modern rooms and a huge two-level central lobby. The suites are particularly spacious.		AE DC MC V	●	▓	●	329
BAIXA: *Avenida Palace* @ hotel.av.palace@mail.telepac.pt €€€€€ Rua 1° de Dezembro 123, 1200-359. **Map** 7 B3. **(** 21-346 01 51. **FAX** 21-342 28 84. The Avenida Palace hotel, with its Neo-Classical façade and enviable central location, offers both elegance and convenience. The luxurious interior decoration retains many charming original details.		AE DC MC V				82
BAIXA: *Sofitel Lisboa* @ h1319@accor-hotels.com €€€€€ Av. da Liberdade 127, 1269-038. **Map** 4 F1. **(** 21-322 83 00. **FAX** 21-322 83 10. The comfortable, modern Sofitel features an attractive piano bar called the "Molière", situated just off the lobby.		AE DC MC V	●			170
BAIXA: *Tivoli Jardim* €€€€€ Rua J. César Machado , 1250-135. **Map** 4 F1. **(** 21-353 99 71. **FAX** 21-355 65 66. The rooms of this smart hotel are well appointed with spacious bathrooms and a mini-bar. An unusual round pool graces the garden behind the hotel and there is use of extensive sports facilities.		AE DC MC V	●	▓	●	119
CAMPO PEQUENO: *Lar do Areeiro* €€ Praça Francisco Sá Carneiro 4, 1000-159. **Map** 6 E1. **(** 21-849 31 50. Conveniently located close to many shops, this *pensão* offers good-value accommodation that is clean and comfortable.		AE DC MC V				44
CASTELO: *Ninho das Águias* €€ Costa do Castelo 74, 1100-179. **Map** 7 C3. **(** 21-855 40 70. The simple "Eagle's Nest" *pensão* sits below the castle walls. A stuffed eagle greets visitors on the terrace that has amazing views. No breakfast.				▓		16
CASTELO: *Solar do Castelo* w www.heritage.pt €€€€€ Rua das Cozinhas 2, 1100-181. **Map** 7 C3. **(** 21-321 82 00. **FAX** 21-347 16 30. This small, luxurious hotel occupies a recently renovated 18th-century mansion located within the castle walls.		AE DC MC V		▓		14
ENTRECAMPOS: *Quality Hotel Lisboa* €€€€ Campo Grande 7, 1700-087. **(** 21-791 76 00. **FAX** 21-795 75 00. A pleasant hotel that caters for the business traveller. Features include a health club, gymnasium and jacuzzi.		AE DC MC V	●			84

For key to symbols see back flap

<table>
<tr><td colspan="2">

Price categories in Euros for a standard double room per night, including breakfast:

€ under 35
€€ 35–60
€€€ 60–100
€€€€ 100–150
€€€€€ over 150

</td><td colspan="6">

RESTAURANT
The hotel has one or more restaurants open for lunch and supper, sometimes reserved for residents.
GARDEN
A garden, courtyard or large terrace for the use of hotel guests.
SWIMMING POOL
The hotel has its own indoor or outdoor pool.
CREDIT CARDS
Major credit cards accepted: *AE* American Express, *DC* Diners Club, *MC* MasterCard and *V* Visa.

</td></tr>
<tr><th colspan="2"></th><th>CREDIT CARDS</th><th>RESTAURANT</th><th>GARDEN</th><th>SWIMMING POOL</th><th>NUMBER OF ROOMS</th></tr>

<tr><td colspan="2">

ESTEFÂNIA: *Caravela*   €€
Rua Ferreira Lapa 38, 1150-159. **Map** 6 D4. 🅲 *21-353 90 15.* **FAX** *21-357 17 51.*
The rooms in this *pensão* have a slightly old-fashioned ambience. Each room has a direct outside line and there is a bar and TV room. 🛏 📺

</td><td>AE
DC
MC
V</td><td></td><td></td><td></td><td>45</td></tr>

<tr><td colspan="2">

GRAÇA: *Mundial* @ mundial.hot@mail.telepac.pt   €€€€
Rua Dom Duarte 4, 1100-198. **Map** 7 B3. 🅲 *21-884 20 00.* **FAX** *21-884 21 10.*
This hotel, located centrally off Praça da Figueira, has plain but comfortable rooms. The restaurant offers marvellous views. 🛏 📺 📗 🅿 ♿

</td><td>AE
DC
MC
V</td><td>●</td><td></td><td></td><td>255</td></tr>

<tr><td colspan="2">

GRAÇA: *Senhora do Monte*   €€€€
Calçada do Monte 39, 1170-250. **Map** 7 D1. 🅲 *21-886 60 02.* **FAX** *21-887 77 83.*
This *albergaria* is somewhat off the beaten track, but it is well worth the effort to find it. The rooms are fairly plain but the views, especially from the rooftop bar and garden, are simply the best in town. 🛏 📺 📗

</td><td>AE
DC
MC
V</td><td></td><td></td><td></td><td>28</td></tr>

<tr><td colspan="2">

LAPA: *As Janelas Verdes* Ⓦ www.heritage.pt   €€€€€
R. das Janelas Verdes 47, 1200-690. **Map** 4 D3. 🅲 *21-396 81 43.* **FAX** *21-396 81 44.*
A delightful *pensão* housed in an 18th-century ivy-covered mansion, once owned by the Portuguese novelist Eça de Queirós *(see p55)*. It has Neo-Classical decor and a peaceful, charming patio. 🛏 📺 📗 🅿

</td><td>AE
DC
MC
V</td><td></td><td>■</td><td></td><td>29</td></tr>

<tr><td colspan="2">

LAPA: *Lapa Palace* Ⓦ www.orient-express.com   €€€€€
R. do Pau da Bandeira 4, 1249-021. **Map** 3 C3. 🅲 *21-394 94 94.* **FAX** *21-395 06 65.*
A gracious and charming hotel located in the city's diplomatic area. Each room in the Palace Wing is uniquely decorated in its own Portuguese style – from 18th-century Neo-Classical to Art Deco. 🛏 📺 📗 🅿 ♿

</td><td>AE
DC
MC
V</td><td>●</td><td>■</td><td>●</td><td>94</td></tr>

<tr><td colspan="2">

LAPA: *York House*   €€€€€
Rua das Janelas Verdes 32, 1200-691. **Map** 4 D4. 🅲 *21-396 24 35.* **FAX** *21-397 27 93.*
This enchanting *pensão* is housed in the 17th-century Convento dos Marianos. Set around a shady, plant-filled patio, the elegant rooms have wooden or terracotta floors and elegant antique furniture. 🛏 📺

</td><td>AE
DC
MC
V</td><td>●</td><td>■</td><td></td><td>34</td></tr>

<tr><td colspan="2">

RATO: *13 da Sorte*   €€
Rua do Salitre 13, 1250-198. **Map** 4 F1. 🅲 *21-353 18 51.* **FAX** *21-353 18 51.*
This well located *pensão* is situated close to Avenida da Liberdade and the Jardim Botanico. Breakfast is not included. 🛏 📺

</td><td>MC
V</td><td></td><td></td><td></td><td>22</td></tr>

<tr><td colspan="2">

RATO: *Amazónia*   €€€
T. da Fábrica dos Pentes 12–20, 1250-106. **Map** 5 B5. 🅲 *21-387 70 06.* **FAX** *21-387 90 90.*
Conveniently close to the city centre, this mid-range hotel has elegant public rooms, large bedrooms and a piano bar. 🛏 📺 📗 🅿 ♿

</td><td>AE
DC
MC
V</td><td></td><td></td><td>●</td><td>192</td></tr>

<tr><td colspan="2">

RATO: *Lisboa Plaza* Ⓦ www.heritage.pt   €€€€
Travessa do Salitre 7, 1250-205. **Map** 4 F1. 🅲 *21-321 82 18.* **FAX** *21-347 16 30.*
Built in 1953, and situated off Praça da Alegria and Av. da Liberade, with decor by the Portuguese interior designer, Graça Viterbo. 🛏 📺 📗

</td><td>AE
DC
MC
V</td><td>●</td><td></td><td></td><td>112</td></tr>

<tr><td colspan="2">

RATO: *Altis* @ reservations@hotel-altis.pt   €€€€€
Rua Castilho 11, 1269-072. **Map** 4 F1. 🅲 *21-310 60 00.* **FAX** *21-310 62 62.*
This huge hotel has every expected facility, including a rooftop grill and well-equipped health club with an indoor pool. 🛏 📺 📗 🅿 ♿

</td><td>AE
DC
MC
V</td><td>●</td><td></td><td>●</td><td>303</td></tr>

<tr><td colspan="2">

RATO: *Ritz Four Seasons* Ⓦ www.fourseasons.com   €€€€€
Rua R. da Fonseca 88, 1099-039. **Map** 5 B5. 🅲 *21-381 14 00.* **FAX** *21-383 17 83.*
The legendary Ritz is an elegant, comfortable hotel. Many of the rooms have balconies that overlook the Parque Eduardo VII. 🛏 📺 📗 🅿 ♿

</td><td>AE
DC
MC
V</td><td>●</td><td>■</td><td></td><td>283</td></tr>

<tr><td colspan="2">

ROTUNDA: *Castilho*   €€
Rua Castilho 57 4°, 1250-068. **Map** 4 F1. 🅲 *21-386 08 22.* **FAX** *21-386 29 10.*
An excellent-value *pensão* on the fourth floor of a building. Good facilities and comfortable rooms, some with three or four beds. 🛏 📺 ♿

</td><td>DC
MC
V</td><td></td><td></td><td></td><td>25</td></tr>

</table>

ROTUNDA: *Jorge V* W www.hoteljorgev.com   €€€   AE DC MC V   51
Rua Mouzinho da Silveira 3, 1250-165. **Map** 5 C5. 21-356 25 25. **FAX** 21-315 03 19.
This pleasant, comfortable hotel offers good value for the area. Roughly half the rooms have balconies, so request one when checking in.

ROTUNDA: *Nacional* @ hotelnacional@mail.telepac.pt   €€€   AE DC MC V   61
Rua Castilho 34, 1250-070. **Map** 5 B5. 21-355 44 33. **FAX** 21-356 11 22.
This interesting glass-fronted hotel has comfortable rooms and extensive facilities. There are also two suites available.

ROTUNDA: *Britânia* W www.heritage.pt   €€€€   AE DC MC V   30
Rua R. Sampaio 17, 1150-278. **Map** 5 C5. 21-315 50 16. **FAX** 21-315 50 21.
Housed in a building designed by the architect Cassiano Branco in 1944, this delightful hotel has a beautiful marble lobby.

ROTUNDA: *Capitol* @ sanaclassic.capitol@sanahotels.com   €€€€   AE DC MC V   57
Rua Eça de Queirós 24, 1050-096. **Map** 5 C4. 21-353 68 11. **FAX** 21-352 61 65.
A comfortable hotel just off Avenida de Duque de Loulé. All the rooms are equipped with satellite television and mini bars.

ROTUNDA: *Diplomático* W www.diplomatico.com   €€€€   AE DC MC V   90
Rua Castilho 74, 1250-071. **Map** 5 B5. 21-383 90 20. **FAX** 21-386 21 55.
The Diplomático has spacious rooms with modern facilities and offers complimentary tea, coffee and chocolate in the rooms.

ROTUNDA: *Rex* @ sanaclassic.rex@sanahotels.com   €€€€   AE DC MC V   68
Rua Castilho 169, 1070-051. **Map** 5 B4. 21-388 21 61. **FAX** 21-388 75 81.
The Rex is located close to the Parque Eduardo VII. The top floor conference room has good views.

ROTUNDA: *Veneza* W www.3khotels.com   €€€€   AE DC MC V   36
Avenida da Liberdade 189, 1250-141. **Map** 5 C5. 21-352 26 18. **FAX** 21-352 66 78.
The ornate staircase decorated with modern murals by Pedro Luiz-Gomes is the highlight of this spacious and comfortable hotel.

ROTUNDA: *Le Méridien Lisboa* W www.lemeridien-lisbon.com   €€€€€   AE DC MC V   330
Rua Castilho 149, 1099-034. **Map** 5 B4. 21-381 87 00. **FAX** 21-389 05 05.
Overlooking the Parque Eduardo VII from one of the city's seven hills, this hotel has comfortable rooms and spectacular views.

SALDANHA: *Marisela*   €   AE MC V   19
Rua Filipe Folque 19, 1050-111. **Map** 5 C3. 21-353 32 05. **FAX** 21-316 04 23.
A good-value *pensão* with rather basic rooms, in a quiet street between the gardens of Parque Eduardo VII and Praça do Duque de Saldanha.

SALDANHA: *Horizonte*   €€   AE DC MC V   52
Av. António A. de Aguiar 42, 1050-017. **Map** 5 B4. 21-353 95 26. **FAX** 21-353 84 74.
This large *pensão* offers good value for money for this area. The rooms at the front can be noisy.

SALDANHA: *VIP*   €€€   AE DC MC V   54
Rua Fernão Lopes 25, 1000-132. **Map** 5 C3. 21-356 86 00. **FAX** 21-315 87 73.
A simple hotel built over shops in a busy part of the city, the VIP is neat and tidy, although the decor is somewhat old-fashioned.

SALDANHA: *Hotel Marquês de Sá* @ marquessahotal@mail.telepac.pt   €€€   AE DC MC V   97
Av. Miguel Bombarda 130, 1050-167. **Map** 6 B2. 21-791 10 14. **FAX** 21-793 69 86.
A pleasant hotel located in one of the most elegant areas of Lisbon, and a short walk from the Museu Calouste Gulbenkian (*see p76–9*).

SALDANHA: *Príncipe* @ confortprincipe@mail.telepac.pt   €€€   AE DC MC V   67
Avenida Duque de Ávila 201, 1050-082. **Map** 5 B3. 21-353 61 51. **FAX** 21-353 43 14.
Most of the rooms in this modern hotel have their own balcony. There is a small bar and lounge just off the lobby.

SALDANHA: *Real Parque* @ info@hoteisreal.com   €€€€€   AE DC MC V   153
Avenida L. Bivar 67, 1069-146. **Map** 5 C3. 21-319 90 00. **FAX** 21-382 29 30.
This impressive modern hotel, located on a quiet side street, has six rooms specially designed for the disabled.

SALDANHA: *Sheraton Lisboa*   €€€€€   AE DC MC V   375
Rua L. Coelho 1, 1069-025. **Map** 5 C3. 21-312 00 00. **FAX** 21-354 71 64.
Lisbon's Sheraton offers spacious rooms, a top-floor restaurant and bar with fine views, a communications centre and a health club.

Price categories in Euros for a standard double room per night, including breakfast:
€ under 35
€€ 35–60
€€€ 60–100
€€€€ 100–150
€€€€€ over 150

RESTAURANT
The hotel has one or more restaurants open for lunch and supper, sometimes reserved for residents.

GARDEN
A garden, courtyard or large terrace for the use of hotel guests.

SWIMMING POOL
The hotel has its own indoor or outdoor pool.

CREDIT CARDS
Major credit cards accepted: *AE* American Express, *DC* Diners Club, *MC* MasterCard and *V* Visa.

	CREDIT CARDS	RESTAURANT	GARDEN	SWIMMING POOL	NUMBER OF ROOMS

THE LISBON COAST

ALCÁCER DO SAL: *Pousada Dom Afonso II* W www.pousadas.pt €€€€€
Alcácer do Sal, 7850. **(** 265-61 30 70. **FAX** 265-61 30 74.
This atmospheric and historic *pousada* occupies a converted castle on a hilltop, overlooking the town and surrounding countryside.

AE DC MC V	●	■		35

CARCAVELOS: *Praia-Mar* W www.almeidahotels.com €€€€
Rua do Gurué 16, 2775-581. **(** 21-458 51 00. **FAX** 21-457 31 30.
This delightful hotel overlooks the Estoril coast's largest sandy beach. Modern and elegant throughout, the rooms are spacious and comfortable. The famed wines from Buçaco *(see p210)* are also available.

AE DC MC V	●	■	●	158

CASCAIS: *Solar Dom Carlos* €€€
Rua Latino Coelho 8, 2750-408. **(** 21-482 81 15. **FAX** 21-486 51 55.
This delightful hotel, the former summer residence of King Carlos I, has a garden, historic chapel and comfortable rooms.

AE DC MC V		■		18

CASCAIS: *Casa da Pérgola* €€€€
Avenida Valbom 13, 2750-508. **(** 21-484 00 40. **FAX** 21-483 47 91.
This grand 19th century house has rooms with stucco ceilings and ornate furniture. It is closed from 15 Dec-31 Jan.

		■		11

CASCAIS: *Cidadela* €€€€
Avenida 25 de Abril, 2750. **(** 21-482 76 00. **FAX** 21-486 72 26.
A short walk from the town centre, the Cidadela is surrounded by gardens. Most of the rooms have spectacular views over the bay.

AE DC MC V	●	■	●	113

CASCAIS: *Albatroz* €€€€€
Rua F. Arouca 100, 2750-353. **(** 21-484 73 80. **FAX** 21-484 48 27.
Built in the 19th century as a retreat for the Portuguese royal family, the Albatroz sits perched on the rocks directly overlooking the ocean. Inside, the luxurious decoration is matched by excellent service.

AE DC MC V	●	■	●	46

CASCAIS: *Estoril Sol* €€€€€
Parque Palmela, 2750-461. **(** 21-483 90 00. **FAX** 21-483 22 80.
The high-rise Estoril Sol has marvellous views over the bay of Cascais, a sea-water pool and a health club with Turkish baths.

AE DC MC V	●		●	310

COSTA DA CAPARICA: *Praia do Sol* €€
Rua dos Pescadores 12, 2825-386. **(** 21-290 00 12. **FAX** 21-290 25 41.
A small hotel, the Praia do Sol offers well-appointed rooms conveniently located close to the beach in this popular resort town.

AE DC MC V				53

COSTA DA CAPARICA: *Costa da Caparica* €€€€
Av. Gen. Delgado 47, 2829-506. **(** 21-291 89 00. **FAX** 21-291 06 87.
This hotel, with an unusual semi-circular entrance, overlooks the beach. It has seven rooms adapted for the disabled.

AE DC MC V	●	■	●	353

ERICEIRA: *Vilazul* €€€
Calçada da Baleia 10, 2655-238. **(** 261-86 00 00. **FAX** 261-86 29 27.
Only 500 m (550 yds) from the sea, this bright and airy hotel has panoramic views from the terrace and some of the bedrooms.

AE DC MC V	●			21

ESTORIL: *São Cristóvão* €€
Av. Marginal 7079, 2765-480. **(** 21-468 09 13. **FAX** 21-468 09 13.
This charming *pensão* is housed in an interesting old villa. Located on the ocean side of the Avenida Marginal, it offers spectacular views.

		■		14

ESTORIL: *Hotel Alvorada* €€€
Rua de Lisboa 3, 2765-240. **(** 21-464 98 60. **FAX** 21-468 72 50.
Only a few minutes' walk from the beach and opposite the casino, this hotel offers friendly service and bright, well-appointed rooms.

AE DC MC V				52

ESTORIL: *Hotel da Inglaterra* €€€€ AE DC MC V 52
Rua do Porto 1, 2765-271. **(** 21-468 44 61. **FAX** 21-468 21 08.
Some rooms in this impressive early 20th-century mansion have lovely
views over the bay of Cascais or the Sintra hills. ▦ TV ▤

ESTORIL: *Palácio* @ palacioestoril@mail.telepac.pt €€€€€ AE DC MC V 162
Rua do Parque, 2769-504. **(** 21-464 80 00. **FAX** 21-468 48 67.
An elegant hotel located between the sea and the casino. Guests have
access to an 18-hole golf course and tennis courts. ▦ TV ▤ P &

GUINCHO: *Fortaleza do Guincho* w www.guinchotel.pt €€€€€ AE DC MC V 29
Estrada do Guincho, 2750-642. **(** 21-487 04 91. **FAX** 21-487 04 31.
Perched on a clifftop overlooking the ocean, this atmospheric hotel with
arched ceilings and medieval decor was once a fortress. ▦ TV ▤ P &

GUINCHO: *Senhora da Guia* €€€€€ AE DC MC V 42
Estrada do Guincho, 2750-374. **(** 21-486 92 39. **FAX** 21-486 92 27.
Set in its own grounds with a sea-water pool, this charming *estalagem*
is housed in a comfortable and relaxing manor house. ▦ TV ▤ P

MAFRA: *Castelão* €€ AE DC MC V 35
Avenida 25 de Abril, 2640-456. **(** 261-81 60 50. **FAX** 261-81 60 59.
Convenient as a base when visiting the fabulous monastery in Mafra,
this hotel is comfortable and clean. ▦ TV P

PALMELA: *Pousada do Castelo de Palmela* w www.pousadas.pt €€€€€ AE DC MC V 28
Castelo de Palmela, 2950-997. **(** 21-235 12 26. **FAX** 21-233 04 40.
The fortified walls of this 12th-century castle now enclose a tranquil
pousada with whitewashed rooms and many plants. ▦ TV ▤ P

QUELUZ: *Pousada Dona Maria I* w www.pousadas.pt €€€€€ AE DC MC V 26
L. do Palácio Nacional, 2745-191. **(** 21-435 61 58. **FAX** 21-435 61 89.
Once used by staff of the marvellous 18th-century Palácio de Queluz,
today the "Clock Tower" is an impressive *pousada*. ▦ TV ▤ P &

SESIMBRA: *Hotel do Mar* w www.hoteldomar.pt €€€€ AE DC MC V 168
R. Gen. Humberto Delgado 10, 2970-628. **(** 21-228 83 00. **FAX** 21-223 38 88.
This hotel, built on different levels on the cliffside, is surrounded by lush
gardens. The presidential suite has a private pool. ▦ TV ▤ P &

SETÚBAL: *IBIS Setúbal* €€ AE DC MC V 102
Rua Alto da Guerra, 2914-518. **(** 265-77 22 00. **FAX** 265-77 24 47.
Featuring the usual combination of IBIS comforts and economy, this
hotel is surrounded by its own peaceful gardens. ▦ TV ▤ P &

SETÚBAL: *Pousada de São Filipe* w www.pousadas.pt €€€€€ AE DC MC V 16
Castelo de São Filipe, 2900-300. **(** 265-55 00 70. **FAX** 265-53 25 38.
This historic castle, built by Philip II of Spain *(see p50)* in 1590, is an
friendly pousada with fine views over the estuary. ▦ TV ▤ P

SINTRA: *Central* €€€ AE DC MC V 10
Praça da República 35, 2710-625. **(** 21-923 09 63.
Heavy furniture and peeling paint give this hotel an old-fashioned atmos-
phere. It has an excellent position opposite the Palácio Nacional. ▦

SINTRA: *Residencial Sintra* @ pensao.residencial.sintra@clix.pt €€€ MC V 10
T. dos Avelares 12, 2710-506. **(** 21-923 07 38. **FAX** 21-923 07 38.
Located just east of Sintra town centre, in the residential area of São Pedro,
this rambling old *pensão* is friendly and full of character. ▦ P

SINTRA: *Tivoli Sintra* w www.fivolihotels.com €€€€ AE DC MC V 76
Praça da República, 2710-616. **(** 21-923 35 05. **FAX** 21-923 15 72.
The modern Tivoli Sintra, tucked away in a corner of Sintra's main square,
has wonderful views across the valley, a bar and a boutique. ▦ TV ▤ P &

SINTRA: *Caesar Park* w www.caesarparkpenhalonga.com €€€€€ AE DC MC V 177
Estr. da Lagoa Azul, Linhó 2714-511. **(** 21-924 90 11. **FAX** 21-924 90 07.
This huge, luxurious complex in the Sintra hills has a 9 and an 18-hole golf
course, designed by Robert Trent Jones Jr, and a health club. ▦ TV ▤ P &

SINTRA: *Palácio de Seteais* w www.fivolihotels.com €€€€€ AE DC MC V 30
Av. B. du Bocage 8, 2710-517. **(** 21-923 32 00. **FAX** 21-923 42 77.
Just outside town, this elegant hotel occupies a delightful 18th-century
palace with tastefully decorated interiors and a topiary garden. ▦ TV P

RESTAURANTS, CAFÉS AND BARS

PARTICULARLY IN Lisbon and along the coast, there are many restaurants dedicated to cooking all manner of freshly caught fish and seafood. It may be grilled, pan-fried or turned into soup or a stew. However, meat dishes are also plentiful, some of the most popular being made of pork and lamb. Lisbon has an abundance of cheap restaurants and cafés, as well as more expensive ones. There are not

Drinks waiter at the Palácio de Seteais *(see p133)*

only typically Portuguese restaurants in Lisbon, but also Chinese, Indian, Indonesian, Brazilian and African, all of which reflect Portugal's colonial past. This section gives tips on the different types of restaurants and cafés, as well as advice on menus, drinks and ordering your meal. The listings found on pages 128–33 are a selection of the best restaurants in all price ranges to be found throughout the capital and in the Lisbon Coast area.

TYPES OF RESTAURANT

EATING VENUES in Lisbon come in all shapes and sizes and at all price levels. Among the most reasonable is the local *tasca* or tavern, often just a room with half-a-dozen tables presided over by a husband-and-wife team. *Tascas* are often frequented by locals and professionals at lunchtime, which is a good indication of quality food. The *casa de pasto* offers a budget three-course meal in a large dining room, while a *restaurante* is more formal and offers a wider choice of dishes. At a typical *marisqueira*, the emphasis is on seafood and fresh fish. A *churrasqueira*, originally Brazilian, specializes in spit-

roasted foods. A *cervejaria* is the ideal place to go for a beer and snack, maybe of delicious seafood. The restaurants in better hotels are generally of good quality. *Pousadas (see p112)*, found mainly in country areas, offer a network of traditional restaurants, with the focus on local gastronomic specialities.

EATING HOURS

LUNCH is usually served between 1 and 3pm, when many restaurants get very crowded. Dinner is served from 7pm until at least 10pm in most places, and can

The pleasant courtyard of Lautasco *(p128)* **along Beco do Azinhal in the Alfama**

often be later. An alternative for a late dinner would be a *fado* house *(see pp142–3)*, usually open from about 9:30pm to 3 or 4am. However, a meal here will be somewhat more expensive as the price includes a show.

RESERVATIONS

IT IS A GOOD IDEA to book ahead for expensive restaurants, and for those in popular locations in high season. Disabled people should certainly check in advance on facilities and access. Special facilities are generally lacking but most places will try to be helpful.

THE MENU

SOME restaurants, in tourist areas particularly, offer an *ementa turística*, a cheap, daily-changing menu. This is served with coffee and a drink (a glass of wine or beer, a soft drink or water) and provides a full meal at a good price with no hidden costs. Lunch

The impressive interior of Cozinha Velha *(see p133)* **at Queluz**

Eating outside in Cascais along the Lisbon coast

(*almoço*) generally consists of a soup or starter and a fish or meat dish with potatoes or rice. To sample a local speciality, you should ask for the *prato do dia* – dish of the day. The choice of sweets can be limited, but there is usually a good selection of fresh fruits in season or you can try a pastry such as a *pastel de nata*.

Dinner (*jantar*) may be two or more courses, perhaps rounded off with ice cream, fruit, a simple dessert or cheese. Casserole-style dishes, such as *cataplana* (a kind of tightly sealed wok in which the food steams in its own juice, often used for fish) or *porco à alentejana* (pork with clams), are brought to the table in a pot for diners to share. This is similarly done with large fish, such as sea bass, which are sold by weight. One serving is large and can easily be shared by two people, and it is perfectly acceptable to ask for a *meia dose* or half-portion. If requested, Portuguese restaurants will be more than happy to supply these half-portions for adults as well as for any children present.

Peculiar to Portugal is the plate of assorted appetizers – perhaps olives, cheese and sardine pâté – which are served with bread at the start of a meal. However, these are not usually included in the price of the meal and an extra charge will be made for each item consumed.

Pastéis de nata (custard pastries)

VEGETARIANS

VEGETARIANS WILL not eat as well as fish lovers, although local cheeses and breads can be excellent. Chefs are usually happy to provide something meatless, although this will probably mean just a salad or omelette. A greater variety of vegetarian dishes can be found in ethnic restaurants.

WHAT TO DRINK

IT WOULD BE a pity to visit Portugal without sampling port *(see pp124–5)* and Madeira, the country's two most famous drinks. Some restaurants may suggest a glass of white port as an aperitif while you wait for your meal. As far as house wine is concerned, it is usually of an acceptable quality to wash down your meal whatever the standard of the restaurant. Otherwise, ask for the wine list *(carta de vinhos)* and choose one of the native Portuguese wines *(see pp124–5)*. As an alternative to wine, the mineral water is recommended. This is either *com gás* (sparkling) or *sem gás* (still). If you prefer to drink beer, Sagres and Super Bock are both good lagers. *Cervejarias*, such as the lively Cervejaria Trindade in the Bairro Alto *(see pp48–59)*, are ideal places to get a snack late at night and enjoy an excellent range of beers, from lagers to dark beers, many of which are draught.

PAYING

IT IS COMMON PRACTICE to add a ten per cent tip to bills where service is not included. The cover charge is extra, and you may need to check that the restaurant takes credit cards if this is how you want to pay.

CHILDREN

THE PORTUGUESE view children as a blessing rather than a nuisance, so Lisbon is an ideal city for families to eat out together. Children's portions at reduced prices are advertised in restaurants or will be provided on request.

SMOKING

SMOKING IS COMMON and permitted in all public places in Portugal, unless there is a sign saying *proibido fumar*. No-smoking areas in restaurants are very rare.

DRINKING COFFEE IN LISBON

Coffee is widely drunk in Lisbon and served in many forms. The most popular, *uma bica*, is a small cup of strong black coffee like an espresso. For a weaker version, ask for *uma carioca de café*. A strong *bica* is called *uma italiana*. *Uma meia de leite* is half coffee, half milk. Strong coffee with a dash of milk is known as *um garoto escuro* (*um garoto claro* is quite milky). If you like coffee with plenty of milk, ask for *um galão* (a gallon). It is served in a glass, and again you can order *um galão claro* (very milky) or *escuro* (strong).

Uma bica   **Um galão**

What to Eat in Lisbon

Serra cheese

GASTRONOMICALLY, the Lisbon region is immensely varied, incorporating many different foods from all over Portugal. Situated near the Atlantic, Lisbon and its coast enjoy a proliferation of excellent seafood, in particular shellfish, dried cod *(bacalhau)* and grilled sardines. A popular dish is *porco à alentejana*, a mixture of pork and clams, originating from southern Portugal. Milk from sheep and goats is turned into a variety of cheeses, one of the most popular being the buttery Serra, which becomes harder as it ages. Sweet dishes include a vanilla flavoured rice pudding and a rich, dark chocolate mousse.

Fresh fruit *is plentiful in Lisbon and grapes and oranges from the Algarve are delicious when in season.*

Pastéis de bacalhau *are a national addiction. These little salt-cod cakes are eaten cold as a snack or hot as a main dish.*

Caldo verde, *Portugal's most famous soup, gets its vibrant colour from its main ingredient, couve galega, a type of kale.*

Paio, sausage made from pork loin

Spiced **chouriço** (sausage)

Cured ham

Cured meats *play an important role in Portuguese cuisine. The chouriços are flavoured with paprika and often wine.*

Leitão à Bairrada, *roasted sucking pig with crisp crackling, is relished hot or cold, and can be bought in good delicatessens.*

Frango à piri-piri, *a great favourite from Portugal's former colonies in Africa, is barbecued chicken with chilli.*

Bife à café, *café-style steak, is tender steak with a creamy sauce, served with chips and topped with a fried egg.*

Bacalhau à Gomes de Sá *is a creation from Oporto, in northern Portugal, made of layers of salt cod, potato and onion, and garnished with egg and olives.*

Pãezinhos

Papo seco

Queijo de ovelha (ewe's milk cheese)

Requeijão

Porco à alentejana, *a curious marriage of pork and clams, is usually cooked with white wine, garlic and parsley, as well as spices such as paprika.*

Fresh cheeses *made from ewe's or goat's milk are enjoyed with a variety of fresh rolls. Especially prized is Requeijão.*

Shellfish is plentiful and much enjoyed in Portugal. Lisbon is full of specialist seafood restaurants artfully displaying lobsters, crayfish, oysters, prawns of all sizes, crabs and other lesser known delicacies. Cockles and clams find their way into many dishes, such as the rich seafood rice, arroz de marisco.

Oysters

Crab

Lobster

Shrimps

Mussels

Prawns

Açorda de marisco is a special and unusual dish: shellfish are added to a thick soup of mashed bread, oil, garlic and coriander.

Sardinhas assadas, charcoal-grilled sardines, are a seaside tradition – a feast in summer when they are at their best.

Mousse de chocolate can be spectacular when made with really good dark chocolate.

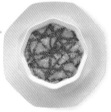

Arroz doce, creamy rice pudding rich with egg, is flavoured with lemon rind and vanilla.

Queijadas de Sintra (cheese tarts spiced with cinnamon)

Pastéis de nata (custard-cream tartlets)

Pastel de feijão (almonds, eggs and beans)

Broas (flour, honey and spices)

Tartlets such as pastéis de nata *epitomize the region's infinite variety of cakes, many based on egg yolks, almonds and spices.*

DRINKS

Portugal produces many fine wines *(see pp124–5)*, from which houses such as JM da Fonseca distil *aguardente* (brandy). Mineral waters, such as Luso, from the spa in central Portugal, are widely available. A tradition of beer-making thrives in the Lisbon area, with many *cervejarias* (beer houses) in the city. *Licor de Amêndoa Amarga* is a bitter almond liqueur.

Aguardente Velha Reserva

Mineral water from Luso

Licor de Amêndoa Amarga

Sagres beer

The Wines of Portugal

ALTHOUGH STILL overshadowed by the excellence and fame of port, Portuguese wine deserves to be taken seriously. After a decade of investment in the industry, many of the reds, such as the full-bodied wines from the Douro (made with some of the same grapes as port), have established an attractive style all their own. Great whites are fewer, but most regions have some. And of course there is *vinho verde*, the usually white, light, slightly carbonated wine from the north.

Sparkling rosés, *such as Mateus and Lancers, have been Portugal's great export success. They may have, however, inhibited a wider appreciation of the country's more ambitious table wines.*

WINE REGIONS

Many of Portugal's wine regions maintain their individual style by specializing in particular Portuguese grape varieties. The introduction of modern wine-making techniques has improved overall quality, and as yet the increasing use of imported grape varieties seems no threat to Portuguese individuality.

OPORTO

LISBON

KEY

▢	Vinhos Verdes
▢	Douro
▢	Dão
▢	Bairrada
▢	Estremadura
▢	Ribatejo
▢	Setúbal
▢	Alentejo

0 kilometres   50

0 miles   25

Vinho verde **vineyards in the village of Lapela, near Monção in the Minho**

Cellar of the Buçaco Palace Hotel, in Coimbra, famous for its red wine

HOW TO READ A WINE LABEL

Tinto is red, *branco* is white, *seco* is dry and *doce* is sweet. Other essential information is the name of the producer, the region and the year. At least 80 per cent of the grape variety on the front label will have been used. *Denominação de Origem Controlada* (DOC) indicates that the wine has been made according to the strictest regulations of a given region, but, as elsewhere, this need not mean higher quality than the nominally simpler *Vinho Regional* appellation. The back label often contains useful information about grape varieties and wine-making techniques used.

DOURO
DENOMINAÇÃO DE ORIGEM CONTROLADA
ENCOSTAS DO TUA
Reserva de 2000
VINHO TINTO
PRODUZIDO E ENGARRAFADO POR
SOCIEDADE AGRÍCOLA E COMERCIAL DOS VINHOS
VALE DA CORÇA, LDA
RESENDA - CARRAZEDA DE ANSIÃES - PORTUGAL
PRODUTO DE PORTUGAL
75 cl e   12,5% VOL.

The Sociedade Agrícola e Comercial dos Vinhos Vale da Corça, Lda, produced and bottled this wine.

This wine is from the Douro and is made according to DOC regulations for the region.

The name of this wine means "banks of the River Tua", further specifying its geographical origin.

Reserva **means** that the wine has probably been aged in oak casks. It also implies that the wine is of higher quality than non-reserva wine from the same producer.

Vinho verde, *"green wine" from the Minho region, can be either red or white, but the fizzy, dry reds are generally consumed locally. Typical white* vinho verde *is bone dry, slightly fizzy, low in alcohol and high in acidity. It should be drunk in the year after the vintage. A different, weightier style of white* vinho verde *is made from the Alvarinho grape, near the Spanish border.*

Bairrada *is a region where the small and thick-skinned Baga grape dominates. It makes big, tannic wines, sometimes with smoky or pine-needle overtones and like the older Dão wines, they need time to soften. Modern winemaking and occasional disregard for regional regulations have meant more approachable reds (often classified as Vinho Regional das Beiras) and crisper whites made from Bical and Maria Gomes among other grapes.*

Ribatejo *is the fertile valley of the Tagus to the north and east of Lisbon. After Estremadura, it is Portugal's biggest wine region measured by volume, but its potential for quality wines has only just begun to be realized. Most of the best wine is made in the central district of Almeirim, but as in Estremadura,* Vinho Regional *bottlings are frequently better than DOC ones.*

The Douro *region is best known as the source of port wine, but in most years about half of the wine produced is fermented dry to make table wine, and these wines are now at the forefront of Portuguese wine-making. The pioneer, Barca Velha, was launched half a century ago and is both highly regarded and the most expensive. Other quality producers are Calheiros Cruz, Domingos Alves de Sousa, Quinta das Castas, Quinta do Crasto and Ramos-Pinto.*

Picking grapes for *vinho verde*

Setúbal, *to the south of Lisbon, is best known for its sweet, fortified Muscat wine, Moscatel de Setúbal. In addition, the region also produces excellent, mostly red, table wine. Two big quality producers dominate the region: José Maria da Fonseca (see p107) and J.P. Vinhos. The co-operative at Santo Isidro de Pegões makes good-value wines, while interesting smaller producers include Venâncio Costa Lima, Hero do Castanheiro and Ermelinda Freitas.*

The Dão region *now offers some of Portugal's best wines. Small producers, such as Quinta dos Roques, Quinta da Pellada and Quinta de Cabriz, and the large Sogrape company make fruity reds for younger drinking, fresh, dry whites and richer reds which retain their fruit with age – a far cry from the heavy, hard-edged, and often oxidized wines of the past.*

Estremadura *is Portugal's westernmost wine area and has only recently emerged as a region in its own right. Several producers now make modern* Vinho Regional *wines with character; look for wines by DFJ, Casa Santos Lima, Quinta de Pancas and Quinta do Monte d'Oiro. The most interesting DOC is Alenquer. Bucelas in the south of the region, produces some light, fragrant white wines.*

Alentejo *produced wine has possibly made the biggest leap in quality in the last decade. Long dismissed as a region of easy-drinking house reds for restaurants, this area now produces some of Portugal's most serious red wines and a surprising number of excellent whites. Among the best producers are Herdade do Esporão, Herdade dos Coelheiros, Cortes de Cima and João Portugal Ramos.*

The Story of Port

THE "DISCOVERY" OF PORT dates from the 17th century when British merchants added brandy to the wine of the northern Douro region to prevent it souring in transit. They found that the stronger and sweeter the wine, the better flavour it acquired. Methods of maturing and blending continue to be refined by the main port producers. Croft was one of the first big shippers, followed by other English and Scottish firms. Despite the consolidation of the global drinks industry, much of the port trade is still in British hands, and some firms are still family-run.

Barco rabelo ferrying port down the Douro river

THE PORT REGION

Port comes only from a demarcated region of the upper Douro valley, stretching 100 km (62 miles) to the Spanish border. Régua and Pinhão are the main centres of production, but most top-quality vineyards lie on estates or *quintas* in the harsh eastern terrain.

STYLES OF PORT

There are essentially two categories of quality port. Bottle-aged port is deeper in colour and will develop after bottling. Wood-aged port is ready to drink when bottled. Ruby and unaged tawny are simpler styles of port, while white port is in a category of its own.

Vintage, the star of any shipper's range, is made from wines of a single year, from the best vineyards. It is blended and bottled after two years in wood, and may then mature for a very long time in the bottle.

Vintage

Late Bottled Vintage (LBV) is wine of a single year, bottled between four and six years after the harvest. Filtered LBV does not require decanting but may have less flavour than unfiltered, "traditional" LBV.

LBV

Aged tawny port is blended from top-quality wines that have been aged in wood for a long time. The age on the label is not precise, but the older it is, the paler, more delicate, less fruity and more expensive the port is likely to be.

Aged Tawny

Tawny port without indication of age may not have been in wood for long enough to develop the complex flavours of aged tawny; its style is light and its price fairly low. It may be a blend of red and white ports.

Tawny

Ruby port is deep red and should be full of lively fruit flavour. It has been aged for two or three years, sometimes in wood, sometimes not. It is less complex than either LBV or Vintage, but costs considerably less.

Ruby

White port is made from white grapes and may be sweet or not so sweet. It is mainly drunk chilled as an aperitif. Some types of white port have a slightly lower alcohol content than the normal 20% for port.

White

Collecting grapes in tall wicker baskets for transport to the wineries

HOW PORT IS MADE

The climax of the Douro farmers' year comes in late September when bands of pickers congregate to harvest the grapes. More than 40 varieties are used for making port, but there are five recommended top varieties.

Treading the grapes *in stone tanks or* lagares *to extract the juice is a feature of very traditional* quintas. *Some shippers believe it adds a special quality.*

Fermentation *in cement or steel tanks is a more common method. Carbon dioxide builds up within the tank, forcing the fermenting must (juice from the grapes) up a tube into an open trough at the top. The gas is released and the must sprays back over the pips and skins, in a process similar to treading.*

In the fortification *process, the semi-fermented must is run into a second vat where brandy – actually grape spirit – is added. This arrests the fermentation, leaving the wine sweet from natural grape sugar.*

Thousands of bottles *of Graham's vintage port from 1977 await full maturation in the cellars of the Vila Nova de Gaia lodge.*

Quality tawny port *is matured in oak casks in the port lodges. Once bottled, it is ready for drinking and does not require decanting.*

VINTAGE PORT

In the interests of maintaining the highest standards of quality – and of not saturating the market – port producers do not "declare" a vintage every year. Each year, the wine from the best vineyards is closely monitored for 18 months, other producers are consulted about their quality, and then a decision is taken. If a vintage is not declared, the wine may remain in wood to be blended as tawny or LBV in future, or it may be bottled as a "single quinta" port – a kind of second-label vintage. On average, producers declare a vintage three times in a decade, though not always in the same years.

A good vintage needs time in bottle to reveal itself. Fifteen years is regarded as a minimum, although many impatient drinkers do not actually wait that long; there is even a fashion for drinking young vintage port. The nature of vintage port's aging process results in a continuously evolving list of truly great vintages. Most connoisseurs agree, however, that no vintage has equalled that produced in 1963.

Pre-war vintages
1927, 1931, 1935:
All great and now very rare.

Post-war vintages
1945, 1947, 1948, 1955:
 For the very rich and extremely lucky.
1963 Perhaps the greatest post-war vintage.
1970 Its reputation has been rising and is now on par with 1963.
1994 A fine vintage, particularly from producers Dow, Taylor and Quinta do Noval.
1997 Another fine vintage.
2000 A very promising year.

Taylor's 1994 vintage

Choosing a Restaurant

THE RESTAURANTS in this guide have been selected for their good value, exceptional food or interesting location. This chart highlights some of the factors which may influence your choice. This chart lists the restaurants by areas within Lisbon. Restaurants in the Lisbon Coast area are listed separately on pages 132–33.

	CREDIT CARDS	LATE OPENING	OUTDOOR TABLES	GOOD WINE LIST

LISBON

ALCÂNTARA: *Espalha Brasas* €€€
Doca de Santo Amaro, Armazém 12. **Map** 3 A5. 🄲 *21-396 20 59.*
Located in Lisbon's lively Docas area, this restaurant specializes in fish and
serves cocktails. Enjoy eating outside in the summer. ● *lunch (Aug); Sun.*

	AE DC MC V	■	●	

ALFAMA: *Hua-Ta-Li* €€
Rua dos Bacalhoeiros 109–115. **Map** 7 C4. 🄲 *21-887 91 70.*
This is a large Chinese restaurant close to the docks that serves all the
regular rice and noodle favourites. Fast and efficient service. 🗏

ALFAMA: *Lautasco* €€
Beco do Azinhal 7a (off Rua de São Pedro). **Map** 8 E4. 🄲 *21-886 01 73.*
Rustically decorated with wooden panelling and wagon-wheel chandeliers,
Lautasco specializes in typical Portuguese cuisine. ● *Sun; 20 Dec–15 Jan.*

	AE DC MC V	■	●	

ALFAMA: *Mestre André* €€€
Calçadinha de Santo Estevão 6. **Map** 8 E3. 🄲 *21-887 14 87.*
Lively Portuguese restaurant offering delicious pork and fish dishes as well as
excellent *churrasco* (spit-roasted meat) *(see p120).* ● *Sun.* ♿

	AE	■	●	

ALFAMA: *Restô do Chapitô* €€€
Costa do Castelo 7. **Map** 7 C3. 🄲 *21-886 73 34.*
The extensive menu includes a wide range of international dishes. A cheerful
restaurant with a bar and fine views over the harbour. ● *Mon.*

		■	●	■

ALFAMA: *Sol Nascente* €€€
Rua de São Tomé 86. **Map** 8 D3. 🄲 *21-887 72 13.*
On the main road up to the castle from Alfama, this restaurant has fine views
over the Tagus. Try the seafood rice or the pork with clams. ● *Mon.* 🗏

	AE DC MC V	■	●	

ALFAMA: *Casa do Leão* €€€€
Castelo de São Jorge. **Map** 8 D3. 🄲 *21-887 59 62.*
Beneath arched brick ceilings, inside part of Castelo de São Jorge *(see pp78–9),*
this restaurant offers superb service and excellent traditional Portuguese
cuisine. Sit outside to enjoy the magnificent views. 🗏 🎵 *Wed–Fri.*

	AE DC MC V		●	■

ALFAMA: *Faz Figura* €€€€
Rua do Paraíso 15b. **Map** 8 F2. 🄲 *21-886 89 81.*
A smart restaurant, where panoramic views of the river and city can be
enjoyed from the covered terrace. Specialities include *cataplana* dishes *(see
p121)* and *picanha* (steak grilled over an open fire). ● *Sat lunch; Sun.* 🗏

	AE DC MC V		●	■

ALMADA: *Atira-te ao Rio* €€€
Cais do Ginjal 69–70. 🄲 *21-275 13 80.*
View Lisbon from the other bank of the Tagus and enjoy the restaurant's
Brazilian specialities, including *feijoada à Brasileira* (bean stew). ● *Mon.*

		■	●	

BAIRRO ALTO: *Bota Alta* €€€
Travessa da Queimada 35-37. **Map** 7 A3. 🄲 *21-342 79 59.*
The "High Boot" is an attractive restaurant with original paintings on the
walls. The menu consists of traditional Portuguese dishes. ● *Sat lunch; Sun.*

	AE DC MC V			

BAIRRO ALTO: *Casanostra* €€€
Travessa do Poço da Cidade 60. **Map** 7 A3. 🄲 *21-342 59 31.*
Within the green, white and black interior of this Italian restaurant you
can choose from a six-page menu full of delicacies. ● *Mon, Sat lunch.* 🗏

	AE DC MC V			

BAIRRO ALTO: *El Último Tango* €€€
Rua Diário de Notícias 62. **Map** 7 A4. 🄲 *21-342 03 41.*
In this Argentinian restaurant the most popular choice is meat grilled over an
open fire. It also has cocktails. ● *Sun; lunch; 2 weeks in Jun; 2 weeks in Oct.* 🗏

	MC V	■	●	

Price categories are for a three-course meal for one with half a bottle of wine, including cover charge, service and VAT:

€ under 10
€€ 10–15
€€€ 15–20.5
€€€€ 20.5–30
€€€€€ over 30

LATE OPENING
The kitchen stays open after 10pm, and you can usually have a meal up until at least 11pm.

OUTDOOR TABLES
Tables for eating outdoors, in a garden or on a balcony, often with a pleasant view.

GOOD WINE LIST
The restaurant will have a good selection of quality wines.

CREDIT CARDS
This indicates which of the major credit cards are accepted: *AE* American Express, *DC* Diners Club, *MC* MasterCard and *V* Visa.

	CREDIT CARDS	LATE OPENING	OUTDOOR TABLES	GOOD WINE LIST
BAIRRO ALTO: *Massima Culpa* €€€ Rua da Atalaia 35–7. **Map 4 F2.** 21-342 01 21. This restaurant has a simple, uncomplicated decor with a very Italian atmosphere, and offers numerous antipasti and pasta dishes. ● *lunch; Mon.* ▤	AE DC MC V	■		
BAIRRO ALTO: *Canto do Camões* €€€€ Travessa da Espera 38. **Map 7 A4.** 21-346 54 64. This small, tiled *fado (see pp66–7)* restaurant serves traditional Portuguese food and a range of international dishes. ● *Sun (Nov–Mar).* ▤ ♫	AE DC MC V	■		
BAIRRO ALTO: *Pap'Açorda* €€€€ Rua da Atalaia 57. **Map 4 F2.** 21-346 48 11. Both Lisboetas and tourists come here for the *açorda de mariscos* (bread stew and seafood). The menu is traditional Portuguese with some novel touches. ● *Mon lunch; Sun; 2 weeks in Jul; 2 weeks in Oct.* ▤	AE DC MC V			■
BAIRRO ALTO: *Tavares* €€€€€ Rua da Misericórdia 35-37. **Map 7 A4.** 21-342 11 12. Lisbon's oldest restaurant, Tavares, dates from 1784. Its reputation is maintained with dishes such as breast of partridge on toast with *foie gras* and fillets of sea bass *au gratin* with prawn sauce. ● *Sat; Sun lunch.* ▤ ♿	AE DC MC V			■
BAIXA: *Casa do Alentejo* €€ Rua das Portas de Santo Antão 58. **Map 7 A2.** 21-346 92 31. Set in a fine 19th-century house, this restaurant specializes entirely in Alentejan food such as *açorda alentejana* (coriander and bread soup). ● *1–19 Aug.*	MC V			
BAIXA: *Ribadouro* €€ Rua do Salitre 2–12. **Map 4 F1.** 21-354 94 11. On the corner of the Avenida da Liberdade in a long, pointed building. Like most, this cervejaria specializes in seafood. ▤	AE DC MC V	■		
BAIXA: *Lagosta Real* €€€ Rua das Portas de Santo Antão 37. **Map 7 A2.** 21-342 39 95. Fish, and particularly shellfish, is the order of the day here. Shellfish casserole, lobster stew and a grilled seafood platter are house specialities. ▤	AE DC MC V	■	●	■
BAIXA: *Paris* €€€ Rua dos Sapateiros 126. **Map 7 B4.** 21-346 97 97. Open for nearly half a century, Paris offers a delicious mixture of Portuguese and Galician cuisine. Try the swordfish steak or the Alentejan pork. ▤ ♿	AE DC MC V			
BAIXA: *Solar dos Presuntos* €€€ Rua das Portas de Santo Antão 150. **Map 7 A2.** 21-342 42 53. An enticing window display of fish and shellfish draws diners inside. Caricatures of famous footballers adorn the walls. ● *Sun; 2 weeks in Aug; 1 week at Christmas.* ▤	AE DC MC V			
BAIXA: *Gambrinus* €€€€€ Rua das Portas de Santo Antão 23. **Map 7 A2.** 21-342 14 66. Renowned throughout Portugal, this is an exceptional and expensive restaurant. The service is impeccable, the cuisine delectable and the extensive wine list includes an array of vintage ports. ● *1 May.* ▤	AE V	■		■
BELÉM: *Já Sei* €€€ Avda Brasilia 202. **Map 1 A5.** 21-301 59 69. This has a beautiful location, right on the river, so it is pleasant in the summer; the seafood-based menu is good all-year-round. ● *Sun dinner; Mon.* ▤ ♫	AE DE MC V		●	■
BELÉM: *São Jerónimo* €€€€ Rua dos Jerónimos 12. **Map 1 C4.** 21-364 87 97. São Jerónimo is an elegant, spacious restaurant with 1930s decor. The excellent mixed menu of Portuguese and French cuisine includes skate in peach sauce and duck with nuts in wine sauce. ● *Sat lunch; Sun.* ▤	AE DC MC V			■

For key to symbols see back flap

<table>
<tr><td colspan="2">

Price categories are for a three-course meal for one with half a bottle of wine, including cover charge, service and VAT:

€ under 10
€€ 10–15
€€€ 15–20.5
€€€€ 20.5–30
€€€€€ over 30

</td>
<td colspan="4">

LATE OPENING
The kitchen stays open after 10pm, and you can usually have a meal up until at least 11pm.

OUTDOOR TABLES
Tables for eating outdoors, in a garden or on a balcony, often with a pleasant view.

GOOD WINE LIST
The restaurant will have a good selection of quality wines.

CREDIT CARDS
This indicates which of the major credit cards are accepted: *AE* American Express, *DC* Diners Club, *MC* MasterCard and *V* Visa.

</td>
</tr>
</table>

	CREDIT CARDS	LATE OPENING	OUTDOOR TABLES	GOOD WINE LIST
BELÉM: *Vela Latina* €€€€ Doca do Bom Sucesso. **Map** 1 B5. ☏ 21-301 71 18. On the waterfront, this restaurant has a bar and terrace overlooking the Torre de Belém. The speciality is *cataplana rica do mar* (seafood). ● Sun. ▤ &	AE DC MC V	■	●	■
BELÉM: *O Nobre* €€€€€ Rua das Mercês 71a–b. **Map** 2 D3. ☏ 21-363 38 27. Worth searching out on a day trip to Belém, O Nobre serves crab soup, game stew, partridge, fish with olives and roast pork with grapes. ● Sun; Sat lunch.	AE MC V	■		■
CAMPO PEQUENO: *Chimarrão* €€€ Campo Pequeno 79. **Map** 5 C1. ☏ 21-793 97 60. This Brazilian restaurant specializes in dishes grilled on an open fire. Try *rodízio* (unlimited amount of grilled meat) with salad, rice and black beans. ▤ ♫	AE DC MC V	■		
CAMPO PEQUENO: *António Clara – Clube dos Empresários* €€€€ Avenida da República 38. **Map** 5 C1. ☏ 21-799 42 80. This wonderful old mansion offers a French-influenced menu in dining areas that were once individual rooms in the house. ● Sun. ▤	AE DC MC V	■		■
CHIADO: *Adega do Ribatejo* €€€ Rua Diário de Notícias 23. **Map** 7 A4. ☏ 21-346 83 43. This charming tavern, whose menu is strong on steak and fried fish, offers frequent and unmissable *fado* extravaganzas. ● Sun. ▤ ♫	MC V	■		
CHIADO: *Tágide* €€€€€ Largo da Academia Nacional de Belas Artes 18–20. **Map** 7 B5. ☏ 21-342 07 20. An elegant restaurant with 18th-century tiles, a 17th-century fountain and a superb view over the Tagus. Luxurious dishes include marinated salmon, baby octopus in red wine sauce and partridge in port sauce. ● Sat lunch; Sun. ▤	AE DC MC V	■		■
ENTRECAMPOS: *A Gôndola* €€€ Avenida de Berna 64. **Map** 5 B2. ☏ 21-797 04 26. A Gôndola is a charming restaurant offering a wide choice of dishes including Italian as well as Portuguese specialities. In the summer enjoy your meal in the pleasant surrounding gardens. ● Sun. ▤	AE MC V		●	■
ESTEFÂNIA: *Espiral* € Praça da Ilha do Faial 14a. **Map** 6 D3. ☏ 21-357 35 85. This vegetarian restaurant, set in a pleasant square, has a plain interior but a large menu, with fresh juice drinks and organic wine. ● 1 Jan; 1 May. ▤	AE MC V			
ESTEFÂNIA: *Clara Restaurante* €€€€€ Campo dos Mártires da Pátria 49. **Map** 6 D5. ☏ 21-885 30 53. This is a spacious and luxurious restaurant in a green-tiled mansion, complete with garden terrace, fountain and fireplace. The excellent menu is predominantly traditional Portuguese. ● Sat lunch; Sun; 1–15 Aug. ▤ ♫	AE DC MC V		●	■
ESTRELA: *Conventual* €€€€ Praça das Flores 44-45. **Map** 4 E2. ☏ 21-390 91 96. Decorated with religious antiques, this restaurant has an interesting menu that includes fried baby eels and ox tongue in egg sauce. ● Sat lunch; Sun; Mon. ▤	AE DC MC V			■
GRAÇA: *Via Graça* €€€ Rua Damasceno Monteiro 9b. **Map** 8 D1. ☏ 21-887 08 30. Via Graça offers some fine views of the castle and the Baixa, and well-presented Portuguese cuisine. ● Sat lunch; Sun. ▤	AE DC MC V	■		■
LAPA: *Café d'Arte* € Rua das Janelas Verdes, Museu de Arte Antiga. **Map** 4 D4. ☏ 21-396 09 30. This establishment provides an excellent opportunity to combine lunch with a museum trip in a fantastic riverside setting. ● Mon; Tue & evenings (closes with museum). ▤ &	AE MC V		●	

LAPA: *Picanha*   €€€
Rua das Janelas Verdes 96. **Map 4 D4.** 📞 *21-397 54 01.*
Picanha sells one dish: *picanha*, which is rump steak grilled on an open fire,
served with potatoes, rice, salad and beans. ● *Sat; Sun lunch.* 🍴

LAPA: *Nariz de Vinho Tinto*   €€€€   AE
Rua do Conde 75. **Map 4 D3.** 📞 *21-395 30 35.*   V
This restaurant offers top-class cooking and is famous for its casseroles and
choice of regional dishes, including wild game in season. ● *Mon.* 🍴 ♿

LAPA: *A Confraria*   €€€€€   AE
Pensão York House, Rua das Janelas Verdes 32. **Map 4 D4.** 📞 *21-396 24 35.*   DC
This delightful hotel restaurant has a varied menu. Sit inside and admire the   MC
tiled walls, or outside below a palm in the flower-laden courtyard. 🍴   V

LAPA: *Ristorante Hotel Cipriani*   €€€€€   AE
Lapa Palace, Rua do Pau da Bandeira 4. **Map 3 C3.** 📞 *21-394 94 34.*   DC
This restaurant offers modern Italian and Mediterranean food in an elegant   MC
setting. There is a non-smoking section. 🍴 ♿   V

LAPA: *Sua Excelência*   €€€€€   AE
Rua do Conde 34. **Map 4 D3.** 📞 *21-390 36 14.*   DC
The owner here can recite the menu in five languages. Classical Portuguese   MC
dishes served in a relaxed atmosphere. ● *Sat & Sun lunch; Wed; Sep.* 🍴 ♿   V

RATO: *Os Tibetanos*   €€   AE
Rua do Salitre 117. **Map 4 F1.** 📞 *21-314 20 38.*   MC
This vegetarian restaurant, in a Tibetan Buddhist centre, has much character   V
and offers a tasty and inexpensive Tibetan menu. No smoking. ● *Sat; Sun.* 🍴

RATO: *Casa da Comida*   €€€€€   AE
Travessa das Amoreiras 1. **Map 5 B5.** 📞 *21-388 53 76.*   DC
A refined Lisbon restaurant with a charming patio, and an exquisite menu   MC
offering caviar, frogs' legs, goat, duck and pheasant. ● *Sat lunch; Sun.* 🍴   V

ROTUNDA: *Restaurante 33A*   €€€€   AE
Rua Alexandre Herculano 33a. **Map 5 C5.** 📞 *21-354 60 79.*   DC
Offering traditional Portuguese cuisine, this restaurant also has a small lounge   MC
with a country ambience and decor to match. ● *Sat lunch; Sun.* 🍴 🎵 ♿   V

ROTUNDA: *Pabe*   €€€€€   AE
Rua Duque de Palmela 27a. **Map 5 C5.** 📞 *21-353 74 84.*   DC
Pabe looks like a Tudor house and serves Portuguese food. A medieval   MC
atmosphere is accentuated by wooden-beamed ceilings and copper tables. 🍴 ♿   V

ROTUNDA: *O Terraço*   €€€€€   AE
Hotel Tivoli Lisboa, Avenida da Liberdade 185. **Map 4 F1.** 📞 *21-319 89 61.*   DC
This top-floor restaurant serves an innovative lunchtime special each day   MC
of the week. There are great views from the terrace. 🍴 🎵 ♿   V

SALDANHA: *António*   €€   V
Rua Tomás Ribeiro 63. **Map 5 C3.** 📞 *21-353 87 80.*
This restaurant is a good stop for lunch. The cooking is straightforward,
and includes steak and fries and roast chicken. ● *Sun.* 🍴

SALDANHA: *Cervejaria Portugalia*   €€   AE
Avenida Almirante Reis 117. **Map 6 E5.** 📞 *21-314 00 02.*   DC
This atmospheric beer hall is the original of a small chain *(see p135)*, the   MC
restaurant is popular with families and serves excellent shellfish and steaks. ♿   V

SALDANHA: *Café Creme*   €€€   AE
Avenida Conde de Valbom 52a. **Map 5 B2.** 📞 *21-796 43 60.*   DC
An attractive, open and airy restaurant, Café Creme offers a wide choice of   MC
pastas, salads, cod, beef and grilled dishes. ● *Sat lunch; Sun.* 🍴   V

SALDANHA: *O Polícia*   €€€   AE
Rua Marquês Sá da Bandeira 112a. **Map 5 B3.** 📞 *21-796 35 05.*   MC
A pleasant restaurant with an attractive bar, so named because the owner's   V
grandfather was a policeman. The menu changes daily. ● *Sat eve; Sun.* 🍴

XABREGAS: *D'Avis*   €€€   AE
Rua do Grilo 96-98. 📞 *21-868 13 54.*   DC
Specialities at this restaurant, located east of the city centre, include cod with   MC
coriander and *migas* (bread dish with spare ribs). ● *Sun.* 🍴 ♿   V

Price categories are for a three-course meal for one with half a bottle of wine, including cover charge, service and VAT:
€ under 10
€€ 10–15
€€€ 15–20.5
€€€€ 20.5–30
€€€€€ over 30

LATE OPENING
The kitchen stays open after 10pm, and you can usually have a meal up until at least 11pm.

OUTDOOR TABLES
Tables for eating outdoors, in a garden or on a balcony, often with a pleasant view.

GOOD WINE LIST
The restaurant will have a good selection of quality wines.

CREDIT CARDS
This indicates which of the major credit cards are accepted: *AE* American Express, *DC* Diners Club, *MC* MasterCard and *V* Visa.

	CREDIT CARDS	LATE OPENING	OUTDOOR TABLES	GOOD WINE LIST

THE LISBON COAST

CASCAIS: *Dom Manolo* €€
Avenida Marginal 11. ☎ 21-483 11 26.
A good-value mixed menu; the house speciality is *frango no churrasco* (spit-roast chicken). *Pastéis de bacalhau* (cod croquettes) are also good. ● Jan. 🍽

| | | | ● | |

CASCAIS: *Estrela da India* €€
Rua Freitas Reis 15b. ☎ 21-484 65 40.
Some distance from the waterfront, this unpretentious Indian restaurant has a good choice of vegetarian dishes and a takeaway service. 🍽

| AE MC V | | | | |

CASCAIS: *Os Navegantes* €€
Travassa dos Navegantes 13. ☎ 21-486 86 31.
This Portuguese restaurant is very popular with locals and is famous for its fresh fish and spit-roasted meats. ● Sun.

| AE V | ▪ | | ▪ |

CASCAIS: *Esplanada Santa Marta* €€€
Travassa do Enviado de Inglaterra 1d, e, f. ☎ 21-352 11 94.
Known for its wide range of fish and shellfish dishes, as well as for a good choice of traditional Portuguese fare. During the summer the food is also served outside on a small terrace overlooking the sea. 🍽 ♿

| AE MC V | ▪ | ● | ▪ |

CASCAIS: *Buchanan's Café, Bar and Restaurant* €€€€
Travessa da Alfarrobeira 2. ☎ 21-484 75 90.
Located on the top floor of a building with stunning views over the new marina. High-quality modern European cuisine is served, with a choice of vegetarian dishes and fine wines. The café/bar has a fireplace. ● Mon (Oct–Mar). 🍽

| AE MC V | ▪ | ▪ | |

CASCAIS: *Casa Velha* €€€€
Avenida Valbom 1. ☎ 21-483 25 86.
With a recommended regional menu and charming rustic decor, Casa Velha also boasts a table always reserved for the president. ● Wed. 🍽 ♿

| AE MC V | ▪ | | |

CASCAIS: *Eduardo's* €€€€
Largo das Grutas 3. ☎ 21-483 19 01.
Tucked away in a quiet corner, Eduardo's serves a mix of Belgian cuisine and Portuguese dishes, many of which are flambéed at the table. ● Wed.

| AE MC V | | ● | ▪ |

CASCAIS: *O Pescador* €€€€€
Rua das Flores 10b. ☎ 21-483 20 54.
A well-known seaside restaurant, decorated with old boats, nets and pictures of famous people who have eaten here. Specializes in seafood. ● Sun. 🍽

| AE DC MC V | ▪ | ▪ | ▪ |

ERICEIRA: *O Barco* €€€
Rua Capitão João Lopes 14. ☎ 261-86 27 59.
O Barco has sea views. The fish specialities include *feijoada de marisco* (seafood and bean stew) and seafood curry. ● Thu; 2 weeks in Jul & Dec. 🍽

| AE DC MC V | | | |

ESTORIL: *Pinto's* €€
Arcadas do Parque 18b. ☎ 21-468 72 47.
Close to the Palácio Hotel, Pinto's is a mix of bar, cafeteria and restaurant. It serves pizzas and pastas, as well as a large selection of shellfish. 🍽

| AE DC MC V | ▪ | ● | |

ESTORIL: *Four Seasons* €€€€€
Hotel Palácio Estoril, Rua do Parque. ☎ 21-464 80 00.
Exposed beams and leather seats furnish this luxurious restaurant. Try the flambéed prawns with Pernod, cream and hollandaise sauce. 🍽 🎵 ♿

| AE DC MC V | | | ▪ |

GUINCHO: *Estalagem Muchaxo* €€€€
Praia do Guincho. ☎ 21-487 02 21.
Overlooking Cabo da Roca, Muchaxo offers a good seafood menu. A popular dish is lobster in a tomato, cream and port sauce. 🍽 🎵 Sat & Sun lunch. ♿

| AE DC MC V | ▪ | ● | ▪ |

GUINCHO: *Porto de Santa Maria* €€€€€ | AE MC DC V
Estrada do Guincho. **(** 21-487 94 50.
This is one of the best seafood restaurants in the area. Choose your meal from
the fish tanks and marble table where the best fish is displayed. ● *Mon.* 🗐 &

MONTE ESTORIL: *O Sinaleiro* €€ | AE MC DC V
Avenida de Sabóia 595. **(** 21-468 54 39.
O Sinaleiro serves excellent food and is popular with locals. Try *escalopes à
Zíngara* (in Madeira wine sauce with cream). ● *Wed; 2 weeks in Apr & Oct.* & 🗐

MONTE ESTORIL: *O Festival* €€€€ | AE MC DC V
Avenida de Sabóia 515d. **(** 21-468 85 63.
This delightful restaurant serves an essentially French menu. Try the duck à
l'orange or the sole filled with salmon mousseline. ● *Mon; Tue lunch.* 🗐

PAÇO D'ARCOS: *La Cocagne* €€€€€ | AE DC MC V
Avenida Marginal (Curva dos Pinheiros). **(** 21-441 42 31.
One of the best French restaurants in Portugal, La Cocagne has refined decor,
impeccable service, exquisite dishes and magnificent views of the ocean. 🗐

PALMELA: *Pousada de Palmela* €€€€€ | AE DC MC V
Pousada de Palmela, Castelo de Palmela. **(** 21-235 12 26.
The converted refectory of the 15th-century monastery offers such delicacies as
oyster soup or salt cod filled with bacon and coated in corn bread. 🎵 *Fri & Sat.*

PORTINHO DA ARRÁBIDA: *Beira-Mar* €€€ | AE DC MC V
Portinho da Arrábida. **(** 21-218 05 44.
Enjoy specials such as *arroz de tamboril* (monkfish rice) and *arroz de marisco*
(seafood rice) in this stunning seaside setting. ● *Wed (Oct–Mar); 15 Dec–15 Jan.*

QUELUZ: *Cozinha Velha* €€€€€ | AE DC MC V
Largo Palácio Nacional de Queluz. **(** 21-435 61 58.
Set in the old kitchens of the Queluz Royal Palace, this spacious restaurant is
famous for its typical Portuguese fare, such as pork with clams. 🗐 🎵

SESIMBRA: *Ribamar* €€€€ | AE MC V
Avenida dos Náufragos 29. **(** 21-223 48 53.
Right next to the sea and offering fantastic views, Ribamar serves some
unusual specialities; try fish with seaweed, or cream of sea-urchin soup. 🗐 &

SETÚBAL: *Copa d'Ouro* €€ | AE MC V
Rua João Soveral 17. **(** 265-52 37 55.
A superb fish menu here features *caldeirada à Setubalense* (seafood stew)
and *cataplana de tamboril* (monkfish steamed *a cataplana*). ● *Tue; Sep.* 🗐

SETÚBAL: *Pousada de São Filipe* €€€€ | AE DC MC V
Pousada de São Filipe, Castelo de São Filipe. **(** 265-55 00 70.
This restaurant is part of a *pousada* that overlooks Setúbal and the Sado estuary.
Its regional dishes include pumpkin cream soup and fried red mullet. 🗐

SINTRA: *Tulhas* €€ | AE DC MC V
Rua Gil Vicente 4–6. **(** 21-923 23 78.
This rustic restaurant, decorated with blue and yellow Sintra *azulejos*, serves
superb traditional dishes such as veal steaks in Madeira sauce. ● *Wed.* 🗐

SINTRA: *Lawrence's* €€€€ | AE V
Rua Consiglieri Pedroso 39–40, Sintra. **(** 21-910 55 00.
Set in the Lawrence's Hotel, this restaurant has a wide-ranging international
and Portuguese menu that changes daily. 🗐 &

SINTRA: *Panorâmico* €€€€ | AE DC MC V
Hotel Tivoli Sintra, Praça da República. **(** 21-923 35 05.
Overlooking the lush, verdant Sintra valley, this restaurant offers a different
speciality as a main dish each evening, as well as a regular menu. 🗐 &

SINTRA: *Restaurante Palácio de Seteais* €€€€€ | AE DC MC V
Avenida Barbosa du Bocage 8, Seteais. **(** 21-923 32 00.
Set in an 18th-century palace, which is now a hotel, this restaurant has a daily-
changing menu of international and traditional Portuguese cuisine. 🎵 &

VILA FRESCA DE AZEITÃO: *O Manel* $$ | AE MC V
Largo Dr Teixeira 6a. **(** 21-219 03 36.
A family-run restaurant with a good-value menu. Specialities here are cod in
cream sauce and *feijoada de gambas* (seafood and bean stew). ● *Sun; Oct.* 🗐

Cafés and Bars

THE PORTUGUESE LOVE COFFEE, and an entire culture has developed around it *(see p121)*. Relaxing over a coffee and a pastry in a café is a way of life in Lisbon.

Some of the most famous and delicious pastries served include *travesseiros* (almond pastries) and *bolos de arroz* (rice cakes). Belém is famous for its *pastéis de nata*, custard pastries, while Sintra is renowned for its *queijadas*, cinnamon cheesecakes *(see p123)*. Most of the bars and restaurants are in Bairro Alto and along the riverfront, and most offer a pleasant view.

Evening drinking is equally popular, and Lisbon and its coast offer a range of night-time venues, from sophisticated bars serving wine and cocktails to brasher venues pumping out beer and live music.

On the Lisbon Coast, there are many bars in central Cascais and plenty of cafés along the seafront promenade. In the countryside, Sintra's cafés are famous for their fine selections of mouthwatering pastries.

LISBON

ALCÂNTARA: *Alcântara Café*
Rua Maria Luísa Holstein 15. **Map** 3 A4.
『 21-363 71 76.
Catering to a fashionable clientele, the decor of this bar/restaurant is trendy and sophisticated in style. Food is only served during the evenings. 🍴

ALFAMA: *Bar Cerca Moura*
Largo das Portas do Sol 4. **Map** 8 D3.
『 21-887 48 59.
A pleasant place for a drink, the bar has a wonderful panoramic view of Alfama and the river below. Mainly serves snacks such as salads and finger food. 🖼

ALFAMA: *Bar das Imagens*
Calçada Marquês de Tancos 1b.
Map 7 C3. 『 21-888 46 36.
This bar and restaurant serves delicious African dishes and has a superb view over Lisbon. The atmosphere is trendy but pleasantly relaxed.
🍴 🎵 🖼

ALFAMA: *Restô do Chapitô*
Costa do Castelo 7. **Map** 7 C3.
『 21-886 73 34.
With superb of the Alfama and the river, this lively bar also has a restaurant that serves exciting and innovative cuisine.
🍴 🖼

BAIRRO ALTO: *Clube da Esquina*
Rua da Barroca 30. **Map** 4 F2.
『 21-342 71 49.
Situated on two floors, the Clube da Esquina is a lively bar with wooden interiors. It serves cocktails.

BAIRRO ALTO: *Mesón El Gordo Tapas Bar*
Rua São Boaventura 16–18.
Map 4 F2. 『 21-342 42 66.
This tastefully decorated bar and restaurant has a selection of 73 different *tapas*. Fine Portuguese wines are served by the glass. 🍴

BAIRRO ALTO: *Pavilhão Chinês*
Rua Dom Pedro V 89. **Map** 4 F2.
『 21-342 47 29.
One of Lisbon's best-known bars is decorated with collections of both mundane and curious artefacts from all over the world.

BAIRRO ALTO: *Solar do Vinho do Porto*
Rua de São Pedro de Alcântara 45.
Map 4 F2. 『 21-347 57 07.
Set in an old mansion *(see p54)*, this establishment serves a wide range of different ports, including some fine vintages.

BAIRRO ALTO: *Tertúlia*
Rua do Diário de Notícias 60. **Map** 7 A4. 『 21-346 27 04.
This tranquil café and bar has reasonably priced drinks and offers a selection of newspapers and magazines. Art exhibitions are also held here. 🎵

BAIXA: *A Ginjinha*
Largo de São Domingos 8. **Map** 7 B3.
『 21-388 08 50.
The smallest bar in Lisbon, off Rossio, is dedicated entirely to serving shots of a *ginjinha* (cherry liqueur) and nothing else.

BAIXA: *Café Martinho da Arcada*
Praça do Comércio 3. **Map** 7 C5.
『 21-886 62 13.
A traditional Lisbon café under the arches of Praça do Comércio, it was once frequented by Fernando Pessoa *(see p53)*. 🖼

BAIXA: *Café Nicola*
Praça Dom Pedro IV 24–25.
Map 7 B3. 『 21-346 05 79.
One of Lisbon's oldest and most famous terraced cafés, this is a charming spot for breakfast, served by smart waiters. It is famous as the haunt of the satirical poet Manuel du Bocage (1765–1805). Wall paintings inside the café illustrate his life. 🍴 🖼

BAIXA: *Chiadomel Restaurant Bar*
Alto do Elevador de Santa Justa.
Map 7 B3. 『 21-346 95 98.
Situated at the top of the Santa Justa lift, the Chiadomel serves a variety of foreign beers and snacks. 🍴 🖼

BAIXA: *Confeitaria Nacional*
Praça da Figueira 18b. **Map** 7 B3.
『 21-342 44 70.
This classic café has wonderful Art Nouveau decor. Pastries and cakes baked on the premises include good *pastéis de nata* and *bolo rei*.

BAIXA: *Pastelaria Suiça*
Praça Dom Pedro IV 96–101. **Map** 7 B3. 『 21-321 40 90.
A good place to have breakfast outdoors before a day of sightseeing, this café serves a wide variety of pastries. Overlooking the square, it is popular with Lisboetas stopping off on their way to work. 🍴 🖼

BELÉM: *Antiga Casa dos Pastéis de Belém*
Rua de Belém 84–88. **Map** 1 C4.
『 21-363 74 23.
A trip to Belém is not complete without visiting this charming tiled café to sample its delicious *pastéis de nata* and excellent coffees.

CAIS DO SODRE: *O'Gilins*
Rua dos Remolares 8.
Map 7 A5. 『 21-342 18 99.
This Irish-style pub has a wooden interior. The atmosphere is lively, especially on band nights. Irish stouts and other beers are available. 🍴 🎵

CAMPO PEQUENO: *Galeto*
Avenida da República 14. **Map** 5 C1.
『 21-354 44 44.
A restaurant and snack bar on two floors, Galeto is a good place to visit for a late night snack as it serves food into the early hours.
🍴 🖼

CAMPO PEQUENO: *Versailles*
Avenida da República 15a. **Map** 5 C1.
[21-354 63 40.
A well-known, turn-of-the-century restaurant café, the Versailles is ornately decorated in the Parisian style. Smartly attired waiters serve lunches, teas and dinners to a well-heeled clientele. [11]

CHIADO: *A Brasileira*
Rua Garrett 120. **Map** 7 A4.
[21-346 95 41.
This is one of Lisbon's oldest and best-known cafés. Founded in 1895, it became a haunt for artists and poets and continues to draw artists and media types. [11] [symbol]

CHIADO: *Bar Pintái*
Largo da Trindade 22. **Map** 7 A3.
[21-342 48 02.
There is live Brazilian music daily in this large cavernous bar and plentiful *caipirinha*, a drink made of *cachaça* (sugar cane spirit), lime, sugar and crushed ice. [symbol]

CHIADO: *Café Pastelaria Bénard*
Rua Garrett 104. **Map** 7 A4.
[21-347 31 33.
This café serves an excellent selection of cakes and pastries. It also has an outdoor terrace. [symbol]

CHIADO: *Café Rosso*
Galerias Garrett Rua Ivens 53-61.
Map 7 A4. [21-347 15 24.
This pleasant courtyard café serves pizzas and other dishes. [symbol]

CHIADO: *Cervejaria Trindade*
Rua Nova da Trindade 20c.
Map 7 A4. [21-342 35 06.
A huge beer hall-style restaurant with beautiful *azulejo* panels, it specializes in seafood. [11]

DOCAS: *Doca de Santo*
Doca de Santo Amaro. **Map** 3 A5.
[21-396 35 22.
This is one of several warehouses along the marina which have been converted into a bar. The terrace has a wonderful view of the marina and river. [11] [symbol]

DOCAS: *Rock City*
Rua Cintura do Porto de Lisboa 225.
[21-342 86 36.
A huge atmospheric American bar, Rock City has live music and a restaurant. [11] [symbol] [symbol]

DOCAS: *Salsa Latina*
Gare Marítima de Alcântara 30. **Map** 3 B4. [21-395 05 55.
This smart bar and restaurant with a terrace overlooking the river, caters to an affluent crowd. Salsa and Latin music are played most evenings. [11] [symbol] [symbol]

GRAÇA: *Bar da Graça*
Travessa da Pereira 43. **Map** 8 E2.
[21-886 37 44.
A trendy bar with live music, art exhibitions and theatre shows. Serves an excellent variety of foreign beers. [symbol]

PENHA DA FRANÇA: *Portugália*
Avenida Almirante Reis 117.
Map 6 E5. [21-314 00 02.
Although there are now several Portugalias in Lisbon, this is the original. Popular with families, this is a classic beer-hall with a bar offering snacks and a restaurant with reasonably priced hearty meals in the back (*see p131*). [11]

RATO: *Real Fábrica*
Rua da Escola Politécnica 275.
Map 4 E1. [21-385 20 90.
A tastefully renovated old ceramic factory on two floors. The bar on the ground floor serves beers and snacks. There is a smart restaurant on the upper floor. [11] [symbol]

THE LISBON COAST

CASCAIS: *Bar 24*
Rua Marquês Leal Pancada 24.
[21-482 12 71.
One of the tiniest bars in town, with trendy decor, Bar 24 attracts a young crowd and can get quite packed. It offers a great range of alcoholic drinks.

CASCAIS: *Bar Trem Velho*
Alameda Duquesa de Palmela.
[21-486 73 55.
This relaxed bar is in a converted train carriage next to Cascais train station. Serves snacks and litre mugs of beer called *girafas*. [11]

CASCAIS: *Beefeaters*
Rua Visconde da Luz 1a.
[21-484 06 96.
This bar serves English ales, Dutch beer and Guinness among other beers. Also offers traditional British pub food. [11] [symbol]

CASCAIS: *Casa do Largo*
Largo da Assunção 6.
[21-483 18 56.
The Casa do Largo is a favourite haunt of the fashionable Cascais population of all ages. Set in an old house and decorated with pictures of boats and other nautical themes. [11] [symbol]

CASCAIS: *John Bull*
Largo Luís de Camões 4.
[21-483 33 19.
A British institution with wooden interiors on two floors, the John Bull serves a variety of local and foreign, especially British, beers on tap. [11] [symbol]

ESTORIL: *Deck Bar*
Arcadas do Parque 21–22.
[21-468 03 66.
One of Estoril's most popular terraced cafés, the Deck Bar is situated under arches opposite elegant gardens. Serves meals till 1am. Closed Mondays. [11] [symbol]

ESTORIL: *Frolic*
Avenida Clotilde.
[21-468 12 19.
The Frolic is a pleasant bar, restaurant and café serving delicious coffee and cakes. Downstairs there is a popular disco that is open every night until 4am. Tables outside overlook Estoril's park. [11]

ESTORIL: *Tamariz Bar*
Praia do Tamariz.
A lively, terraced bar overlooking Praia do Tamariz, the Tamariz Bar is a venue for live music every weekend. Serves salads, burgers and a variety of drinks including *caipirinhas* and jugs of *sangria*. Only open during summer months. [symbol] [symbol]

SINTRA: *Café da Natália*
Rua 1° de Dezembro 3–5, São Pedro de Sintra. [21-923 56 79.
This old manor house, converted into an airy café, serves local food and wines. Dona Natália is known for her delicious quiches and crepes. Closed Sundays. [11]

SINTRA: *Café Paris*
Largo Rainha Dona Amélia 32.
[21-923 23 75.
An elegant, terraced café located on the main square opposite the Palácio Nacional, Café Paris is also open for lunches and dinners. [11] [symbol]

SINTRA: *Casa da Sapa*
Volta do Duche 12. [21-923 04 93.
A tiny cake shop, it has been baking its famous *queijadas* (cinnamon cheesecakes) since the mid-18th century. Lovely view of the Sintra valley. [symbol]

SINTRA: *Pastelaria Piriquita*
Rua das Padarias 1–3.
[21-923 06 26.
One of Sintra's oldest cafés, it is situated on a narrow street opposite the Palácio Nacional. Serves good *queijadas* and *travesseiros* (almond pastries).

SINTRA: *Restaurante Café Cintia*
Avenida Miguel Bombarda 49.
[21-923 27 12.
A typical Portuguese café with a dark interior, it offers a glorious view of the Sintra valley and serves excellent *travesseiros*. [11] [symbol]

SHOPS AND MARKETS

LISBON offers a wide variety of shops to the visitor, with its combination of elegant high street shops, flea markets and modern shopping centres. The cobbled streets of the Baixa, and the chic Chiado district have traditionally been Lisbon's main shopping areas, but now the new out-of-town shopping centres are becoming increasingly

Portuguese ceramic cockerel

popular. Numerous markets in Lisbon, Sintra and Cascais provide more adventurous shopping. If you are after something typically Portuguese, the handwoven tapestries and lacework are worth buying. Most of all, choose from a range of ceramics, such as *azulejos* or Vista Alegre porcelain. For wine lovers, Lisbon's wine merchants offer the best from all over the country.

A delicatessen in the Bairro Alto

OPENING HOURS

TRADITIONAL SHOPPING hours are Monday to Friday 9am to 1pm and 3pm to 7pm, and Saturday 9am to 1pm.

However, in order to satisfy consumer demand, many shops, especially those in the Baixa, are now staying open during the lunch hour and on Saturday afternoons. Specialist shops such as hardware stores generally close for lunch at 12:30pm and reopen at 2:30pm. Shopping centres are open daily from 10am to midnight with most shops closing at 11pm. Generally, convenience stores, such as the **Select** chain, are open daily from 7am to 2am.

HOW TO PAY

MOST SHOPS in Lisbon accept Visa and, to a lesser extent, American Express and MasterCard. Many smaller shops outside the main shopping areas will

not. An alternative is to obtain a cash advance with a credit card from one of the many Multibanco teller machines (ATMs). Note that these charge interest on the withdrawal from day one, in addition to a currency conversion fee.

VAT AND TAXES

NON-EUROPEAN UNION residents are exempt from IVA (Value Added Tax) in Portugal provided they remain in the country for no longer than 180 days. However, obtaining a rebate may be complicated in small shops or in areas less frequented by tourists. It is much simpler to buy in shops with a Tax Free sign outside.

To get your rebate, ask the shop assistant for an *Isençao na Exportaçao* form. This must then be presented to a customs

officer on your departure from Portugal. The original of the document will be returned to the vendor who is responsible for the reimbursement.

SHOPPING CENTRES

MODERN SHOPPING centres have become increasingly popular in Lisbon. The **Amoreiras Shopping Centre** is a huge complex, with cinema, underground parking and a range of shops and restaurants. **Galerias Monumental** is a smaller complex with four cinemas, a supermarket, restaurant and bar, clothes shops and underground parking. **Armazéns do Chiado** is a trendy centre in the Chiado district; its historic façade masks a modern interior. **El Corte Inglés** at the top of Parque Eduardo VII is the first store from this Spanish chain. **Vasco da Gama** is a newish shopping venue in Parque das Nações and has a variety of shops. **Cascaishopping** is the largest centre outside Lisbon, with 130 shops, seven cinemas and restaurants; it is located between Sintra and Estoril. The large **Centro Colombo** in Benfica also has an amusement park.

The vast Amoreiras Shopping Centre, home to international chain stores

Shoppers browsing among the bric-a-brac in the popular Feira da Ladra

MARKETS

Campo de Santa Clara

THERE ARE markets of every variety in Lisbon, from municipal markets selling fresh produce to the famous **Feira da Ladra** (Thieves' Market), a flea market on the slopes of the Alfama district. Although some stalls just sell junk, some bargains can be found among the array of bric-a-brac, second-hand clothes and general arts and crafts.

For more specialized markets, the **Feira Numismática** in Praça do Comércio has a fascinating selection of old Portuguese coins and notes. Located at Parque das Nações are the **Feira de Antiguidades Velharas**, an antiques market, and the **Feira dos Alfarrabistas**, for old books.

Set in picturesque surroundings outside Lisbon, the **Feira de São Pedro**, in Sintra, is a wonderful market selling everything from new clothes and old bric-a-brac, to maturing cheeses and noisy livestock.

Fresh fish for sale at one of Lisbon's minicipal markets

Along the coast, the **Feira de Cascais** has some good clothes bargains, as does the **Feira de Carcavelos**. Arrive early to beat the crowds.

FOOD SHOPS

IT IS ALMOST IMPOSSIBLE to window shop in Lisbon's delicatessens *(charcutarias)* without buying. Lined with a vast array of mouth watering foods, from superb cheeses to tasty smoked meats and exquisite sweets, establishments such as **Charcutaria Brasil** are a must for all seasoned gourmets. Here you can buy almost all regional specialities, from cheeses such as *serra* and *ilhas* to wild game such as partidge. Smoked hams and spicy sausages are also popular. If you have a sweet tooth, try some delicious *ovos moles* (egg sweets) or an assortment of dried or crystallized fruits, including delicious Elvas plums.

Other good food shops include **Charcutaria Carvalho & Morais** and **Manteigaria Londrina**, which specializes in cheeses. **Celeiro Dieta** is a good health food shop, and is well-known for stocking a wide range of organic foods.

WINES AND SPIRITS

THERE IS PLENTY of choice for the wine connoisseur in Lisbon, from light *vinhos verdes* and rosés to more mature *tintos* (red wines) and fruity Muscatel dessert wines. Fortified wines such as port and Madeira are widely available and vary considerably in taste. Some of the most popular (and very strong) spirits and brandies on the market include Bagaceira Velha and Maceira. **Napoleão**, the best-known wine merchants in Lisbon, has outlets dotted all around the city, with its oldest shop in the Baixa. If you wish to buy port specifically, the best place to visit, though not the cheapest, is the **Solar do Vinho do Porto** *(see p54)*, in the Bairro Alto, where you can sample some superb vintages before deciding what to buy. At **Garrafeira** in Campo de Ourique, the shopkeeper always seems to dig up something interesting. Not the most organized wine merchants, but certainly one of the city's best. Alternatively, visit the cellars of **J.M. da Fonseca** in Azeitão, where you can taste and buy numerous different wines.

MUSIC AND MULTIMEDIA

THE MUSIC SCENE in Portugal has exploded recently and Portuguese rock music, which is influenced by African music from the former colonies has found international fame.

FNAC operates two megastores in the city and are considered to be Lisbon's best equipped music stores. Apart from CDs and cassettes, there are magazines, computer games, laser-discs, CD-ROMs, videos and T-shirts also on sale. **Valentim de Carvalho**, another music store, has outlets all over town with its main store in Rua do Carmo. Both stores stock a variety of Portuguese music, from the latest rock hits to more traditional *fado* and folk music.

Frontage of Livraria Bertrand, one of Lisbon's oldest bookshops

BOOKSHOPS

PORTUGAL ENJOYS a great literary tradition with a range of authors, past and present, such as Luís de Camões, Fernando Pessoa and José Saramago. Translated versions of their works are available in most large bookshops.

Three of Lisbon's oldest bookshops include **Livraria Bertrand** and **Livraria Portugal**, both in the Chiado, and **Livraria Buchholz** near Avenida da Liberdade. Here you can find a wide selection of both English and foreignlanguage books, from travel guides to dictionaries as well as paperback fiction novels and hardbacks on a range of subjects including art, history and literature.

For an interesting selection of second-hand books, try visiting the **Feira dos Alfarrabistas** market, held at Parque das Nações on the last two Sundays of every month.

Terracotta ware for sale in Setúbal

CLOTHES

Lisbon has branches of many international chainstores, most of which can be found in the growing number of purpose built shopping centres in the city (*see p136*).

Amongst the Portuguese stores are a number of exclusive shops, including **Rosa & Teixeira**, a well-established tailors stocking classic menswear. **Loja das Meias** is a clothing store with several outlets in Lisbon. For something special, **Ana Salazar** is one of Portugal's most famous designers, but her prices are high.

CERAMICS

Portugal's ceramics are famous for their quality and variety. In Lisbon you can find everything, from delicate porcelain to rustic terracotta, and from tiles to tableware.

The very fine **Vista Alegre** porcelain tableware is internationally known. Also famous are the hand-painted ceramics, including tiles from **Viúva Lamego**, **Santana** and **Cerâmica Artistica de Carcavelos**. Known as *azulejos*, glazed tiles have long been used in Portugal to brighten up buildings. They are usually sold as complete paintings, 16 or 25 square in size. In Cascais, **Ceramicarte** is one of the largest ceramic centres. Perhaps the most ubiquitous pottery originates from Barcelos, famous for its decoratively painted cockerel which has become the unofficial national symbol.

REGIONAL CRAFTS

Portugal has a rich history of fine regional craftwork (*artesanato*), in particular embroidery and fine lace, hand-knitted woolens, and delicate jewellery made from silver and gold thread. There are plenty of handicraft and gift shops in the Restauradores and Rossio areas of Lisbon, though these can be a little touristy. **Arte Rustica**, in the Baixa, is excellent for genuine crafts.

Regionália, in Estoril, and **Sintra Bazar** in central Sintra, are also both good for arts. Between July and August a wide variety of carafts can be seen at the **Estoril Craft Fair**, at which artisans from all over Portugal gather to exhibit their work. **Casa Quintão** specializes in fine hand-woven carpets and tapestries. Cork carvings and pottery can be found at **Santos Oficios**.

Lisbon offers regional crafts from all over Portugal

ANTIQUES

Antiques often tend to be overpriced in Portugal, especially in Lisbon where the shops are mostly geared to a fairly up-market clientele. You will generally find better value in towns outside the city. Look for shops that are members of APA (*Associação Portuguesa de Antiquários*), often indicated by a sign in the shop window.

The majority of Lisbon's antique shops, such as **Antiguidades Moncada** and **Brique-à-Braque de São Bento**, are located in Rua Dom Pedro V, at the top of the Bairro Alto, in Rua de São Bento, by the Parliament building, and around the cathedral, in the Alfama. There are numerous religious artefacts to be found in the area and **Solar** specializes in 16th–20th-century tiles (*azulejos*).

Beautiful prints (known as *gravuras*), sold at various second-hand bookshops in the Bairro Alto, are usually good value for money. **Livraria Olisipo** stocks books and also old prints of landscapes, fauna and maps. For a good range of quality antiques, it is worth visiting the auctions held at **Cabral Moncada Leilões** (every Monday evening) and also the Antiques Fair, which is held in Lisbon annually during April.

SIZE CHART

Lisbon uses both British and American systems.

Women's dresses, coats and skirts

Portuguese	34	36	38	40	42	44	46
British	8	10	12	14	16	18	20
American	6	8	10	12	14	16	18

Women's shoes

Portuguese	36	37	38	39	40	41
British	3	4	5	6	7	8
American	5	6	7	8	9	10

Men's suits

Portuguese	44	46	48	50	52	54	56	58
British	34	36	38	40	42	44	46	48
American	34	36	38	40	42	44	46	48

Men's shirts

Portuguese	36	38	39	41	42	43	44	45
British	14	15	15½	16	16½	17	17½	18
American	14	15	15½	16	16½	17	17½	18

Men's shoes

Portuguese	39	40	41	42	43	44	45	46
British	6	7	7½	8	9	10	11	12
American	7	7½	8	8½	9½	10½	11	11½

DIRECTORY

SHOPPING CENTRES

Amoreiras
Avenida Eng. Duarte
Pacheco, Amoreiras.
Map 5 A5.
21-381 02 00.

Armazéns do Chiado
Rua do Carmo,
Chiado. **Map** 7 B4.
21-321 06 00.

Cascaishopping
Estrada Nacional 9,
Alcabideche - Estoril.
21-467 90 78.

Centro Colombo
Avenida Lusíada
Colombo.
21-711 36 36.

El Corte Inglés
Avenida António Augusto
Aguiar. **Map** 5 B5.
21-371 17 00.

Galerias Monumental
Avenida Fontes Pereira
de Melo 51e, Saldanha.
Map 5 C4.
21-351 05 00.

Vasco da Gama
Avenida Dom João II,
Parque das Nações.
21-893 06 01.

MARKETS

Feira dos Alfarrabistas
Parque das Nações.

Feira de Antiguidades Velharas
Parque das Nações.

Feira de Carcavelos
Carcavelos.

Feira de Cascais
Cascais.

Feira da Ladra
Alfama. **Map** 8 E3.

Feira Numismática
Praça do Comércio.
Map 7 C5.

Feira de São Pedro
Sintra.

FOOD SHOPS

Celeiro Dieta
Rua 1º de Dezembro 65,
Rossio. **Map** 7 B3.
21-342 24 63.

Charcutaria Brasil
Rua Alexandre Herculano
90–92, Rato. **Map** 5 C5.
21-388 56 44.

Charcutaria Carvalho and Morais
Avenida João XXI 54,
Areeiro.
Map 6 E1.
21-797 34 12.

Manteigaria Londrina
Rua das Portas de Santo
Antão 53–5,
Rossio. **Map** 7 A2.
21-342 74 48.

WINES AND SPIRITS

Garrafira
Rua Tomás de Anunciação
29a, Campo de Ourique.
21-397 34 94.

J.M. da Fonseca
Vila Nogueira de Azeitão,
Azeitão.
21-219 15 00.

Napoleão
Rua dos Fanqueiros 72–6,
Baixa.
Map 7 C4.
21-887 20 42.

Solar do Vinho do Porto
Rua São Pedro de
Alcântara 45 r/c,
Bairro Alto. **Map** 7 A3.
21-347 57 07.

MUSIC AND MULTIMEDIA

FNAC
Rua Nova do Almada 110,
Chiado. **Map** 7 B4
21-322 18 00.

Valentim de Carvalho
Rua do Carmo, Edifício
Grandella. **Map** 7 B4.
21-324 15 70.

BOOKSHOPS

Livraria Bertrand
Rua Garrett 73,
Chiado. **Map** 7 A4.
21-342 19 41.

Livraria Buchholz
Rua Duque de Palmela 4,
Rotunda. **Map** 5 C5.
21-317 05 80.

Livraria Portugal
Rua do Carmo 70–74,
Chiado. **Map** 7 B4.
21-347 49 82.

CLOTHES

Ana Salazar
Rua do Carmo 87,
Chiado. **Map** 7 B3.
21-347 22 89.

Loja das Meias
Praça Dom Pedro IV 1,
Rossio. **Map** 7 B3.
21-347 41 81.

Rosa & Teixeira
Avenida da Liberdade 204,
Liberdade. **Map** 5 C5.
21-311 03 50.

CERAMICS

Cerâmica Artistica de Carcavelos
Avenida Loureiro 47b,
Carcavelos.
21-456 32 67.

Ceramicarte
Largo da Assunção 3–4,
Cascais.
21-484 01 70.

Santana
Rua do Alecrim 95,
Chiado. **Map** 7 A5.
21-342 25 37.

Vista Alegre
Largo do Chiado 18,
Chiado. **Map** 7 A4.
21-346 14 01.

Viúva Lamego
Calçada do Sacramento 29,
Chiado. **Map** 7 B4.
21-346 96 92.

REGIONAL CRAFTS

Arte Rústica
Rua Áurea 246–8,
Baixa. **Map** 7 B4.
21-342 11 27.

Casa Quintão
Rua Serpa Pinto12,
Chiado. **Map** 7 A4.
21-346 58 37.

Regionália
Arcadas do Parque 27,
Estoril.
21-468 16 19.

Santos Ofícios
Rua da Madalena 87,
Baixa. **Map** 7 C4
21-887 20 31.

Sintra Bazar
Praça da República 37,
Sintra.
21-924 82 45.

ANTIQUES

Antiguidades Moncada
Rua Dom Pedro V 34,
Bairro Alto. **Map** 4 F2.
21-346 82 95.

Brique-à-Braque de São Bento
Rua São Bento 542,
São Bento. **Map** 4 E1.
21-390 70 01.

Cabral Moncada Leilões
Rua Miguel Lupi, 12,
Estrela. **Map** 4 E2.
21-395 47 81.

Livraria Olisipo
Largo Trindade Coelho 7–8,
Bairro Alto. **Map** 7 A3.
21-346 27 71.

Solar
Rua Dom Pedro V 68–70,
Bairro Alto. **Map** 4 F2.
21-346 55 22.

ENTERTAINMENT IN LISBON

Though quite small compared to other European capitals, Lisbon boasts an outstanding cultural calendar. Chosen as Cultural Capital of Europe 1994, the city hosts both modern and traditional events from classical music, ballet and opera to street festivals, fairs and bullfights. Pop and rock concerts are held all year round and traditional *fado (see pp142–3)* is widely performed. Football fans can spend an afternoon watching Benfica or Sporting. The city also offers excellent late-night entertainment, focused on lively, fashionable clubs and bars along the waterfront and in the Bairro Alto.

BOOKING TICKETS

Tickets can be reserved by phoning the Agência de Bilhetes para Espectáculos Públicos (**ABEP**). Pay in cash when you collect them from the kiosk. Cinemas and theatres will not take phone or credit card bookings – only the major cultural centres do.

ABEP kiosk selling tickets on Praça dos Restauradores

LISTINGS MAGAZINES

Previews of forthcoming events and listings of bars and clubs appear in several magazines in Lisbon. English-language publications on offer include the monthly *Follow Me Lisboa* and the quarterly *Lisboa Step By Step,* which are available free from tourist offices. The monthly *Agenda Cultural* is in Portuguese.

CINEMA AND THEATRE

Movie-goers are extremely well served in Lisbon. Films are shown in their original language with subtitles in Portuguese, and tickets are inexpensive. There are plenty of cinemas to choose from, and the futuristic **Amoreiras Shopping Centre** *(see p74)* has a multiplex centre with ten screens showing all the latest Hollywood releases. Cult movies and international art-house films can be seen at the

Cinemateca Portuguesa, which has a comprehensive monthly film calendar. Copies are available at the box office or tourist office. Most cinemas offer reductions on Mondays.

Theatre lovers can enjoy Portuguese and foreign language plays at the **Teatro Nacional Dona Maria II** and the **Teatro da Trindade**. For a slightly less formal but entertaining show try Chapitô in the Alfama quarter, a circus school and theatre, which sometimes stages open-air performances.

CLASSICAL MUSIC, OPERA AND DANCE

Lisbon's top cultural centres are the modern **Centro Cultural de Belém** *(see p68)* and the **Fundação Calouste Gulbenkian** *(see pp76–9).* They host a variety of national and international events including concerts, ballet and opera. A calendar of events for each venue is available from the box office or the tourist office. Operas and classical concerts also take place at the **Teatro Nacional de São Carlos** *(see p53)* and the Coliseu dos Recreios.

Performance at the Chapitô circus school, Alfama

WORLD MUSIC, JAZZ, FOLK AND ROCK

Though Lisbon's musical soul is *fado,* the city also swings to a variety of sounds from contemporary jazz and heavy rock through the rhythms of South America and Africa. Venues such as **B. Leza** and **Lontra** are popular for African music.

Every summer the Fundação Calouste Gulbenkian puts on the International Jazz Festival. The **Hot Clube** is a favourite jazz spot and **Speakeasy**

The house orchestra playing at the Fundação Calouste Gulbenkian

Brazilian musician at Pé Sujo

offers live jazz, especially late at night during the week, while up-tempo blues can be heard on evenings at the weekend.

Top pop and rock bands can be found at a variety of large venues such as **Pavilhão Atlântico**, **Praça Sony** and **Coliseu dos Recreios**, as well as in stadiums.

NIGHTCLUBS

THE BAIRRO ALTO remains a lively area for Lisbon nightlife, although its mostly small bars don't usually have dance floors or keep very late hours. There are exceptions, including the doyen of Bairro Alto clubs, **Frágil**.

Among the larger-scale and more mainstream dance venues are **Kremlin** and **Kapital**; the first a nearly historic house club, the second a very middle-of-the-road disco-bar.

Farther westward by the Doca de Santo Amaro marina is the attractively housed **Salsa Latina**, one of Lisbon's few salsa places. Inland, in the Alcântara area, is the ambitious **W**, while eastwards along the river, near the Santa Apolónia railway station, is

Lux, the cream of Lisbon's current club scene.

Details of recommended bars in Lisbon, Estoril, Cascais and Sintra can be found on pages 134–5.

SPORTS

MOST SPORTING action takes place outside the city, but one of Lisbon's two football teams (Benfica and Sporting) plays at home almost every Sunday, Benfica at **Estádio da Luz** and Sporting at **Estádio José Alvalade**. Portugal is hosting the 2004 European championships. Games in Lisbon will be held in these two stadia, which have been specially renovated for the event.

Lisbon's bullfight arena, Campo Pequeno, is closed for works until 2003 (*see p80*).

DIRECTORY

BOOKING TICKETS

ABEP
Praça dos Restauradores.
Map 7 A2.
☎ 21-347 58 24.

CINEMA AND THEATRE

Amoreiras Shopping Centre
Avenida Engenheiro Duarte Pacheco.
Map 5 A5.
☎ 21-381 02 00.

Cinemateca Portuguesa
Rua Barata Salgueiro 39.
Map 5 C5.
☎ 21-354 62 79.

Teatro da Trindade
Rua Nova da Trindade 9
Map 7 A3.
☎ 21-342 32 00.

Teatro Nacional Dona Maria II
Praça Dom Pedro IV.
Map 7 B3.
☎ 21-347 22 46.

CLASSICAL MUSIC, OPERA AND DANCE

Centro Cultural de Belém
Praça do Império.
Map 1 C5.
☎ 21-361 24 00.

Fundação Calouste Gulbenkian
Avenida de Berna 45.
Map 5 B2.
☎ 21-793 51 31.

Teatro Nacional de São Carlos
Rua Serpa Pinto 9.
Map 7 A4.
☎ 21-346 84 08.

WORLD MUSIC, JAZZ, FOLK AND ROCK

B. Leza
Largo do Conde Barão 50.
Map 4 E3.
☎ 21-396 37 35.

Coliseu dos Recreios
Rua das Portas de Santo Antão 92.
Map 7 A2.
☎ 21-324 05 80.

Hot Clube
Praça da Alegria 39.
Map 4 F1.
☎ 21-346 73 69.

Lontra
Rua de São Bento 157.
Map 4 E1.
☎ 21-369 10 83.

Praça Sony
Parque das Nações.
☎ 21-891 90 00

Pavilhão Atlântico
Parque das Nações.
☎ 21-891 84 40.

Speakeasy
Cais das Oficinas, Armazém 115, Rocha Conde d'Óbidos.
Map 4 D4.
☎ 21-395 73 08

NIGHTCLUBS

Frágil
Rua da Atalaia 128.
Map 4 F2.
☎ 21-346 95 78.

Kapital
Avenida 24 de Julho 68.
Map 4 E3.
☎ 21-395 71 01.

Kremlin
Escadinhas da Praia 5.
Map 4 D3.
☎ 21-395 71 01.

Lux
Avenida Infante Dom Henrique.
Map 8 D5.
☎ 21-882 08 90.

Salsa Latina
Gare Marítima de Alcântara.
Map 3 A5/B5.
☎ 21-395 05 55.

W
Rua Maria Luísa Holstein 13.
Map 3 A4.
☎ 21-363 68 30.

SPORTS

Estádio José Alvalade
Rua Francisco Stromp 2.
☎ 21-756 79.30.

Estádio da Luz
Avenida General Norton Matos.
☎ 21-726 61 29.

Fado: the Music of Lisbon

L IKE THE BLUES, *fado* is an expression of longing and sorrow. Literally meaning "fate", the term may be applied to an individual song as well as the genre itself. The music owes much to the concept known as *saudade*, meaning a longing both for what has been lost, and for what has never been attained, which perhaps accounts for its emotional power. The people of Lisbon have nurtured this poignant music in back-street cafés and restaurants for over 150 years, and it has altered little in that time. It is sung as often by women as men,

A guitarra accompanist

always accompanied by the *guitarra* and *viola* (acoustic Spanish guitar). *Fado* from Coimbra has developed its own light-hearted style.

A graphic depiction of the music's low-life associations from the 1920s

Argentina Santos is a legendary singer and fado house owner. All female *fadistas* wear a black shawl in memory of Maria Severa.

The guitarrista plays the melody and will occasionally perform a solo instrumental piece.

CREAÇÃO DE DINA TERESA

FADO DA ESPERA DE TOIROS DO FONOFILME A SEVERA

MÚSICA DE FREDERICO DE FREITAS LETRA DE DR. JÚLIO DANTAS SASSETTI & Cᵃ EDITORES RUA NA CARMO 56-LISBOA

Maria Severa *(1810–36) was the first great* fadista *and the subject of the first Portuguese sound film in 1931. Her scandalous life and early death are pivotal to fado history, and her spiritual influence has been enormous, inspiring* fados, *poems, novels and plays.*

Most instruments have 12 paired strings, like this one. The double strings produce a resonant, silvery-sweet tone.

Delicate mother-of-pearl inlaid flower motifs

Mother-of-pearl finger plate

THE GUITARRA

Peculiar to Portuguese culture, the *guitarra* is a flat-backed instrument shaped like a mandolin, with eight, ten or twelve strings, arranged in pairs. It has evolved from a simple 19th-century design into a finely decorated piece, sometimes inlaid with mother-of-pearl. The sound of the *guitarra* is an essential ingredient of a good *fado*, echoing and enhancing the singer's melody line.

All kinds of themes *may occur in* fado. *This song of 1910, for example, celebrates the dawning of the liberal republic. Such songsheets remained a favoured means of dissemination, even after the first records were made in 1904.*

__Alfredo Duarte__ (1891–1982) was a renowned writer of fado *lyrics dealing with love, death, longing, tragedy and triumph. Affectionately known as O Marceneiro (the master carpenter) because of his skill as a joiner, he is still revered and his work widely performed.*

__A cultural icon__ for the Portuguese, Amália Rodrigues (1921–99) was the leading exponent of fado *for over 50 years. She crystallized the music's style in the postwar years, and made it known around the world.*

The *viola* provides rhythm accompaniment, but the player will never take a solo.

__The music has long inspired__ great writers and painters. O Fado (1910) by José Malhôa (1855–1933) shows it in an intimate setting with the fadista *captivating his listener. The air of abandonment underlines the earthiness of many of the songs.*

THE FADO HOUSE

Lisbon's best *fado* houses, such as the famous Parreirinha de Alfama, which belongs to Argentina Santos *(shown above)*, are run by the *fadistas* themselves for love of the music, not as a tourist attraction. They continue the tradition that began originally in the Alfama, whereby cafés and restaurants gave the music of the people a home. Such authentic venues still provide a good meal and a sense of history as well as entertainment. The oldest is Luso, which has been in existence since the 1930s.

WHERE TO ENJOY FADO IN LISBON

Any of these fado houses will offer you good food, wine and music. Or visit the Casa do Fado for a fascinating exhibition of the history of Fado.

Adega Machado
Rua do Norte 91.
Map 7 A3. (21-322 46 40.

Casa do Fado
Largo do Chafariz de Dentro 1.
(21-882 34 70. ▦ 8, 28,
35, 50, 107. ◯ 10am–6pm
Wed–Mon.

Lisboa à Noite
Rua das Gáveas 69.
Map 7 A3. (21-346 85 57.

Luso
Travessa da Queimada 10.
Map 7 A3. (21-342 22 81.

Parreirinha de Alfama
Beco do Espírito Santo 1.
Map 7 E4. (21-886 82 09.

Senhor Vinho
Rua do Meio à Lapa 18.
Map 4 D3. (21-397 74 56.

SURVIVAL GUIDE

PRACTICAL INFORMATION 146–153
GETTING TO LISBON 154–155
GETTING AROUND LISBON 156–177

PRACTICAL INFORMATION

L ISBON IS becoming increasingly popular as a tourist destination. The best time to visit is in the spring or autumn when the weather is at its best. Lisbon and large towns in the area all have *Postos de Turismo* (tourist information offices) which will provide information about the immediate region,

Tourist information sign

town plans, maps and details on current events as well as accommodation. Check that sights are open before you visit, although most museums are open from Tuesday to Sunday. Banks are open from Monday to Friday and the ATM machines can be used 24 hours a day and accept many international credit and debit cards.

CUSTOMS

O N 30 JUNE 1999, the intra-EU Duty and Tax Free Allowances, better known as Duty-free and mainly affecting such items as alcohol, tobacco, perfumes, were abolished. Consulates will be able to provide up-to-date details on particular customs regulations. For more information on customs and other tax-related matters, see page 136.

VISAS

N ATIONALS of the EU may stay for up to six months before applying for a residence permit. Canadians, Americans, New Zealanders and Australians need a passport and can stay for up to two months without a visa. Check visa requirements with the Portuguese consulate before booking.

TOURIST INFORMATION

T HE TOURIST OFFICES' opening hours are generally the same as those of local shops. Offices in the centre of Lisbon

have been marked on the Street Finder *(see pp170–77)*. Offices may also be found at Portela airport and at Santa Apolónia station. Addresses of offices in the Lisbon Coast area are given in the information at the top of each sight entry. Portuguese tourist offices abroad can provide you with helpful information before you travel that will help you plan your holiday.

Museum tickets

ADMISSION CHARGES

M OST MUSEUMS and monuments, except churches, charge an entrance fee, which often increases in the summer. Entry is often free on Sunday mornings and public holidays. Pensioners and children under 14 are entitled to a 40 per cent discount. Visitors under 26 with a *Cartão Jóvem* (youth card) or an ISIC card (international student identity card) are entitled to half-price entrance. Visitors to Lisbon can buy a LISBOA card, which

permits free entry to Lisbon's state museums and also free travel on all the city's public transport *(see p158)*.

OPENING TIMES

M OST MUSEUMS open from 10am–5pm daily with many closing for lunch from 12–2pm or from 12:30–2:30pm. Smaller museums, or privately-owned ones, may have different opening times. Note that state-run museums and some sights close on Mondays and public holidays. Major churches are open all day although some may close from 12–4pm. Smaller ones may only open for services.

FACILITIES FOR THE DISABLED

D ISABLED FACILITIES in Lisbon are slowly improving. Adapted toilets are available at airports and the main stations and reserved car-parking is now more evident. Ramps and lifts are gradually being installed in public places.

LANGUAGE

P ORTUGUESE is very similar to Spanish, so if you are familiar with Spanish you should have little difficulty reading Portuguese. However, the pronunciation of the language is very different. The Portuguese are proud of their language, and do not take kindly to being addressed in Spanish. A phrasebook containing useful words and phrases is on pages 191–2.

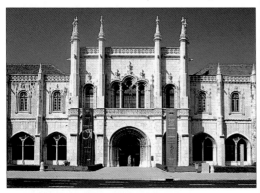

Façade of the Museu Nacional de Arqueologia in Lisbon

◁ **View across Lisbon's skyline, with the Elevador de Santa Justa in the foreground**

Respectably dressed Portuguese leaving church

ETIQUETTE

THE PORTUGUESE appreciate efforts by visitors, however small, to communicate in their language. A simple *bom-dia* (good day) will work wonders and earn a grateful smile. Generally open and friendly, the Portuguese are unerringly polite. It is considered courteous to address people as *senhor* or *senhora* and you are expected to shake hands when introduced to anyone, although a kiss on each cheek between females and among the young is more commonplace. Dress is relaxed but decorum should

Portuguese newspapers

be observed especially when visiting churches; arms and legs should be covered.

PORTUGUESE TIME

PORTUGAL follows Britain in adopting Greenwich Mean Time (GMT) in winter and moving the clocks forward one hour in summer. The 24-hour clock is commonly used.

ELECTRICITY

VOLTAGE IN PORTUGAL is 220 volts. Plugs have two round pins and most hotel bathrooms offer built-in adaptors for shavers only.

NEWSPAPERS, RADIO AND TELEVISION

ENGLISH-LANGUAGE newspapers printed in Europe are widely available on the day of publication. Various other European newspapers and periodicals are on sale the day after home publication. Portuguese daily newspapers include *Diário de Notícias* and *Público*. The *Anglo-Portuguese News* (APN) is Lisbon's main English-language publication. Published weekly, it provides information for the British expatriates in Lisbon. There are two state-owned television channels in Portugal, RTP1 and RTP2, and two privately-owned channels, SIC and TVI. Satellite television is also available, broadcasting in several languages. Listings of television programmes broadcast in English can be found in the *Anglo-Portuguese News*. Portuguese radio has programmes in English, French and German with information for tourists, but these only operate during the summer.

Newspaper stall in the Café Brasiliera (p53)

CONVERSION CHART

Imperial to Metric
1 inch = 2.54 centimetres
1 foot = 30 centimetres
1 mile = 1.6 kilometres
1 ounce = 28 grams
1 pound = 454 grams
1 pint = 0.6 litres
1 gallon = 4.6 litres

Metric to Imperial
1 millimetre = 0.04 inches
1 centimetre = 0.4 inches
1 metre = 3 feet 3 inches
1 kilometre = 0.6 miles
1 gram = 0.04 ounces
1 kilogram = 2.2 pounds
1 litre = 1.8 pints

Personal Health and Security

I N GENERAL, Lisbon is relatively free of crime, but simple precautions should always be taken. When parked, do not leave any valuable possessions in the car, and watch out for pickpockets in crowded areas and on public transport. Should you have serious medical problems, ring the emergency service number given in this section. For minor complaints, consult a pharmacist, who should be able to help.

Motorway SOS telephone

WHAT TO DO IN AN EMERGENCY

T HE NUMBER to contact in the event of an emergency is 112. Dial the number and then indicate which service you require – the police *(polícia)*, an ambulance *(ambulância)* or the fire brigade *(bombeiros)*. If you need medical treatment, the casualty department *(serviço de urgência)* of the closest main hospital will treat you. On motorways and main roads, use the orange SOS telephone to call for help should you have a car accident. The service is in Portuguese; press the button and then wait for an answer. The operator will put you through.

HEALTH PRECAUTIONS

N O VACCINATIONS are needed for visitors, although it is a sensible precaution to have had a typhoid shot and a current polio booster. Tap water is safe to drink throughout the country. If you are visiting during the summer, it is advisable to bring insect repellent, as mosquitoes, while they do not present any serious health problems, can be a nuisance.

PHARMACIES

P HARMACIES *(farmácias)* in Lisbon can diagnose simple health problems and suggest appropriate treatment. Pharmacists can dispense a range of drugs that would normally only be available on prescription in many other countries. The sign for a *farmácia* is a green cross on a white background. They are open from 9am to 1pm and 3pm to 7pm. Each pharmacy displays a card in the window

showing the address of the nearest all-night pharmacy and a list of those that are open until late (10pm).

MEDICAL TREATMENT

S OCIAL SECURITY coverage is available for all EU nationals, but you may have to pay first and reclaim later. You must have an E111 form before travelling which is available at post offices or from the Department of Health. The E111 covers emergencies only, so visitors should obtain insurance for all other types of medical treatment.
US visitors should check with their insurance carriers before leaving home to ensure that they are covered. Many medical facilities will require that treatment is paid in full at the time of service. Be sure to get an itemized bill for your carrier.
The **British Hospital** in Lisbon has English-speaking doctors, as do the international health centres in Estoril and Cascais on the Lisbon Coast.

Pharmacy sign

PORTUGUESE POLICE

I N LISBON and other main towns, the police force is the *Polícia de Segurança Pública* (PSP). In rural areas, law and order is kept by the *Guarda Nacional Republicana* (GNR). The *Brigada de Trânsito* (traffic police) are a division of the GNR, and are recognizable by their red armbands. They are responsible for patrolling roads.

PERSONAL SECURITY

V IOLENT CRIME is extremely rare in Lisbon and in Portugal generally, and the vast majority of visitors to the country will experience no problems whatsoever, but sensible precautions should be taken. It is advisable to arrange travel insurance for your possessions before you

Traffic policeman   **Male PSP officer**

Female PSP officer

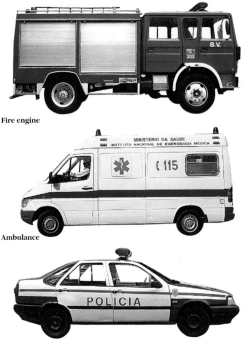

Fire engine

Ambulance

Police car

DIRECTORY

EMERGENCY NUMBERS

General Emergency (Fire, Police, Ambulance)
📞 *112*.

Assistentes Intérpretes de Portugal
Avenida da República 41, 3°,
1269-098 Lisbon.
📞 *21-799 43 60*.

British Hospital
Rua Saraiva de Carvalho 49,
1269-098 Lisbon.
📞 *21-395 50 67*.

Ordem dos Advogados
Largo de São Domingos 14, 1°,
1169-060 Lisbon.
📞 *21-882 35 50*.

leave for Lisbon. Thieves do operate in certain areas in particular, and care should be taken after dark in the Alfama, Bairro Alto and Cais do Sodré districts of Lisbon, as well as in some areas of the coastal resorts. Personal belongings should be protected as much as possible and leaving anything inside a car, particularly a radio, is not recommended. When out walking, be sure to conceal wallets, and carry bags and cameras on your side away from the road so as not to tempt snatchers in cars or on motorbikes. If you are unfortunate enough to encounter thieves during your visit, you are advised not to attempt to resist and hand over your possessions immediately.

REPORTING A CRIME

IF YOU HAVE any property stolen, you should immediately contact the nearest police station. Theft of documents, such as a passport, should also be reported to your

consulate. Many insurance companies insist that policy holders report any theft within 24 hours. The police will file a report which you will need in order to claim from your insurance company on your return home. Contact the PSP in towns or cities, or the GNR in rural areas. In all situations, keep calm and be polite to the authorities to avoid delays. The same applies should you be involved in a car accident. In rural areas you may be asked to accompany the other driver to the nearest police station to complete the necessary paperwork. Ask for an interpreter if no one there speaks English.

Ladies' toilet sign

Men's toilet sign

LEGAL ASSISTANCE

AN INSURANCE POLICY that covers the costs of legal advice, issued by companies such as Europ Assistance or Mondial Assistance, will help with the legal aspects of your insurance claim should you have an accident. If you have not arranged this cover, call your nearest consulate or the **Ordem dos Advogados** (lawyers' association) who can give you names of English-speaking lawyers and help you with obtaining representation. Lists of interpreters, if you require one, are given in the local Yellow Pages (*Páginas Amarelas*) under *Tradutores e Intérpretes*, or can be contacted through the **Assistentes Intérpretes de Portugal**, which is based in Lisbon.

PUBLIC CONVENIENCES

THE PORTUGUESE for toilets is *casa de banho*. If the usual figures of a man or woman are not shown, look for *homens* (men) and *senhoras* (ladies). Toilet facilities are provided at service areas every 40 km (25 miles) and at drive-in rest areas on the motorways. In some cases you may have to pay to use ladies' toilets, but men's facilities are always free.

Banking and Local Currency

BPI Bank Logo

YOU CAN TAKE any amount of foreign currency into Portugal but sums worth more than 12,450 euros should be declared at customs when entering the country. Traveller's cheques are the safest way to carry money in Lisbon, but credit and debit cards are the most convenient. They can be used to withdraw currency, for a fee, from ATMs (automatic teller machines) displaying the appropriate sign.

A 24-hour bank at Lisbon airport

BANKING HOURS

BANK OPENING HOURS are from 8:30am to 3pm, Monday to Friday, although the major branches in Lisbon and those in the resorts close at 6pm. Banks are closed at weekends and on public holidays.

CHANGING MONEY

MONEY CAN be changed at banks, at a bureau de change (câmbio) and in many hotels. The most convenient of these methods is to use banks as they are more common than bureaux de change and offer a better rate of exchange than hotels. However, service in banks can sometimes be slow and usually involves filling in a number of forms. In addition, some banks restrict currency exchange to their customers.

The quickest and most practical way of changing money is to use the electronic currency exchange machines found outside the branches of most major banks, and at railway stations and the airport. They have the added advantage of allowing you to change money outside normal banking hours. The screen in the centre of the machine displays the current exchange rates and gives instructions for use in several languages.

CHEQUES AND CARDS

TRAVELLER'S CHEQUES are available from most banks or from branches of Thomas Cook and American Express offices. They are a safe way of carrying money, but in Lisbon they are expensive to cash. Commission rates vary from bank to bank, so it is wise to shop around first.

Although Eurocheques are less expensive than traveller's cheques, they are no longer accepted by many banks and shops. Visitors now find it more convenient simply to use their debit card to withdraw cash from an ATM.

The credit cards that are most commonly accepted for payment are Visa, American Express and MasterCard. These cards can also be used to withdraw currency at banks and bureaux de change.

CASH DISPENSERS

A PRACTICAL WAY of obtaining cash advances using your credit card is to use the MB (Multibanco) ATM located outside banks, at railway stations and shopping centres. Cards accepted include Visa, Master-Card and American Express. A transaction tax may be charged as well as a commission. Checking the rates is worthwhile as tax and commission will vary. The cost of using a debit card for cash withdrawals may be less. Most ATMs accept Cirrus and Star debit cards.

Exchange rates and instructions are shown on this screen.

Euro bank notes and coins emerge from these slots.

Language and currency is selected using these buttons.

Foreign currency is inserted here.

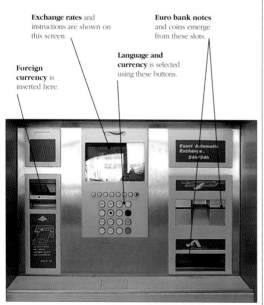

Currency Exchange Machine at Lisbon Airport
These machines provide a convenient way of changing foreign notes into euros at any time of day or night.

THE EURO

TWELVE COUNTRIES have replaced their traditional currencies with a single European currency called the euro. Austria, Belgium, Finland, France, Germany, Greece, Ireland, Italy, Luxembourg, Netherlands, Portugal and Spain chose to join the new currency; the UK, Denmark and Sweden stayed out, with an option to review their situation. The euro was introduced on 1 January, 1999, but only for banking purposes. Notes and coins came into circulation on 1 January 2002. A transition period allowed euros and escudos to be used simultaneously, with national notes and coins phased out in March 2002. Euros can be used anywhere within the participating member states.

Bank Notes

Euro bank notes have seven denominations. The 5-euro note (grey in colour) is the smallest, followed by the 10-euro note (pink), 20-euro note (blue), 50-euro note (orange), 100-euro note (green), 200-euro note (yellow) and 500-euro note (purple). All notes show the stars of the European Union.

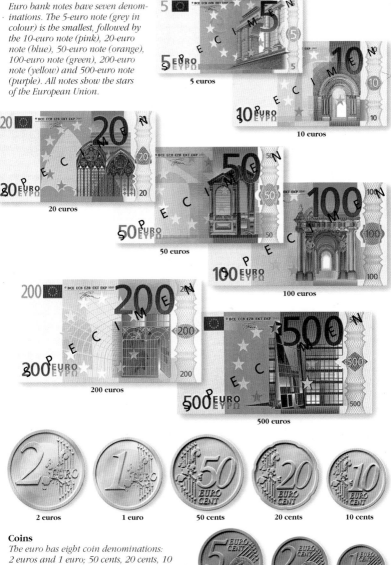

5 euros

10 euros

20 euros

50 euros

100 euros

200 euros

500 euros

Coins

The euro has eight coin denominations: 2 euros and 1 euro; 50 cents, 20 cents, 10 cents, 5 cents, 2 cents and 1 cent. The 2- and 1-euro coins are both silver and gold in colour. The 50-, 20- and 10-cent coins are gold. The 5-, 2- and 1-cent coins are bronze.

2 euros   1 euro   50 cents   20 cents   10 cents

5 cents   2 cents   1 cent

Using the Telephone

English-style phone box

RECENT YEARS have seen a dramatic improvement in the Portuguese telecommunications system. Formerly, the antiquated equipment caused all manner of problems for visitors. Thankfully, it has been updated with the help of the latest technology, and visitors should now find that using the telephone in Lisbon is relatively free of complications. Public telephones may be used for phoning internally or abroad, either with coins or cards. It is generally much more convenient, especially when making international or long-distance calls, to use card phones instead of coin phones.

Post office *cabine* phone

USING A COIN PHONE

1 Lift receiver and wait for the dialling tone.

2 Insert coins in this slot one at a time.

3 The display shows amount of credit. If more money is required the message *"Inserir mais moedas por favor"* appears.

4 Key in telephone number and wait to be connected.

5 To make another call, press the follow-on call button.

6 Replace receiver after call. Unused coins will be refunded.

USING A TELECOM CARD PHONE

1 Lift receiver and wait for the dialling tone.

2 Insert phonecard arrow side up, or credit card magnetic strip down.

3 The screen will display number of units available, then tell you to key in telephone number.

4 Key in number and wait to be connected.

5 If phonecard runs out in the middle of a call, it will re-emerge. Remove it and insert another one.

6 Replace receiver after call. When card re-emerges, remove it.

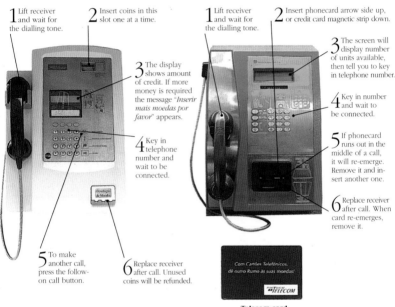

Telecom card

TELEPHONING IN LISBON

THERE ARE SEVERAL different types of pay phone in Lisbon. Some use coins and others take cards. Coin-operated telephones may be found in the street, as well as in most bars, cafés, newsagents and other shops. During 2002 all phones will be adapted to accept the new euro coins, and are likely to accept denominations from

Portugal Telecom logo

10 cents to 2 euros *(see p151)*. However, if you wish to call abroad it is far more convenient to use a card phone. These phones tend to be either red or blue and accept phone cards as well as credit cards. Telephone cards are available in different denominations from post offices, and telecom company outlets, tobacconists and newsagents.

You can also call from post offices without having to have change or a card. Simply

queue at the cashier's window and you will eventually be directed to a booth *(cabine)*. Make your call first and then pay at the counter. The cost is based on how many units you have used and the rate is much better than in hotels. Some cafés, restaurants and bars now also use this method of paying for phone calls.

If you are going to make an international call, bear in mind that it is usually much cheaper to phone in the evening after 9pm or at weekends, when you will benefit from the off-peak rates.

Reverse Charge Calls

Reverse charge calls can be made from any telephone. Dial the *país directo* number or 172 for the country you wish to call. This number is listed in the opening pages of any telephone directory, after the list of city dialling codes for that country. This number will put you in contact with the local telephone operator. There are also separate numbers for calls to the USA using services such as AT&T, MCI and Sprint.

A beige coin telephone outside a café, covered by a shelter

Dialling Codes

- All numbers in Portugal now have nine digits, including the area code, regardless of where you are calling from.
- To call Portugal use the country code 351.
- To phone Lisbon, and most places in the Lisbon Coast area from abroad, first dial 00 35 121 and then the local number.
- To call abroad from Lisbon, dial 00 and then the country code. The code for Australia is 61; Ireland: 353; New Zealand: 64; UK: 44 and US and Canada: 1.
- Lisbon's directory enquiries number is 118. For international directory enquiries dial 179.
- The Algarve is covered by Portimão (282), Faro (289), and Tavira (281). Madeira's code is 291.

Postal Services

***Correios* (postal service) logo**

The postal service is known as the *Correios*. It is reasonably efficent: a letter sent to a country within the EU should take five to seven days, and a letter sent to the USA or further afield should take about seven to ten days. The *Correios* sign features a horse and rider in white on a red background.

Sending a Letter

First-class mail is known as *correio azul* and second-class mail is called *normal*. First-class letters are posted in blue postboxes and second-class post in red ones. At post offices there may be separate slots for national and international mail. There is also an express mail service called EMS and, for valuable letters, a recorded delivery service *(correio registado)* is available. Stamps *(selos)* can be bought from post offices or from any shop displaying the *Correios* sign. You can also buy stamps from vending machines that are found in airport terminals and railway stations, as well as on the streets of large towns.

Portuguese stamps

Poste Restante

A mail-holding service *(posta restante)* is also available at most major post offices. The envelope should carry the name of the recipient in block capitals, underlined, followed by *posta restante* together with the postcode and the name of the destination town. To collect the mail, take your passport and look for the counter that is marked *encomendas*. A small fee is charged for this service.

Post Offices

Post offices are usually open from 9am until 6pm from Monday to Friday. The main post office in Praçk dos Restuaradores is open between 8:30am and 10pm, Monday to Friday and 9am–6pm on Saturdays and Sundays.

Lisbon's Addresses

Lisbon's addresses often include both the storey of a building and the location within that floor. The ground floor is the *rés-do-chão* (r/c), first floor *primeiro andar* (1°), the second floor is expressed as 2°, and so on. Each floor is divided into left, *esquerdo* (E or Esq^{do}), right, *direito* (D or D^{to}).

Lisbon's Postboxes
First-class letters should be posted in blue (Correio Azul) *boxes and second-class letters in red boxes.*

Information on collection times · First-class postbox

Second-class postbox

TRAVEL INFORMATION

LISBON IS SERVED by an international airport as well as good road and rail links; it is also a popular port with cruise liners. Road networks into Lisbon have improved significantly in the last decade with the construction of new ring roads and motorways while a second bridge across the Tagus was completed in 1998 to alleviate traffic congestion into the city. Trams provide fascinating trips through Lisbon's old neighbourhoods which are

TAP, the Air Portugal logo

also worth exploring on foot. However, travel in the city during peak hours can be frustrating. Despite modernization of the city's public transport system, many still commute by car, creating endless traffic jams. Lisbon's surroundings offer an escape from the hubbub as well as some wonderful sightseeing opportunities – either by train to the resort of Cascais, across the Tagus by ferry to Caparica's beaches or by road to romantic Sintra.

AIR TRAVEL

LISBON HAS regular scheduled flights from European capitals and major cities, including Paris, Frankfurt, Madrid, Milan and Zurich. Daily scheduled flights by TAP, the national airline of Portugal, and British Airways from London, and by TAP from Dublin, serve Lisbon. Travellers from North America can pick up a direct TWA, Delta or TAP flight to Lisbon from New York. TAP and its partner Varig also link major South American cities, such as Rio de Janeiro, São Paulo and Caracas, to the Portuguese capital.

There are no direct flights to Lisbon from Canada, Australia or New Zealand, and the usual connecting point is London. Domestic flights also operate to destinations including Porto, Faro, Madeira and the Azores.

Airlines offer a host of options on flights to Lisbon. BA offers some of the cheapest scheduled flights from the UK with four daily depatures from Heathrow and one daily flight from Gatwick.

However, BA's timetables, European routes and pricing structures are in a state of flux and this may change in the near future. One significant development is the airline's

Signs at Lisbon's Portela airport

intention to offer more tickets at reduced prices to people using its internet web site.

Charter flights are also available to Lisbon, and all have fixed outward and return dates. Young people should consult agencies that specialize in student travel. If you are arranging a long-haul flight, check whether you can take a budget flight to London, and continue to Lisbon from there. In general, tickets cost more in the summer season, Christmas and Easter periods.

LISBON AIRPORT

PORTELA AIRPORT is located only 7 km (4 miles) to the north of Lisbon city centre. Although airy and modern, it remains relatively small by international standards. All the facilities usually associated with an international airport are on offer, including shops,

cafés, bars, restaurants, duty free shops, bureaux de change and car hire agencies.

CONNECTIONS WITH THE AIRPORT

THE AIRPORT'S proximity to the city centre means that it is reasonably cheap to get into to the heart of Lisbon. Taxis are readily available from the taxi rank just outside the International Terminal at Portela airport.

Express shuttle service aerobuses depart every 20 minutes (7am–9pm) from outside the International Terminal to Praça do Comércio, Praça Marquês de Pombal, Praça dos Restauradores and Cais do Sodré station. The ticket is then valid for the rest of the day and can be used on local buses, trams and funiculars in the city. Cheaper local buses (No. 44 and No. 45) stop just outside the airport car park and also offer a service to Praça dos Restauradores and Cais do Sodré station. These buses operate from 6am–1am, but their timetable is less predictable than the aero-bus service.

Shuttle bus waiting to depart from the airport to the city centre

Entrance to the Ponte 25 de Abril, one of the main routes into Lisbon

ARRIVING BY TRAIN

To the east of the Alfama district, on Avenida Infante Dom Henrique, is **Santa Apolónia**, the main station for long distance trains from Coimbra, Porto and the north, as well as from Madrid and Paris. It is 15 minutes' walk east of Praça do Comércio.

For helpful advice about accommodation or to change money, there is a tourist information office (open 9am–7pm Mon–Sat) and a bureau de change inside the station. To get to your hotel, there is a taxi rank outside the station's main entrance.

Since 1998, the impressive, ultra-modern **Gare do Oriente** has provided an alternative international terminus to Santa Apolónia. Although located much further north at the old Expo site Parque das Nações, it has excellent links into the city by both bus and metro routes.

Trains from the south and east of the city arrive at **Barreiro** station on the south bank of the Tagus and connect with the ferry which docks at Terreiro do Paço.

Nearby, **Cais do Sodré** station serves the resort towns of Cascais and Estoril. **Rossio** station, on Praça dos Restauradores, serves Queluz, some 20 minutes away, and Sintra, about 45 minutes from Lisbon. For more details on travelling by train, see page 161.

ARRIVING BY ROAD

There are at present five entry routes into Lisbon; the newest is the Vasco da Gama bridge to the north of the city that opened in 1998.

For those arriving from the Algarve and the south as well as Madrid and the east, the standard route is via the A2 motorway and the very busy toll bridge Ponte 25 de Abril.

From Oporto and the north the A1 motorway brings you to Lisbon's outskirts, where there is a motorway toll to be paid. In order to reach the centre of Lisbon follow the signs indicating *Centro*.

However, if you prefer not to go into Lisbon itself but wish to head straight to the coastal resorts of Cascais and Estoril, or to Sintra, then turn off the motorway on to the A9 at Alverca, 20 km (12 miles) north of Lisbon, where there are signs marked Cascais/C.R.E.L. (the outer ring road).

Those arriving from Cascais and the coast enter Lisbon via the A5 motorway, while the A8 is the main entry point for traffic from Torres Vedras and the coastal region.

The new bridge at Montijo provides better access to the northern end of the city, including the airport, via the A1 C.R.I.L. (the inner ring road).

If you are arriving in Lisbon by bus, the main bus station is centrally located at Avenida Duque de Ávila, and has good transport connections as well as a taxi rank. For further information on bus travel, see page 160.

LISBON'S BRIDGES

One of Lisbon's most famous landmarks, the Ponte 25 de Abril, provides the main link between Lisbon and the southern bank of the Tagus. Built in the 1960s, this bridge is busy with traffic. The best time to cross is outside the rush hours when it is least busy. To improve traffic flow, a toll is charged only on the way into Lisbon, and this covers the exit cost as well.

In order to ease traffic pressure, a second bridge, the Vasco da Gama, near the Parque das Nações, was completed in March 1998. This, and the new Fertagus rail link across the Ponte 25 de Abril, now provide a much needed link between the north of Lisbon and Montijo, on the south side of the Tagus, from where motorways lead south to the Alentejo and Algarve regions.

DIRECTORY

Air France
Lisbon **(** 21-848 21 77.
W www.airfrance.pt

British Airways
London **(** 0845 77 333 77.
W www.britishairways.com

Delta Airlines
New York **(** 800-241 41 41.
W www.delta.com

Lufthansa
Lisbon **(** 21-843 12 00.
W www.lufthansa.pt

TAP-Air Portugal
Lisbon **(** 21-841 69 90.
London **(** 020-87 62 73 76.
Dublin **(** 01-679 88 44.
New York **(** 800-221 73 70.
W www.tap.pt

TWA
New York **(** 800-892 41 41.
W www.twa.com

Varig
Lisbon **(** 21-313 68 30.
W www.varig.com

Getting Around Lisbon

Aⁿ ATTRACTIVE CITY, Lisbon is a pleasure to explore and walking can be one of the best ways to see it. However, it is also hilly and even the fittest of sight-seers will soon tire. The trams, lifts *(elevadores)* and buses come as a welcome rest for the foot-weary tourist and offer some excellent views (see pages 158–60 for information on public transport). Driving around the city can be a hair-raising experience, with its maze of one-way streets and impatient *Lisboeta* drivers, and it is not generally recommended. However, taxis offer the convenience of road travel without the troubles of parking and finding your way around in an unfamiliar city. They are also relatively cheap.

A typical alleyway in the Alfama district, Lisbon

WALKING AROUND LISBON

Lisbon is a delightful city to wander around taking in the sights, especially in the old neighbourhoods such as the Alfama and Bairro Alto. Narrow cobbled streets, picturesque buildings and alleyways provide a charming setting to experience tradi-tional Lisbon life.

However, it is important to remember that Lisbon is built on seven hills, and unless you are fairly fit, it is wise to take advantage of public transport as much as possible for the up-hill climbs. The older trams go almost as far as Castelo de São Jorge, while the new *eléctricos*, run along the river. You can then walk down through the Alfama, and enjoy the views.

The heart of Lisbon's com-mercial area is made up of Chiado and the Baixa, where pedestrianized streets are filled with bustling shoppers and street artists. A wide variety of shops, department stores, outdoor cafés and banks offer plenty of oppor-tunity to buy souvenirs, change money or enjoy a coffee whilst soaking up the atmosphere.

When walking around the old neighbourhoods such as the Alfama, beware of pick-pockets and thieves that may prey on unsuspecting tourists.

DRIVING AROUND LISBON

Using a car to get around the busy city centre of Lisbon is not advisable. Portuguese drivers can be intimidating and parking can often be difficult during the busy rush hours. The city centre is also full of partially hidden one-way traffic signs, which can be frus-trating, if not somewhat expensive, should you come across an unsympathetic policeman who may issue an on-the-spot fine to visitors. Having said this, most police-men in Lisbon are generally

Pay and display sign

understanding of, and tolerant towards confused drivers and puzzled tourists, and will be willing to guide you back in the right direction.

There are relatively few roundabouts in Lisbon; the larger ones, such as Marquês de Pombal and Rotunda do Relógio by the airport, have traffic lights, although many of the smaller ones do not. Cars on roundabouts travel anticlockwise and have priority over waiting traffic. However, unless there are signs to the contrary, traffic from the right has priority at squares, cross-roads, junctions and even minor side roads.

If it is absolutely necessary for you to drive in Lisbon, keep calm and try to avoid the worst of the rush hour traffic (8–10am and 5:30–7:30pm). You should also look out for pedestrian crossings as these are often badly marked.

PARKING

Pressured by the chaotic state of parking on its streets, Lisbon City Council has embarked on a massive underground and outdoor car park construction programme. Since 1998, a total of around 20,000 above- and under-ground parking spaces have become available in the city.

The main underground car parks are located at Avenida 5 de Outubro, Avenida de Roma, Praça de Londres, Praça dos Restauradores, Praça da Figueira and Alameda.

Car parks are signposted by a white P on a blue back-ground and are relatively inexpensive. Most are located in the city centre. The largest, and newest, is situated in Praça Marquês de Pombal and has over 1,000 spaces.

Central Lisbon also has pay and display zones on weekdays between 8am and 8pm. They are iden-tified by the car park sign plus a hand and a card or a coin. The tickets are bought from machines; unfortunately most do not give out change, so be sure to have coins to

The Marquês de Pombal roundabout in central Lisbon

hand if you intend to park in the city centre. Parking illegally will result in either a hefty fine or your car being towed away. If it is impounded, the car will then only be released upon payment of a large fine.

CAR HIRE

MOST OF THE major hire companies such as Hertz and Avis have offices at the airport inside the International Terminal. To rent a car in Portugal you must have an international driving licence (unless you hold a licence from an EU member state). Drivers must be over the age of 21 and have held their licence for at least one year.

It is usually more expensive to hire a car at an airport, as is renting in summer; most companies offer special off-peak and weekend deals. The price depends on whether unlimited mileage is included and if you want comprehensive insurance *(todos-os-riscos)*. Normally, the car is provided with a full tank of petrol; it is best to return it with the tank full, as the agency will charge to fill it themselves.

A typical Lisbon taxi

PETROL

PETROL, CALLED *gasolina*, is relatively expensive in Portugal and is the same price countrywide. Diesel *(gasóleo)* is the cheapest. There are two types of unleaded *(gasolina sem chumbo)*: *normal* is slightly cheaper than *super*. Leaded petrol is rare.

In order to help differentiate between different fuels at petrol stations, a colour coding system exists: *normal* petrol is marked green, *super* is red, diesel is yellow.

Many petrol stations are located on Lisbon's outskirts so try not to get caught in town with an empty tank. Those outside town are generally self-service and often open 24 hours a day. The few that operate in the city centre are manned but usually close by 11pm. Filling up your tank is referred to as *cheio* and it is customary to give the attendant a small tip.

TAXIS

COMPARED TO THE rest of Europe, taxis in Portugal remain relatively inexpensive and if costs are shared between two or more people they can work out cheaper than travelling by bus or tram. Most taxis are beige but a few of the older black and green cabs still exist. All are metered although costs depend on the time of day.

Taxis have two green lights on their roofs to indicate

which of two rates is being charged. One light illuminated (6am–10pm), means normal rates apply, while two indicates the higher tariff (10pm–6am, weekends, public holidays). A flat extra rate is charged for any luggage. The meter is switched off for trips outside the city, so it is important to agree a price first.

If you try to flag a taxi down in the street check that the "taxi" sign on the roof is on first. Alternatively, you can order a radio taxi from a firm such as **Autocoope**, which costs a little more.

DIRECTORY

CAR HIRE AGENCIES AT LISBON AIRPORT

Auto Jardim
[21-846 29 16.

Avis Rent-a-Car
[21-754 78 00.

Budget
[21-319 55 55.

Guérin
[21-370 34 00.

Hertz
[21-381 24 30.

24-HOUR TAXI SERVICES

Autocoope
[21-793 27 56.

Teletáxis
[21-811 11 00.

Retalis Rádio Táxis
[21-811 90 00.

24-HOUR PETROL PUMPS

Garagem Almeida Navarro
Rua da Palma 256, Almirante Reis. **Map** 7 B2.

Miranda & Ferrão
Avenida António Serpa 22, Campo Pequeno. **Map** 5 C1.

BP Areeiro
Avenida Almirante Gago Coutinho, Areeiro. **Map** 6 E1.

Getting Around by Public Transport

Metro logo

As a result of the ever increasing traffic on its streets, Lisbon City Council has made huge efforts to improve the capital's public transport system. To date, the *Metropolitano* has seen the most significant improvement. A number of larger new trams have also been introduced to replace much loved but ageing predecessors, built at the beginning of the 20th century. Lisbon's orange and yellow buses have a more extensive network than trams and are another good way to get around and see the sights at the same time. Buses, trams and funiculars are all run by Carris, a state-owned company.

only one journey, but a one-day (*bilhete de um dia*) or seven-day ticket (*bilhete de sete dias*) is available and worth buying, as well as a set of ten (*dez*), known as a *caderneta*.

Children between the ages of four and twelve, students and adults over 65 all pay half price on public transport. Children under the age of four are permitted to travel free of charge.

TICKETS

Lisbon's transport system offers a wealth of choice regarding different ticket types. Value for money depends on how long you wish to stay and how many different types of transport you want to use.

If you wish to remain as flexible as possible it is best to buy tickets on boarding. Single tickets on all Carris transport (bus, tram and funicular) are bought from the driver or lift operator. However, if you buy Carris tickets beforehand at one of their kiosks (at Praça da Figueira, Elevador de Santa Justa or Sete Rios) you are entitled to two journeys for the price of one.

For visitors wishing to spend a whole day sightseeing and travelling around Lisbon, it is better to buy a one- or three-day ticket at a Carris kiosk. These allow travel on all Carris transport and are excellent value for money if you intend to make

numerous journeys in a short period. Both tickets must be validated at the beginning of the first journey.

Should you intend to stay longer in the city and wish to use the Metro as well as the bus, tram and funicular, it is more economical to invest in a Tourist Pass. This pass is available for either four or seven days, and is sold at Carris kiosks and Metro stations. You will need to show your passport or some other relevant form of identification in order to buy one. A one-day ticket allowing travel on all Carris transport and the Metro is also available.

If you just want to use the Metro, tickets can be bought either from the ticket office or from an automatic vending machine located at the station. It is cheaper to buy them from the vending machines. Metro tickets usually cover

Metro *obliterador* machine

TRAVELLING BY METRO

The quickest and cheapest way by far to get around town is by the *Metropolitano*. Metro stations are signposted with a red M and the service operates from 6:30–1am each day. Although the Metro becomes quite packed during the morning and evening rush hours, there are frequent trains. The system is safe to travel on, even at night, since the stations and trains are patrolled regularly 24 hours a day by the metro police. Tickets must be validated in the *obliterador*, which is usually located at the entrance to the station. You should do this before boarding a train or you could face a hefty fine of 100 times the value of a single ticket from one the Metro's travelling ticket inspectors.

The Metro first opened in December 1959 and consisted of one Y-shaped line between

BUYING TICKETS

Buses, trams and funiculars accept the same tickets, which can be purchased from Carris kiosks around the city centre. A wide variety of single journey, single day and multi-day tickets are available, some with discounts. The same applies for Metro tickets. The cheapest Metro tickets can be purchased from self-service station machines. Tickets valid for travel on the Carris system and the Metro are also available, while purchasing a special Tourist Pass allows unlimited travel on public transport throughout the city.

One-day Metro ticket

Half-price Carris ticket

THE LISBON METRO SYSTEM

Falagueira
Alfornetos
Pontinha
Carnide
Colégio Militar/Luz
Laranjeiras
Jardim Zoológico
Praça De Espanha
Alto dos Moinhos
Telheiras
Quinta das Mouras
Campo Grande
São Sebastião
Cidade Universitária
Entre Campos
Campo Pequeno
Ameixeira
Lumiar
Alvalade
Odivelas
Senhor Roubado
Roma
Oriente
Cabo Ruivo
Olivais Sul
Chelas
Bela Vista
Areeiro
Olaias
Saldanha
Picoas
Parque
Marquês De Pombal
Rato
Avenida
Restauradores
Cais do Sodré
Alameda
Arroios
Anjos
Intendente
Martim Moniz
Rossio
Terreiro do Paço
Santa Apolónia
Baixa-Chiado

KEY

- Linha da Gaivota
- Linha da Girassol
- Linha da Caravela
- Linha do Oriente
- Under construction

Jardim Zoolológico, Entre-campos and Restauradores. Today, there are some 37 stations operating on four lines: the Gaivota (Seagull line), the Girassol (Sunflower line), the Caravela (Caravel line) and the Oriente (Orient line). These lines link the Metro to major bus, train and ferry services, and provide transport from Lisbon's suburbs to the commercial heart of the city, along the north bank of the river. Plans are underway to greatly extend the city's Metro system and a number of stations are currently under construction.

TRAVELLING BY TRAM

TRAMS *(eléctricos)* are one of the most pleasant ways of sightseeing in Lisbon. However, they only operate in a very limited area of the city, along the river to Belém and around the hilly parts of Lisbon. There are presently two types of tram operating in Lisbon: the charming, old, pre-World War I models, and the much longer new trams with sleek interiors.

Single tickets for all rides are very cheap except for those on the red *Colinas* or *Tejo* trams, which provide special sightseeing rides for tourists and are much more

expensive than the ordinary routes. These sightseeing services operate throughout the year and take you through the hilly parts of Lisbon and along the Tagus. However, it is better value to catch one of the following trams:

No. 12 starts from Praça da Figueira and follows a route to São Tomé, in the picturesque Alfama district *(see p30–9).*

No. 15 goes from Praça da Figueira along the river to Belém where you can admire

the beautiful architecture of the Torre de Belém and the Mosteiro dos Jerónimos, and also visit the new Cultural Centre of Belém (CCB).

No. 28 starts at Praça de Martim Moniz and provides a fascinating trip through some of the oldest parts of Lisbon. The route follows the tight corners and narrow streets of Alfama and passes close to the Castelo de São Jorge. This enjoyable journey also includes Graça and Estrela.

New-style tram

Sightseeing tram

Lisbon's Elevador da Glória ascending to the Bairro Alto

FUNICULARS AND LIFTS

D UE TO LISBON'S hilly terrain, funiculars and lifts are a convenient and popular means of getting from river level to the upper parts of the city, namely Bairro Alto, Alfama and Graça. Although expensive in relation to the distance covered, this form of transport certainly helps take the effort out of negotiating Lisbon's hills, and in addition offers some superb views over the city.

Elevador da Bica climbs from the São Paulo area up to the lower end of Bairro Alto. **Elevador da Glória** goes from Praça dos Restauradores to the upper end of Bairro Alto. Closure of the walkway at **Elevador de Santa Justa,** means it does not currently link the Baxia with the Bairro Alto *(see p52).* **Elevador da Lavra,** climbs from Praça dos Restauradores up to the Hospital São José.

TRAVELLING BY BUS

B US TRANSPORT in Lisbon is more expensive than travelling by metro and less reliable. Although buses are fairly frequent, they are often packed. However, the service is presently more extensive than either the metro or the tram system and offers better access to sights for visitors.

Lisbon buses *(autocarros)* are orange. All services run about every 15 minutes from 5:30am to 1am. There is also a less extensive night bus system between 1am and 5:30am.

Stops are indicated by a sign marked *paragem* where details of the specific route are shown. The final destination is always displayed on the front of the bus. Tickets bought at Carris kiosks need to be validated in an *obliterador* machine on the bus, although those purchased from the driver do not. A set of ten tickets can be bought for half price at news stands. They are valid on buses and trams.

Orange and white Lisbon bus heading for Praça do Comércio

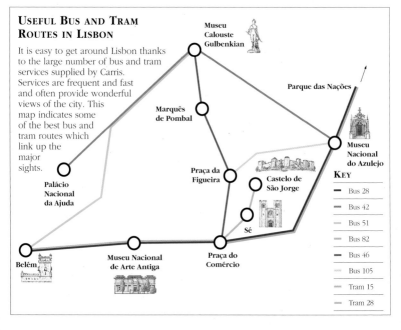

USEFUL BUS AND TRAM ROUTES IN LISBON

It is easy to get around Lisbon thanks to the large number of bus and tram services supplied by Carris. Services are frequent and fast and often provide wonderful views of the city. This map indicates some of the best bus and tram routes which link up the major sights.

Museu Calouste Gulbenkian

Parque das Nações

Marquês de Pombal

Praça da Figueira

Castelo de São Jorge

Museu Nacional do Azulejo

Palácio Nacional da Ajuda

Sé

Belém

Museu Nacional de Arte Antiga

Praça do Comércio

KEY

— Bus 28
— Bus 42
— Bus 51
— Bus 82
— Bus 46
— Bus 105
— Tram 15
— Tram 28

Travelling Around the Lisbon Coast

Logo for Caminhos de Ferro Portugueses

L ISBON AND ITS surroundings offer numerous sightseeing opportunities and the good road network means that most sights are only 30 minutes or so from the city centre. Buses, coaches and local trains are available for visiting Cascais and Estoril. Although no public buses go to Sintra, there are organized coach tours to the palaces and the glorious countryside around the town. A frequent rail service operates from Rossio station to Sintra. To visit Sesimbra and other areas to the south of the Tagus, ferries depart from Praça do Comércio, in Lisbon, and offer a more leisurely way to cross the river than the busy Ponte 25 de Abril. Alternatively, the Fertagus train also crosses the bridge on the lower level. Trains and buses can then be picked up on the south bank of the river.

High-speed Alfa train at Santa Apolónia station in Lisbon

TRAVELLING BY TRAIN

THE STATE-OWNED railway company, Caminhos de Ferro Portugueses (CP), operates all trains in Portugal.

There are four main rail lines out of Lisbon. Most popular with tourists is the line which runs from Cais do Sodré to Cascais on the coast, and the line linking Rossio station to the town of Sintra. Rossio station (metro Restauradores) is situated next to Praça dos Restauradores. There are regular trains from there to Sintra (departing every 15 minutes at peak hours) and the journey takes about 45 minutes. Santa Apolónia is the main station for trains travelling north as well as for most international arrivals. For those travelling east or south of Lisbon, a ferry departs from Fluvial station, on the north bank of the Tagus, to Barreiro station on the south side, from where train services depart. A new station, the Gare do

Façade of Rossio station

Oriente near the Parque das Nações, opened in 1998. It serves as an alternative international terminus as well as an interchange for local destinations.

To reach Estoril and Cascais take the train from Cais do Sodré station. The journey follows the coastline and takes about 45 minutes. Check destinations on the screens at the station before you travel as some trains terminate at Oeiras. You can also catch the train to Alcântara from Cais do Sodré, only five minutes away, or to Belém, ten minutes away.

TICKETING SYSTEM

DISCOUNTS of 50 per cent are available on all CP tickets for children aged from four to twelve years, students (you will need to show your student ID), and adults over 65. Children under the age of four travel free. However, there are no special discounts available for groups travelling together.

Return tickets can be bought on the Cais do Sodré-Cascais and Rossio-Sintra lines; however this will only save time rather than money, as returns are simply double the cost of single tickets.

If you wish to take a bicycle on these trains you will only be permitted to do so outside rush hours and an additional fee will be charged. Never get on a train without a ticket as you will be liable to a fine.

Departures board in Santa Apolónia station giving times and destinations

TRAVELLING BY CAR

W HEN DRIVING, always carry your passport, licence, car insurance and rental contract. Failure to produce these *documentos* if the police stop you will incur a fine.

The road network in and around Lisbon has seen significant improvements in the last decade, with the construction of new ring roads as well as motorways. If you are heading west out of Lisbon towards the coast and Estoril and Cascais, the quickest route is to take the A5 motorway.

Local signs giving directions to Estoril, the south via the bridge and Sete Rios

However, try to avoid rush hour traffic (8–10am and 5:30–7pm). To get on to the A5, follow the road out from Praça de Espanha or from Rotunda past Amoreiras.

Alternatively, if you prefer to take the scenic coastal route (N6), follow the A5 out of Lisbon for 8 km (5 miles), and turn off at the sign to Avenida Marginal.

To get to Sintra, the best route to take is either the A5 motorway, or to follow the IC19 past Queluz. Parts of the A5 motorway pass through picturesque countryside.

To reach Caparica, Tróia and Setúbal, south of the Tagus, you can either cross the Ponte 25 de Abril at Alcântara or catch the car ferry which departs regularly from Cais do Sodré port to Cacilhas. Once across the river, follow the A2 motorway south.

MOTORWAYS

M OTORWAYS AROUND Lisbon have toll charges since they are privately owned by a company called **Brisa**.

In general, they are the quickest way to travel around Portugal, as they have better surfaces than minor roads. There are also motorway rest areas where you can have something to eat and fill the car up with petrol.

There are two systems for paying tolls on motorways. Most drivers take a ticket *(título)* at the entrance and pay at the exit where the fee is displayed at the toll booth. The other system, known as the Via Verde, is primarily for residents in the area and is not intended for general use. Drivers subscribing to the system drive through the Via Verde channel without stopping. Their passage is registered automatically and billed later. It is strictly forbidden for anyone who does not subscribe to drive through the *Via Verde*, so make sure that you are in the correct lane as you approach the toll booths.

BREAKING DOWN

T HE LOCAL motoring association, **ACP** (Automóvel Club de Portugal), has a reciprocal breakdown service with most other international motoring organizations. To qualify, drivers should take out European cover with their own organization.

Should you suffer a road accident, the emergency services number is 112. If you have simply broken down, call the ACP. There are SOS phones at regular intervals along motorways. Unless you state that you are a member of an ACP-affiliated organization, a private tow truck will be sent to help you.

Breakdown assistance will try to repair your car on the spot, but if it is a more serious problem they will tow your car to a garage. Depending on your insurance, the ACP can make arrangements for you to have a hire car until yours is repaired.

In Portugal, international rules apply to breakdowns, including placing a red warning triangle behind the car to alert other drivers. Be sure to check that you have one in your car before you travel.

A sightseeing coach from one of the many tour operators

TRAVELLING BY COACH

F OLLOWING the privatization of the Rodoviária Nacional (RN), concessions have been made available to private enterprise. Competitive pricing has developed between rival coach companies, but the absence of a central coach service can make it difficult to know which company serves which destination.

Each of the companies operates its own ticketing system. As a general rule, however, you buy your ticket from the driver when you board the coach, although it is possible to get cheaper tickets, known as *modulos*, beforehand from the relevant coach company's kiosk. As on the trains, there are no group discounts though children between the ages of four and twelve travel half price.

At present, the only direct coach service operating between Lisbon and Cascais is run by the Scottish bus company **Scotturb** and **Rodoviária de Lisboa**. This hourly service departs from Lisbon airport via Campo Grande to Cascais, returning on an hourly basis as well. The two companies run one bus each, on alternate hours.

TST (Transportes Sul do Tejo) serves destinations south of the Tagus. Buses leave from Praça de Espanha (Metro Praça de Espanha) for destinations such as Costa da Caparica (1hr) and Sesimbra (1hr 45 mins).

For destinations northwest of Lisbon, contact Rodoviária de Lisboa. **Rede Expressos** and **EVA** are two coach companies that operate direct services to destinations all over the country. EVA covers the Algarve particularly well. Both are based at the Arco do Cego bus terminal in Avenida Duque de Ávila, while Rodoviária de Lisboa operates from Campo Grande among other places.

To date there is no coach link between Lisbon and Sintra. However, Scotturb operates three routes to Sintra from Cascais and Estoril. The No. 403 departs from near Cascais railway station every 90 minutes, via Cabo da Roca. The No. 417 runs from Cascais via Alcabideche and the No. 418 departs hourly from outside Estoril train station. Both buses stop at Sintra station and in the town centre. In Sintra, Scotturb also runs a service from the train station to Palácio da Pena and Castelo dos Mouros from Tuesday to Sunday.

COACH TOURS

THERE ARE MANY coach tours operating in the Lisbon area, offering a wide choice of destinations, from a short local trip around the city's sights to longer trips to other cities in Portugal such as Oporto. For those who just wish to tour Lisbon itself, short half-day tours are available. Sintra, Cabo da Roca, Estoril and Cascais are all easily reached in a day trip. Alternatively, you can head southwards to Sesimbra and Arrábida, or north to Mafra. Prices depend on whether meals or special events, such as *fado* or bullfighting, are included. Most tours offer reductions to children under the age of ten.

Tours can be booked directly with the tour operator, through a travel agent or at some hotels. If you are staying at one of Lisbon's major hotels, some tours will provide a pick-up service.

FERRIES ACROSS THE TAGUS

MOST FERRY SERVICES are operated by **Transtejo**. There are several different points at which you can cross the Tagus by ferry. The trips are worth making purely for the fabulous views of Lisbon.

From Terreiro do Paço (Estação Fluvial) there are crossings to Cacilhas (daily from 6am to 10:30pm) which take 15 minutes. Fast new ferries also cross from Terreiro do Paço to Seixal and Montijo (daily from 6am to 10:30pm) and take 15 and 30 minutes respectively. Ferries owned by Soflusa operate a 15 minute service from Terreiro do Paço to Barreiro (daily from 5:45am to 2:45am). From Belém, ferries go to Trafaria (daily from 7am to 9pm), where you can get a bus to the beaches at Caparica.

If you wish to take your car across the river, the regular ferry from Cais do Sodré to Cacilhas only takes about 15 minutes. This service operates daily from 5:30am to 2:30am.

Ferry docking at Terreiro do Paço

LISBON STREET FINDER

MAP REFERENCES given in this guide for sights and entertainment venues in Lisbon refer to the Street Finder maps on the following pages. Map references are also given for Lisbon's hotels *(see pp114–119)* and restaurants *(see pp128–33)*. The first figure in the map reference indicates which Street Finder map to turn to, and the letter and number which follow refer to the grid reference on that map. The map below shows the area of Lisbon covered by the eight Street Finder maps. Symbols used for sights and useful information are displayed in the key below. An index of street names and all the place of interest marked on the maps can be found on the following pages.

KEY TO STREET FINDER

▨	Major sight
▨	Place of interest
🚉	Railway station
Ⓜ	Metro station
🚌	Main coach stop
🚊	Tram stop
🚋	Funicular railway
🚕	Taxi rank
⛴	Ferry boarding point
🅿	Parking
🛈	Tourist information
✚	Hospital with casualty unit
👮	Police station
✝	Church
✡	Synagogue
☪	Mosque
⊠	Post office
❀	Viewpoint
=	Railway line
=	Motorway
→	One-way street
▬	Pedestrianized street
=45	House number

SCALE OF MAP PAGES 1–6

0 metres	250
0 yards	250

SCALE OF MAP PAGES 7–8

0 metres	250
0 yards	250

Street Finder Index

1º de Dezembro, Rua 7 B3
1º de Maio, Rua 3 A4
5 de Outubro, Avenida 5 C1
24 de Julho, Avenida 3 C4

A

Abade Faria, Rua 6 F2
Abílio Lopes do Rego,
  Rua 3 C3
Academia de Belas Artes,
  Largo da 7 B5
Academia das Ciências,
  Rua da 4 F2
Academia Recreativa
  de Santo Amaro, Rua 2 F3
Acesso à Ponte 3 A3
Açores, Rua dos 6 D3
Actor Isidoro, Rua 6 E2
Actor Taborda, Rua 6 D3
Actor Tasso, Rua 5 C4
Actor Vale, Rua 6 F3
Actriz Virgínia, Rua 6 E2
Açucenas, Rua das 1 C2
Adelas, Rua das 4 E2
Adro, Travessa do 7 B2
Afrânio Peixoto, Praça 6 E1
Afonso Costa, Avenida 6 F1
Afonso de Albuquerque,
  Praça 1 C4
Afonso Domingues, Rua 8 F1
Agostinho de Carvalho,
  Calçada de 7 C2
Águas Livres, Travessa 5 A5
Ajuda, Calçada da 2 D2
Ajuda, Calçada da 2 F2
Ajuda, Largo da 2 D2
Alcaide, Travessa do 4 F3
Alcântara, Rua de 3 A4
Alcolena, Rua de 1 A3
Alecrim, Rua do 7 A5
Alegria, Praça da 4 F1
Alegria, Rua da 4 F1
Alexandre Braga, Rua 6 D4
Alexandre Herculano,
  Rua 5 C5
Alexandre de Sá Pinto,
  Rua 2 D4
Alfândega, Rua da 7 C5
Alfredo Cortês, Rua 5 C1
Alfredo da Silva, Rua 2 D3
Alfredo Roque Gameiro,
  Rua 5 A1
Alfredo Soares, Rua 1 B2
Aliança Operária, Rua 2 E3
Almada, Rua do 4 F3
Almada, Travessa do 7 C4
Almas, Travessa das 3 C2
Almeida Brandão, Rua 4 D2
Almeida e Sousa, Rua 3 C1
Almirante Barroso, Rua 6 D3
Almirante Gago
  Coutinho, Avenida 6 E1
Almirante Reis, Avenida 6 E5
Alto do Duque, Rua do 1 A3
Álvaro Coutinho, Rua 6 E5
Álvaro Esteves, Rua 1 B3
Álvaro Pais, Avenida 5 B1
Alves Redol, Rua 6 D2
Alves Torgo,
  Rua (ao Areeiro) 6 E1
Alves Torgo,
  Rua (a Arroios) 6 E3
Alvito, Estrada do 2 F1
Alvito, Rua do 3 A3
Amendoeira, Rua da 8 D2
Américo Durão, Rua 6 F2
Amoreiras, Rua das
  (à Ajuda) 2 D3
Amoreiras, Rua das
  (ao Rato) 5 A5
Amoreiras, Travessa
  das (ao Rato) 5 B5

Amoreiras Shopping
  Center 5 A5
Anchieta, Rua 7 A4
Andaluz, Rua do 5 C4
Andrade, Rua 6 E5
Andrade Corvo, Rua 5 C4
André Brun, Rua 3 B2
Angelina Vidal, Rua 6 F5
Angola, Rua de 6 E4
Anjos, Rua dos 6 E5
Antão Gonçalves, Rua 1 A2
Antero de Quental, Rua 6 E5
António Abreu, Rua 1 A4
António Augusto de
  Aguiar, Avenida 5 B3
António Enes, Rua 5 C3
António Janeiro, Rua 1 A1
António José de Almeida,
  Avenida 6 D2
António Luís Inácio,
  Rua 6 F3
António Maria Cardoso,
  Rua 7 A5
António Pedro, Rua 6 E4
António Pereira
  Carrilho, Rua 6 E3
António de Saldanha,
  Rua 1 A2
António Serpa, Avenida 5 C1
Aqueduto das Águas
  Livres 5 A5
Arco, Rua do
  (a Alcântara) 3 B4
Arco, Rua do
  (a São Mamede) 4 E1
Arco do Cego, Rua do 6 D2
Arco do Chafariz das
  Terras, Rua 3 C3
Arco do Carvalhão,
  Rua do 3 B1
Arco da Graça, Rua do 7 B2
Arco Grande de Cima 8 E2
Armador, Travessa do 2 D2
Arrábida, Rua da 4 D1
Arriaga, Rua da 3 C4
Arrochela, Travessa da 4 E2
Arroios, Calçada de 6 D3
Arroios, Rua de 6 E4
Arsenal, Rua do 7 B5
Artilharia Um, Rua 5 A4
Artur de Paiva, Rua 6 F4
Artur Lamas, Rua 2 E4
Assunção, Rua da 7 B4
Ataíde, Rua do 7 A5
Atalaia, Rua da 4 F2
Augusta, Rua 7 B3
Augusto Gil, Rua 6 D1
Augusto Gomes Ferreira,
  Rua 2 D2
Augusto Machado, Rua 6 E2
Augusto Rosa, Rua 8 D4
Áurea, Rua (Rua
  do Ouro) 7 B4
Azedo Gneco, Rua 3 C1

B

Bacalhoeiros, Rua dos 7 C4
Barão, Rua do 8 D4
Barão de Sabrosa, Rua 6 F2
Barata Salgueiro, Rua 5 C5
Barbadinhos, Calçada
  dos 8 F1
Barbosa du Bocage,
  Avenida 5 C2
Barracas, Rua das 6 E5
Barroca, Rua da 4 F2
Bartolomeu da Costa,
  Rua 8 F1
Bartolomeu Dias, Rua 1 A5
Basílica da Estrela 4 D2
Beatas, Rua das 8 E1

Bela Vista, Rua da
  (à Graça) 8 E1
Bela Vista, Rua da
  (à Lapa) 4 D2
Belém, Rua de 1 C4
Bempostinha, Rua da 6 D5
Beneficência, Rua da 5 A1
Benformoso, Rua do 7 C1
Berna, Avenida de 5 B2
Bernardim Ribeiro, Rua 5 C5
Bernardino Costa, Rua 7 A5
Bernardo Lima, Rua 5 C4
Betesga, Rua da 7 B3
Bica do Marquês, Rua da 2 D3
Boa Hora, Calçada da 2 E3
Boa Hora, Travessa da
  (ao Bairro Alto) 4 F2
Boa Hora, Travessa da
  (à Ajuda) 2 D3
Boavista, Rua da 4 F3
Bombarda, Rua da 7 C1
Bombeiros, Avenida dos 1 B1
Boqueirão do Duro,
  Rua 4 E3
Boqueirão
  de Ferreiros, Rua 4 E3
Borges Carneiro, Rua 4 D3
Borja, Rua do 3 B3
Braamcamp, Rua 5 B5
Brás Pacheco, Rua 6 D2
Brasília, Avenida de 1 A5
Brito Aranha, Rua 6 D2
Brotero, Rua 1 C3
Buenos Aires, Rua de 4 D3

C

Cabo, Rua do 4 D1
Cabo Verde, Rua de 6 E5
Caetano Alberto, Rua 6 D2
Caetanos, Rua dos 4 F2
Cais de Santarém,
  Rua do 8 D4
Calado, Travessa do 6 F4
Calouste Gulbenkian,
  Avenida 5 A2
Camilo Castelo Branco,
  Rua 5 C5
Caminhos de Ferro,
  Rua dos 8 D3
Campo dos Mártires
  da Pátria 6 D5
Campo de Ourique,
  Rua de 4 D1
Campo Pequeno 5 C1
Campo de Santa Clara 8 F2
Campolide, Rua de 5 A4
Capelão, Rua do 7 C2
Capelo, Rua 7 A4
Capitão Afonso Pala, Rua 3 B3
Capitão Humberto de
  Ataíde, Rua 8 F1
Capitão Renato Baptista,
  Rua 6 E5
Cara, Travessa da 4 F2
Cardal à Graça, Rua do 8 E1
Cardal, Rua do 7 A1
Cardeal Cerejeira,
  Alameda 5 B4
Cardeal, Calçada do 8 F2
Cardeal Mercier, Rua 5 A1
Carlos Alberto da Mota
  Pinto, Rua 5 A5
Carlos Calisto, Rua 1 B2
Carlos José Barreiros,
  Rua 6 E3
Carlos da Maia, Rua 3 C1
Carlos Mardel, Rua 6 E3
Carlos Reis, Rua 5 B1
Carmo, Calçada do 7 A3
Carmo, Travessa do 7 A4
Carmo, Rua do 7 B4

Carrião, Rua do 7 A1
Carvalho, Travessa do 4 F3
Carvalho Araújo, Rua 6 F3
Casa dos Bicos 8 D4
Casal Ribeiro, Avenida 6 D3
Casal Ventoso de Baixo 3 B2
Casal Ventoso de Cima 3 B1
Casalinho da Ajuda,
  Rua do 2 E2
Cascais, Rua 3 B4
Cascão, Calçada do 8 F3
Caselas, Estrada de 1 B2
Castelo Branco Saraiva,
  Rua 6 F5
Castelo Picão,
  Calçada do 4 E3
Castelo Picão, Rua do 8 D4
Castilho, Rua 4 F1
  5 A4
Cavaleiro de Oliveira,
  Rua 6 E3
Cavaleiros, Rua dos 7 C2
Cecílio de Sousa, Rua 4 F1
Cemitério da Ajuda 1 C2
Cemitério dos Prazeres 3 B2
Centro de Arte Moderna 5 B3
Centro Cultural de Belém 1 B5
Cesário Verde, Rua 6 F4
Cesteiros, Calçada dos 8 F2
Ceuta, Avenida de 3 A2
Chagas, Rua das 4 F3
Chaminés d'El Rei, Rua 1 A1
Chão da Feira, Rua do 8 D3
Chiado 7 A5
Chiado, Largo do 7 A4
Chile, Praça do 6 E3
Cidade Avintes, Travessa 8 F2
Cidade da Horta, Rua 6 D3
Cidade de Cardiff, Rua 6 E4
Cima dos Quartéis,
  Travessa de 3 C1
Clube Atlético e Recreativo
  do Caramão, Rua 1 C1
Clube de Ténis,
  Estrada de 3 A2
Coelho da Rocha, Rua 3 C1
Colégio de São José,
  Rua do 1 A2
Columbano Bordalo
  Pinheiro, Avenida 5 A2
Combatentes, Avenida
  dos 5 A1
Combro, Calçada do 4 F2
Combro, Travessa do 4 D3
Comércio, Praça do 7 C5
Comércio, Rua do 7 B5
Conceição, Rua da 7 B4
Conceição da Glória,
  Rua da 4 F1
Conde, Rua do 4 D3
Conde Barão, Largo do 4 E3
Conde de Monsaraz,
  Rua 6 F4
Conde de Pombeiro,
  Calçada do 6 E5
Conde da Ponte,
  Travessa do 3 A5
Conde de Redondo,
  Rua do 5 C5
Conde da Ribeira,
  Travessa do 2 F3
Conde de Valbom,
  Avenida 5 B2
Condes, Rua dos 7 A2
Condessa, Rua da 7 A3
Condessa do Rio,
  Travessa da 4 F3
Conselheiro Arantes
  Pedroso, Rua 7 B1
Conselheiro Fernando de
  Sousa, Avenida 5 A4
Conselheiro Martins de
  Carvalho, Rua 1 C2

Convento de Jesus,
Travessa do | 4 F2
Cordeiro de Sousa, Rua | 5 C1
Cordoeiros, Rua dos | 4 F3
Coronel Eduardo
Galhardo, Avenida | 6 F4
Castelo de São Jorge | 8 D3
Coronel Ferreira
do Amaral, Rua | 6 E2
Coronel Pereira da Silva,
Rua | 2 D3
Corpo Santo, Rua do | 7 A5
Correeiros, Rua dos | 7 B4
Correia Teles, Rua | 3 C1
Correio Velho,
Calçada do | 7 C4
Corvos, Rua dos | 8 E3
Costa, Rua da | 3 B3
Costa, Travessa da | 3 B3
Costa do Castelo | 7 C3
Costa Goodolfim, Rua | 6 D2
Costa Pimenta, Rua | 3 B1
Cova da Moura, Rua da | 3 B3
Cozinha Económica,
Rua da | 3 A4
Crucifixo, Rua do | 7 B4
Cruz, Estrada da
(ao Caramão) | 1 B2
Cruz , Rua da
(a Alcântara) | 3 A3
Cruz, Rua da (a Caselas) | 1 A1
Cruz, Travessa da
(do Torel) | 7 B1
Cruz da Carreira, Rua da | 6 D5
Cruz do Desterro,
Travessa | 7 B1
Cruz dos Poiais, Rua da | 4 E2
Cruz Vermelha, Rua da | 5 B1
Cruzeiro, Rua do | 2 E2
Cura, Rua do | 4 D3

D

Damão, Praça de | 1 A4
Damasceno Monteiro,
Rua | 6 E5 / 8 D1
David Melgueiro,
Rua | 1 A4
David de Sousa, Rua | 6 D1
Defensores de Chaves,
Avenida dos | 5 C2
Descobertas,
Avenida das | 1 A2
Desterro, Calçada do | 7 C1
Desterro, Rua do | 7 B1
Diário de Notícias, Rua | 7 A4
Dinis Dias, Rua | 1 A4
Dio, Praça de | 1 A4
Diogo Cão, Rua | 2 E3
Diogo Gomes, Rua | 1 A4
Diogo de Silves, Rua | 1 B2
Diogo de Teive, Rua | 1 B2
Dom Afonso Henriques,
Alameda | 6 E2
Dom Carlos I, Avenida | 4 E3
Dom Constantino de
Bragança, Rua | 1 A3
Dom Cristóvão da Gama,
Rua, | 1 A4
Dom Duarte, Rua | 7 B3
Dom Francisco
de Almeida, Rua | 1 A4
Dom Francisco Manuel
de Melo, Rua | 5 A4
Dom João V, Rua | 4 D1
Dom João de Castro,
Rua | 2 E3
Dom Lourenço
de Almeida, Rua | 1 B4
Dom Luís I, Rua | 4 E3
Dom Luís de Noronha,
Rua | 5 A2
Dom Pedro IV, Praça | 7 B3
Dom Pedro V, Rua | 4 F2
Dom Vasco, Rua de | 2 D3

Dom Vasco, Travessa de | 2 D3
Domingos Sequeira, Rua | 4 D2
Domingos Tendeiro, Rua | 1 C3
Dona Estefânia, Rua de | 6 D3
Dona Filipe de Vilhena,
Rua | 6 D2
Douradores, Rua dos | 7 C4
Doutor Almeida Amaral,
Rua | 6 D5
Doutor Álvaro de Castro,
Rua | 5 A2
Doutor Eduardo Neves,
Rua | 5 C1
Doutor Júlio Dantas, Rua | 5 A3
Doutor Mário Moutinho,
Avenida | 1 B1
Doutor Nicolau
de Bettencourt, Rua | 5 B3
Doutor Oliveira Ramos,
Rua | 6 F3
Doutor Silva Teles, Rua | 5 B2
Doutor Teófilo Braga,
Rua | 4 D2
Duarte Pacheco Pereira,
Rua | 1 A4
Duque, Rua do | 7 A3
Duque de Ávila, Avenida | 5 C3
Duque de Loulé, Avenida | 5 C4
Duque de Palmela, Rua | 5 C5
Duque de Saldanha,
Praça do | 5 C3
Duques de Bragança,
Rua dos | 7 A5

E

Eça de Queirós, Rua | 5 C4
Eduardo Bairrada, Rua | 2 D2
Eduardo Coelho, Rua | 4 F2
Eduardo da Costa, Rua | 6 F4
Egas Moniz, Rua | 6 F2
Elevador de Santa Justa | 7 B3
Elias Garcia, Avenida | 5 C2
Embaixador Teixeira de
Sampaio, Rua | 3 C3
Embaixador, Rua do | 2 D4
Emenda, Rua da | 4 F3
Engenheiro Duarte
Pacheco, Avenida | 5 A5
Engenheiro Miguel Pais,
Calçada | 4 E1
Engenheiro Santos
Simões, Rua | 6 F2
Engenheiro Vieira
da Silva, Rua | 5 C3
Entrecampos, Rua de | 5 C1
Entremuros do Mirante,
Rua de | 8 F2
Ermida de São Jerónimo | 1 A3
Escola Araújo,
Travessa da | 6 D4
Escola do Exército,
Rua da | 6 D5
Escola de Medicina
Veterinária, Rua da | 6 D4
Escola Politécnica,
Rua da | 4 E1
Escolas Gerais, Rua das | 8 E3
Espanha, Praça de | 5 A2
Espera, Travessa da | 7 A4
Esperança, Rua da | 4 E3
Esperança do Cardal,
Rua | 7 A1
Espírito Santo, Beco do | 8 E4
Estádio Municipal
do Restelo | 1 B3
Estrela, Calçada da | 4 E2
Estrela, Praça da | 4 D2
Estrela, Rua da | 4 D2

F

Fábrica dos Pentes,
Travessa da | 5 B5
Fala Só, Travessa do | 7 A2

Fanqueiros, Rua dos | 7 C4
Farinhas, Rua das | 7 C3
Fé, Rua da | 7 A1
Feira da Ladra | 8 E2
Feliciano de Sousa, Rua | 3 A3
Fernandes Tomás, Rua | 4 F3
Fernando Pedroso, Rua | 6 D2
Fernão Gomes, Rua | 1 A3
Fernão Lopes, Rua | 5 C3
Fernão Mendes Pinto,
Rua | 1 A5
Ferragial, Rua | 7 A5
Ferreira Borges, Rua | 3 C1
Ferreira Lapa, Rua | 6 D4
Ferreiro, Travessa do | 3 C3
Ferreiros, Rua dos | 4 E2
Ferreiros, Travessa dos | 1 C4
Fialho de Almeida, Rua | 5 A3
Fiéis de Deus,
Travessa dos | 4 F2
Figueira, Praça da | 7 B3
Filinto Elísio, Rua | 2 F3
Filipe da Mata, Rua | 5 A1
Filipe Folque, Rua | 5 C3
Flores, Rua das | 7 A4
Florindas, Travessa das | 2 D3
Fonseca Benevides, Rua | 2 E2
Fontainhas, Rua das | 3 A4
Fonte do Louro,
Azinhaga da | 6 F1
Fontes Pereira de Melo,
Avenida | 5 C4
Forno, Rua do | 7 B2
Forno do Tijolo, Rua do | 6 E5
Forte, Calçada do | 8 F1
Forte do Alto do Duque,
Estrada de | 1 A2
Fradesso da Silveira, Rua | 3 A4
Francesinhas, Rua das | 4 E3
Francisco de Holanda,
Rua | 5 B1
Francisco Metrass, Rua | 3 C1
Francisco Pedro Curado,
Rua | 6 F4
Francisco Ribeiro, Rua | 6 E5
Francisco Sá Carneiro
Praça, (ao Areeiro) | 6 E1
Francisco Sanches, Rua | 6 E3
Francisco Tomás
da Costa, Rua | 5 B1
Frei Amador Arrais, Rua | 6 D1
Frei Manuel do Cenáculo,
Rua | 6 F5
Frei Miguel Contreiras,
Avenida | 6 E1
Freiras, Travessa das
(a Arroios) | 6 E3
Freiras, Travessa das
(a santa Clara) | 8 F2
Freitas Gazul, Rua | 3 B1
Fresca, Rua | 4 E3
Funil, Travessa do | 8 D3

G

Gaivotas, Rua das | 4 E3
Galé, Travessa da | 3 A5
Galvão, Calçada do | 1 C3
Garcia de Orta, Rua | 4 D3
Garrett, Rua | 7 A4
Garrido, Rua do | 6 F2
Gâveas, Rua das | 7 A4
General Farinha Beirão,
Rua | 6 D4
General Garcia Rosado,
Rua | 6 D4
General João de Almeida,
Rua | 1 C3
General Leman, Rua | 5 A1
General Massano
de Amorim, Rua | 1 C3
General Roçadas,
Avenida | 6 F5
Gervásio Lobato, Rua | 3 B2
Giestal, Rua do | 2 E4

Giestal, Travessa do | 2 E3
Gil Eanes, Rua | 1 A3
Gil Vicente, Rua | 2 F3
Gilberto Rola, Rua | 3 B4
Giovanni Antinori, Rua | 2 E2
Glória, Calçada da | 7 A3
Glória, Rua da | 4 F1 / 7 A2
Glória, Travessa da | 7 A2
Goa, Praça de | 1 A3
Gomes Freire, Rua | 6 D4
Gonçalo Nunes, Rua | 1 B2
Gonçalo Sintra, Rua | 1 B2
Gonçalo Velho Cabral,
Rua | 1 B3
Gonçalves Crespo, Rua | 6 D4
Gonçalves Zarco, Rua | 1 C3
Gorgel do Amaral, Rua | 5 A5
Graça, Calçada da | 8 D2
Graça, Largo da | 8 D2
Graça, Rua da | 8 D1
Gravato, Rua do | 1 A1
Gregório Lopes, Rua | 1 B2
Guarda, Travessa da | 2 F4
Guarda-Jóias, Rua do | 2 D2
Guarda-Jóias,
Travessa do | 2 D3
Guarda-Mor, Rua do | 4 D3
Guerra Junqueiro,
Avenida | 6 E2
Guilherme Braga, Rua | 8 E3
Guilherme Coussul,
Travessa de | 7 A4
Guilherme dos Anjos,
Rua | 3 B1
Guiné, Rua da | 6 E4
Gustavo de Matos
Sequeira, Rua | 4 E1

H

Heliodoro Salgado, Rua | 6 F5
Hellen Keller, Avenida | 1 C2
Henrique Alves, Rua | 5 A3
Henrique Cardoso,
Travessa | 6 D1
Heróis de Quionga, Rua | 6 E4
Horta, Travessa da | 4 F2
Horta e Silva, Rua | 1 B1
Horta Navia, Travessa da | 3 B3
Horta Seca, Rua da | 7 A4

I

Igreja do Carmo | 7 B3
Igreja da Memória | 1 C3
Igreja de Santo António
à Sé | 7 C4
Igreja de São Roque | 7 A3
Igreja de São Vicente
de Fora | 8 E3
Ilha do Faial, Praça da | 6 D3
Ilha da Madeira,
Avenida da | 1 B2
Ilha do Príncipe, Rua da | 6 E4
Ilha de São Tomé,
Rua da | 6 E4
Ilha Terceira, Rua | 6 D3
Império, Praça do | 1 C4
Imprensa, Rua da
(à Estrela) | 4 E2
Imprensa Nacional,
Rua da | 4 E1
Índia, Avenida da | 1 A5
Indústria, Rua da | 2 F3 / 3 A4
Infantaria Dezasseis,
Rua de | 3 C1
Infante Dom Henrique,
Avenida | 8 D5
Infante Dom Pedro,
Rua | 5 C1
Infante Santo, Avenida | 3 C3
Inglesinhos, Travessa
dos | 4 F2

Instituto Bacteriológico,
Rua do   **7 B1**
Instituto Industrial,
Rua do   **4 E3**
Intendente, Largo do   **7 C1**
Ivens, Rua   **7 B4**

J

Jacinta Marto, Rua   **6 D4**
Jacinto Nunes, Rua   **6 F3**
Janelas Verdes, Rua das   **4 D4**
Jardim, Travessa do   **3 C2**
Jardim Agrícola Tropical   **1 C4**
Jardim Botânico   **4 F1**
Jardim Botânico
da Ajuda   **1 C2**
Jardim Botânico,
Rua do   **1 C3**
Jardim Ducla Soares   **1 A4**
Jardim da Estrela   **4 D2**
Jardim do Tabaco, Rua   **8 E4**
Jasmim, Rua do   **4 F2**
Jau, Rua   **2 F3**
Jerónimos, Rua dos   **1 C4**
João XXI, Avenida   **6 E1**
João Afonso de Aveiro,
Rua   **1 A4**
João de Barros, Rua   **2 F3**
João Bastos, Rua   **1 B4**
João de Castilho, Rua   **1 C3**
João Coimbra, Rua   **1 A3**
João Crisóstomo,
Avenida   **5 B3**
João Dias, Rua   **1 B2**
João Fernandes Labrador,
Rua   **1 B3**
João de Menezes, Rua   **6 F2**
João do Outeiro, Rua   **7 C2**
João de Paiva, Rua   **1 B3**
João Penha, Rua   **5 B5**
João das Regras, Rua   **7 B3**
João do Rio, Praça   **6 E2**
João Villaret, Rua   **6 D1**
Joaquim António
de Aguiar, Rua   **5 B5**
Joaquim Bonifácio, Rua   **6 D4**
Joaquim Casimiro, Rua   **3 C3**
Jorge Afonso, Rua   **5 A1**
José Acúrcio das Neves,
Rua   **6 F2**
José Dias Coelho, Rua   **3 A4**
José Estêvão, Rua   **6 E4**
José Falcão, Rua   **6 E3**
José Fernandes,
Travessa   **2 E2**
José Malhôa, Avenida   **5 A2**
José Pinto Bastos, Rua   **1 B1**
José Ricardo, Rua   **6 E3**
Josefa Maria, Rua   **8 D1**
Josefa de Óbidos, Rua   **8 E1**
Julieta Ferrão, Rua   **5 B1**
Júlio de Andrade, Rua   **7 A1**
Júlio Dinis, Avenida   **5 C1**
Junqueira, Rua da   **2 D4**

L

Lagares, Rua dos   **8 D2**
Lagares, Travessa dos   **8 D2**
Lapa, Beco da   **8 E3**
Lapa, Rua da   **4 D3**
Latino Coelho, Rua   **5 C3**
Laura Alves, Rua   **5 C1**
Leão de Oliveira, Rua   **3 A4**
Leite de Vasconcelos,
Rua   **8 F2**
Liberdade, Avenida da   **4 F1**
                                5 C5
                                7 A2
Limoeiro, Rua do   **8 D4**
Livramento, Calçada do   **3 B3**
Lóios, Largo dos   **8 D4**
Londres, Praça de   **6 E2**
Loreto, Rua do   **4 F3**

Luciano Cordeiro, Rua   **5 C4**
Lucília Simões, Rua   **6 E3**
Lucinda do Carmo,
Rua   **6 E2**
Luís Bívar, Avenida   **5 C3**
Luís de Camões, Praça   **7 A4**
Luís de Camões, Rua   **2 F3**
Luís Derouet, Rua   **3 C1**
Luís Monteiro, Rua   **6 F3**
Luís Pedroso de Barros,
Rua   **1 B3**
Luísa Todí, Rua   **2 F3**
Lusíadas, Rua dos   **2 F3**
                                3 A4
Luz Soriano, Rua   **4 F2**

M

Macau, Rua de   **6 E5**
Machadinho, Rua do   **4 E3**
Machado, Rua do
(à Ajuda)   **2 E3**
Machado de Castro,
Rua   **8 F1**
Madalena, Rua da   **7 C4**
Madres, Rua das   **4 E3**
Madrid, Avenida de   **6 E1**
Mãe d'Água, Rua   **4 F1**
Maestro António Taborda,
Rua   **3 C3**
Malaca, Praça de   **1 B4**
Manuel Bento de Sousa,
Rua   **7 B1**
Manuel Bernardes, Rua   **4 E2**
Manuel da Maia,
Avenida   **6 E2**
Manuel Gouveia, Rua   **6 F1**
Manuel Soares Guedes,
Rua   **7 C1**
Manuelzinho d'Arcolena,
Rua   **1 A1**
Marconi, Avenida   **6 D1**
Marcos, Estrada dos   **1 C1**
Marcos, Largo dos   **1 C2**
Marcos, Rua dos   **1 C2**
Marechal Saldanha, Rua   **4 F3**
Margiochis, Rua dos   **1 A1**
Maria, Rua   **6 E5**
Maria Andrade, Rua   **6 E5**
Maria da Fonte, Rua   **6 E5**
Maria Luísa Holstein,
Rua   **3 A4**
Maria Pia, Rua   **3 B1**
Marquês de Abrantes,
Calçada   **4 E3**
Marquês de Fronteira,
Rua   **5 A4**
Marquês de Pombal,
Praça   **5 C5**
Marquês de Ponte de
Lima, Rua   **7 C2**
Marquês de Sá da
Bandeira, Rua   **5 B3**
Marques da Silva, Rua   **6 E4**
Marquês de Subserra,
Rua   **5 A5**
Marquês de Tancos,
Calçada do   **7 C3**
Marquês de Tomar,
Avenida   **5 C2**
Martim Moniz, Rua   **7 C2**
Martim Vaz, Rua de   **7 B2**
Martins Barata, Rua   **1 B4**
Martins Ferrão, Rua   **5 C4**
Martins Sarmento, Rua   **6 F4**
Mastros, Rua dos   **4 E3**
Mato Grosso, Rua   **8 F1**
Meio, Rua do (à Lapa)   **4 D3**
Mem Rodrigues, Rua   **1 B2**
Memória, Calçada da   **1 C3**
Memória, Travessa da   **1 C3**
Mercado 24 de Julho   **4 F3**
Merceeiras, Travessa
das   **8 D4**
Mercês, Rua das   **2 D3**

Mercês, Travessa das`   **4 F2**
Mestre António Martins,
Rua   **6 F4**
Mexico, Avenida do   **6 D2**
Miguel Bombarda,
Avenida   **5 C2**
Miguel Lupi, Rua   **4 E2**
Milagre de Santo António,
Rua do   **7 C4**
Miradouro de São Pedro
de Alcântara   **7 A2**
Mirador, Rua do   **2 E3**
Miradouro da Graça   **8 D2**
Miradouro de
Santa Luzia   **8 D4**
Mirante, Beco do   **8 F2**
Mirante, Calçada do
(à Ajuda)   **2 D2**
Misericórdia, Rua da   **7 A4**
Moçambique, Rua de   **6 E4**
Moeda, Rua da   **4 F3**
Moinho de Vento,
Calçada   **7 A1**
Moinho de Vento,
Travessa do   **3 C3**
Moinho Velho,
Travessa do   **2 E3**
Moinhos, Travessa dos   **2 E3**
Monte, Beco do   **7 C1**
Monte, Calçada do   **7 D1**
Monte, Travessa do   **8 D1**
Monte Olivete, Rua do   **4 E1**
Morais Soares, Rua   **6 F3**
Mosteiro dos Jerónimos   **1 C4**
Mouraria, Rua da   **7 C2**
Mouros, Rua dos   **4 F2**
Mouzinho da Silveira,
Rua   **5 B5**
Mouzinho de Albuquerque,
Avenida   **6 F4**
Município, Praça do   **7 B5**
Museu de Arte Popular   **1 B5**
Museu de Artes
Decorativas   **8 D3**
Museu Calouste
Gulbenkian   **5 B2**
Museu do Chiado   **7 A5**
Museu da Marinha   **1 B4**
Museu da Marioneta   **8 D3**
Museu Militar   **8 F3**
Museu Nacional de
Arqueologia   **1 B4**
Museu Nacional de
Arte Antiga   **4 D4**
Museu Nacional
dos Coches   **2 D4**
Museu de Artilharia,
Rua do   **8 F3**

N

Navegantes, Rua dos   **4 D2**
Nazaré, Travessa de   **7 C1**
Necessidades,
Calçada das   **3 C3**
Necessidades, Rua das   **3 B3**
Newton, Rua   **6 E4**
Noronha, Rua do   **4 E1**
Norte, Rua do   **7 A4**
Nossa Senhora da
Conceição Velha   **7 C4**
Nova do Almada, Rua   **7 B4**
Nova do Calhariz, Rua   **2 D3**
Nova do Carvalho,
Rua   **7 A5**
Nova do Colégio,
Calçada   **7 B2**
Nova do Desterro, Rua   **7 C1**
Nova do Loureiro, Rua   **4 F2**
Nova da Piedade, Rua   **4 E2**
Nova de Santos,
Travessa   **4 D3**
Nova de São Domingos,
Travessa   **7 B3**

Nova de São Mamede,
Rua   **4 E1**
Nova da Trindade, Rua   **7 A3**
Nuno Tristão, Rua   **1 A4**

O

Ocidental, Largo   **1 B1**
Olaias, Rotunda das   **6 F2**
Olarias, Largo das   **7 C2**
Olarias, Rua das   **7 C1**
Olival, Rua do   **3 C4**
Olival, Travessa do
(à Graça)   **8 F1**
Oliveira, Rua da   **7 A3**
Oliveira Martins, Rua   **6 D1**
Oliveirinha, Rua   **8 D3**
Óscar Monteiro Torres,
Avenida   **6 D1**

P

Paço da Rainha, Largo   **6 D5**
Padre António Vieira,
Rua   **5 A4**
Padre Francisco Rua   **3 C2**
Padre Luís Aparício, Rua   **6 D5**
Padre Manuel Alves
Correia, Rua   **2 E2**
Padre Manuel de
Nóbrega, Avenida   **6 E1**
Padrão dos
Descobrimentos   **1 C5**
Paiva de Andrade, Rua   **7 A4**
Paiva Couceiro, Praça   **6 F4**
Palácio de Belém   **1 C4**
Palácio Nacional da
Ajuda   **2 D2**
Palácio de São Bento   **4 E2**
Palma, Rua da   **7 B2**
Palma, Travessa da   **7 B2**
Palmeira, Rua da   **4 F2**
Palmeira, Travessa da   **4 E2**
Palmira, Rua   **6 E5**
Pampulha, Calçada da   **3 C4**
Paraíso, Rua do   **8 F2**
Pardal, Travessa do   **2 E2**
Paris, Avenida de   **6 E1**
Parque Eduardo VII   **5 B4**
Parque Florestal de
Monsanto   **1 B1**
Particular, 2ª Rua   **3 A4**
Páscoa, Rua da   **4 D1**
Pascoal de Melo, Rua   **6 D3**
Passadiço, Rua do   **5 C5**
                                7 A1
Passos Manuel, Rua   **6 E4**
Pasteur, Praça   **6 E2**
Patrocínio, Rua do   **3 C2**
Pau da Bandeira, Rua do   **3 C3**
Paulo da Gama, Rua   **1 A3**
Paulo Martins, Travessa   **1 C3**
Paz, Rua da   **4 E2**
Paz do Laranjal, Rua da   **1 C3**
Pedras Negras, Rua das   **7 C4**
Pedreiras, Rua das   **1 C3**
Pedro Alexandrino, Rua   **8 F1**
Pedro Álvares Cabral,
Avenida   **4 D1**
Pedro Augusto Franco,
Rua   **1 B1**
Pedro de Barcelos, Rua   **1 B3**
Pedro Calmon, Rua   **2 F3**
Pedro Escobar, Rua   **1 A4**
Pedro Fernandes
Queirós, Rua   **1 A3**
Pedro Nunes, Rua   **5 C3**
Pedro de Sintra, Rua   **1 B2**
Pedro Teixeira,
Estrada de   **1 C1**
Pedrouços, Rua de   **1 A5**
Pena, Travessa da   **7 B2**
Penha de França, Rua da   **6 E4**
Pereira, Travessa da   **8 E2**

Pereira e Sousa, Rua   3 C1
Pero da Covilhã, Rua   1 B3
Pero de Alenquer, Rua   1 A3
Picoas, Rua das   5 C3
Pinheiro, Travessa do   4 D2
Pinheiro Chagas, Rua   5 C3
Pinto, Travessa do   2 F4
Pinto Ferreira, Rua   2 E4
Pinto Quartin, Rua   2 D2
Planetário Calouste
  Gulbenkian   1 B4
Poço da Cidade,
  Travessa do   7 A3
Poço dos Mouros,
  Calçada dos   6 F3
Poço dos Negros, Rua do   4 E3
Poiais de São Bento,
  Rua dos   4 E3
Ponte 25 de Abril   3 A5
Ponte, Avenida da   3 A4
Ponta Delgada, Rua   6 D3
Portas de Santo Antão,
  Rua das   7 A2
Portas do Sol, Largo   8 D3
Portugal Durão, Rua   5 A1
Possidónio da Silva, Rua   3 B2
Possolo, Rua do   3 C2
Possolo, Travessa do   3 C2
Praças, Rua das   4 D3
Praia, Escadinhas da   4 E3
Praia, Travessa da   2 F4
Praia de Pedrouços,
  Rua da   1 A5
Praia da Vitrouços,
  Rua da   1 A5
Prata, Rua da   7 B4
Prazeres, Estrada dos   3 B4
Prazeres, Rua dos   4 E2
Presidente Arriaga, Rua   3 C4
Pretas, Rua das   7 A1
Príncipe Real, Praça do   4 F1
Prior, Rua do   3 C3
Prior do Crato, Rua   3 B4
Professor Armando de
  Lucena, Rua   2 D2
Professor Cid dos Santos,
  Rua   2 D1
Professor Gomes
  Teixeira, Rua   3 C2
Professor Lima Basto,
  Rua   5 A2
Professor Sousa da
  Câmara, Rua   5 A5

Q

Quartéis, Rua dos   2 D3
Quatro de Infantaria, Rua   3 C1
Queimada, Travessa da   7 A3
Quelhas, Rua do   4 D3
Queluz, Estrada de   1 C1
Quinta do Almargem,
  Rua da   2 E3
Quinta do Jacinto,
  Rua da   3 A3
Quintinha, Rua da   4 E2
Quirino da Fonseca,
  Rua   6 E3

R

Rafael de Andrade, Rua   6 E5
Ramalho Ortigão, Rua   5 B1
Rato, Largo do   4 E1
Rebelo da Silva, Rua   5 B1
Regueira, Rua da   8 E4
Regueirão dos Anjos, Rua   6 E5
Remédios, Rua dos
  (a Alfama)   8 E3
Remédios, Rua dos
  (à Lapa)   4 D3

Remolares, Rua dos   7 A5
República, Avenida da   5 C1
Ressano Garcia, Avenida   5 A3
Restelo, Avenida do   1 A4
Restauradores, Praça dos   7 A2
Ribeira das Naus,
  Avenida da   7 B5
Ribeira Nova, Rua da   4 F3
Ribeiro Santos, Calçada   4 D3
Ribeiro Sanches, Rua   3 C3
Ricardo Espírito Santo,
  Rua   3 C3
Rio Seco, Rua do   2 E3
Rodrigo da Fonseca,
  Rua   5 A4
Rodrigo Rebelo, Rua   1 A2
Rodrigues Faria, Rua   3 A4
Rodrigues Sampaio, Rua   5 C5
Roma, Avenida da   6 D1
Rosa Araújo, Rua   5 C5
Rosa Damasceno, Rua   6 E3
Rosa, Rua da   4 F2
Rossio (Praça Dom
  Pedro IV)   7 B3
Rotunda das Olaias   6 F2
Rovisco Pais, Avenida   6 D3
Roy Campbell, Rua   2 E2
Rui Barbosa, Rua   8 F1
Rui Pereira, Rua   1 B3

S

Sá de Miranda, Rua   2 F3
Sabino de Sousa, Rua   6 F3
Sacadura Cabral, Avenida   6 D1
Saco, Rua do   7 B1
Sacramento, Calçada do   7 B4
Sacramento, Rua do
  (à Lapa)   3 C3
Sacramento, Rua do
  (a Alcântara)   3 B4
Sacramento, Travessa do
  (a Alcântara)   3 B4
Salitre, Rua do   4 F1
Salitre, Travessa do   4 F1
Salvador, Rua do   8 D3
Sampaio Bruno, Rua   3 B1
Sampaio e Pina, Rua   5 A4
Santa Bárbara, Rua de   6 E5
Santa Catarina, Rua de   4 F3
Santa Catarina,
  Travessa de   4 F3
Santa Cruz do Castelo,
  Rua   8 D3
Santa Engrácia   8 F2
Santa Justa, Rua de   7 B3
Santa Marinha, Rua de   8 D3
Santa Marta, Rua de   5 C5
Santa Marta,
  Travessa de   5 C5
Santa Quitéria,
  Travessa de   4 D1
Santana, Calçada   7 B2
Santana, Rua de
  (à Lapa)   3 C2
Santo Amaro, Calçada de   2 F3
Santo Amaro, Rua de   4 E2
Santo André, Calçada de   8 D2
Santo António, Rua de
  (à Estrela)   3 C2
Santo António,
  Travessa de (à Graça)   8 E1
Santo António da Glória,
  Rua   4 F1
Santo António da Sé,
  Rua de   7 C4
Santo Estêvão, Rua de   8 E3
Santos, Largo de   4 E3
Santos Dumont, Avenida   5 A2
Santos-o-Velho, Rua de   4 D3
São Bento, Rua de   4 E1

São Bernardino,
  Travessa   6 D5
São Bernardo, Rua de   4 D2
São Boaventura, Rua de   4 F2
São Caetano, Rua de   3 C3
São Ciro, Rua de   4 D2
São Domingos, Largo de   7 B3
São Domingos, Rua de   4 D3
São Félix, Rua de   4 D3
São Filipe Neri, Rua de   5 B5
São Francisco Xavier,
  Rua   1 A4
São Francisco,
  Calçada de   7 B5
São Gens, Rua de   8 D1
São João de Deus,
  Avenida   6 E1
São João da Mata,
  Rua de   4 D3
São João da Praça,
  Rua de   8 D4
São Jorge, Rua de   4 D2
São José, Rua de   7 A1
São Julião, Rua de   7 B4
São Lázaro, Rua de   7 B1
São Mamede, Rua de   7 C4
São Marçal, Rua de   4 E2
São Martinho, Largo de   8 D4
São Miguel, Rua de   8 E4
São Nicolau, Rua de   7 B4
São Paulo, Rua de   4 F3
                              7 A5
São Pedro, Rua de   8 E4
São Pedro de Alcântara,
  Rua de   7 A3
São Pedro Mártir, Rua de   7 C3
São Plácido, Travessa de   4 E2
São Sebastião da Pedreira,
  Rua de   5 C4
São Tiago, Rua de   8 D4
São Tomé, Rua de   8 D3
São Vicente, Calçada de   8 E3
São Vicente, Rua de   8 E3
São Vicente, Travessa de   8 D2
Sapadores, Rua dos   6 F5
Sapateiros, Rua dos   7 B4
Saraiva de Carvalho, Rua   3 C2
Sarmento de Beires, Rua   6 F1
Saudade, Rua da   8 D4
Sé   8 D4
Sebastião Saraiva Lima,
  Rua   6 F4
Sebeiro, Travessa do   3 A3
Século, Rua do   4 F2
Senhora da Glória, Rua   8 E1
Senhora da Graça,
  Travessa da   8 E1
Senhora da Saúde,
  Rua da   7 C2
Senhora do Monte,
  Rua da   8 D1
Serpa Pinto, Rua   7 A4
Sidónio Pais, Avenida   5 B4
Silva Carvalho, Rua   4 D1
                              5 A5
Silva Porto, Rua   2 E3
Silva, Rua da   4 E3
Sítio ao Casalinho
  da Ajuda, Rua do   2 D2
Soares de Passos, Rua   2 F3
Sociedade Farmacêutica,
  Rua da   5 C5
Soeiro Pereira Gomes,
  Rua   5 A1
Sol, Rua do (a Chelas)   6 F3
Sol, Rua do (à Graça)   8 E1
Sol, Rua do (ao Rato)   4 D1
Sol, Rua do (a Santana)   7 B1
Solar do Vinho do Porto   4 F2
Sousa Lopes, Rua   5 B1
Sousa Martins, Rua   5 C4

T

Taipas, Rua das   4 F1
Tapada da Ajuda   3 A1
Tapada das Necessidades   3 B3
Tapada, Calçada da   2 F3
                              3 A3
Teatro de São Carlos   7 A4
Teixeira Júnior,
  Travessa de   3 A4
Teixeira Pinto, Rua   6 F4
Telhal, Rua do   7 A1
Tenente Espanca, Rua   5 B2
Tenente Ferreira Durão,
  Rua   3 C1
Tenente Valadim, Rua   3 B4
Terra, Calçada   6 F2
Terreirinho, Rua do   7 C2
Terreirinho, Travessa do   8 D2
Terreiro do Trigo,
  Rua do   8 E4
Tesouro, Travessa do   3 B3
Tijolo, Calçada de   4 F2
Tijolo, Calçadinha de   8 E3
Timor, Rua de   6 E5
Tomás da Anunciação,
  Rua   3 C1
Tomás Ribeiro, Rua   5 C3
Torel, Travessa do   7 B1
Torre de Belém   1 A5
Torre de Belém,
  Avenida da   1 A4
Torre, Largo da   2 D2
Torre, Rua da   2 D2
Torrinha, Azinhaga da   5 B1
Touros, Praça de   5 C1
Trabuqueta, Travessa da   3 B4
Triângulo Vermelho, Rua   6 F5
Trinas, Rua das   4 D3
Trindade, Largo da   7 A3
Trindade, Rua da   7 A3
Tristão da Cunha, Rua   1 A4
Tristão Vaz, Rua   1 C2

V

Vaga-Lumes, Rua dos   1 B1
Vale de Santo António,
  Rua do   8 F1
Vale do Pereiro, Rua do   4 E1
Vale, Rua do   4 E2
Veloso Salgado, Rua   5 A1
Verónica, Rua da   6 F4
Vicente Borga, Rua   4 E3
Vicente Dias, Rua   1 A2
Vieira da Silva, Rua   3 B4
Vigário, Rua do   8 E3
Vila Berta   8 E2
Vila Correia   1 B4
Vinha, Rua da   4 F2
Viriato, Rua   5 C4
Visconde de Santarém,
  Rua   6 D3
Visconde de Seabra, Rua   5 C1
Visconde de Valmor,
  Avenida   5 C2
Vítor Cordon, Rua   7 A5
Vítor Hugo, Rua   6 E1
Vitória, Rua da   7 B4
Voz do Operário, Rua da   8 E2

W

Washington, Rua   8 F1

X

Xavier Cordeiro, Rua   6 D2

Z

Zagalo, Travessa do   8 F3
Zaire, Rua do   6 E4

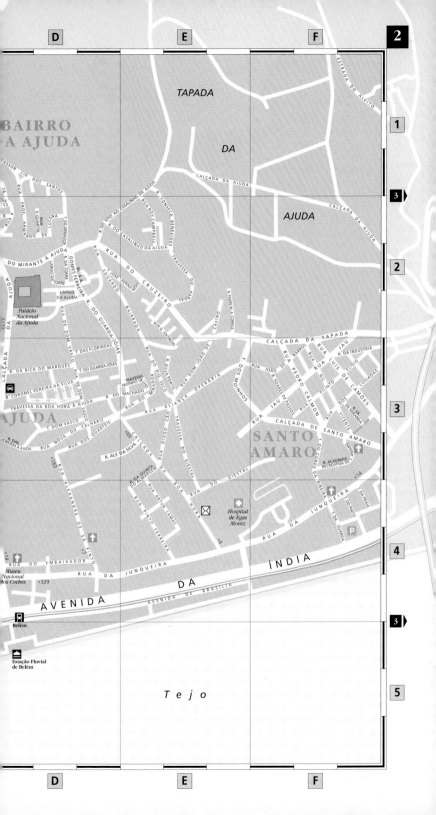

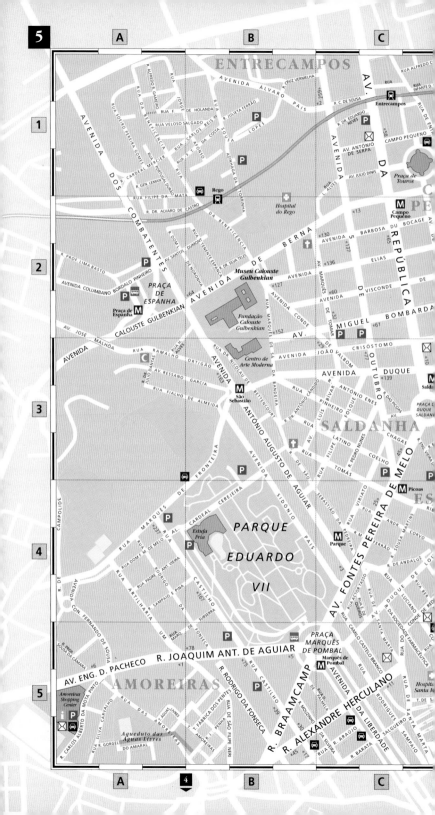

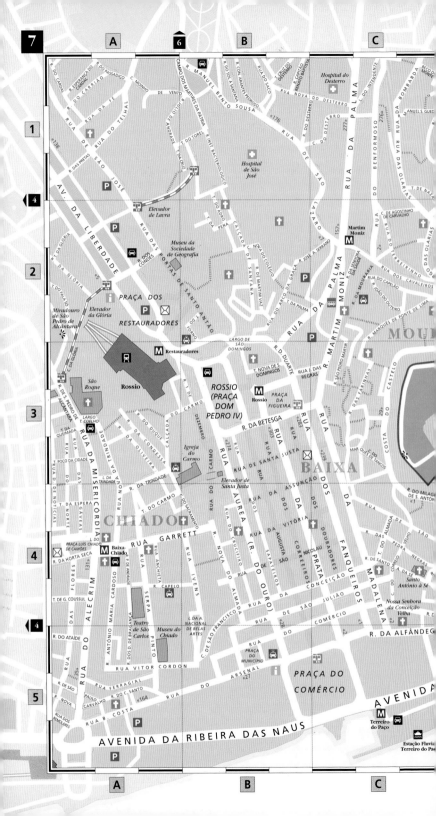

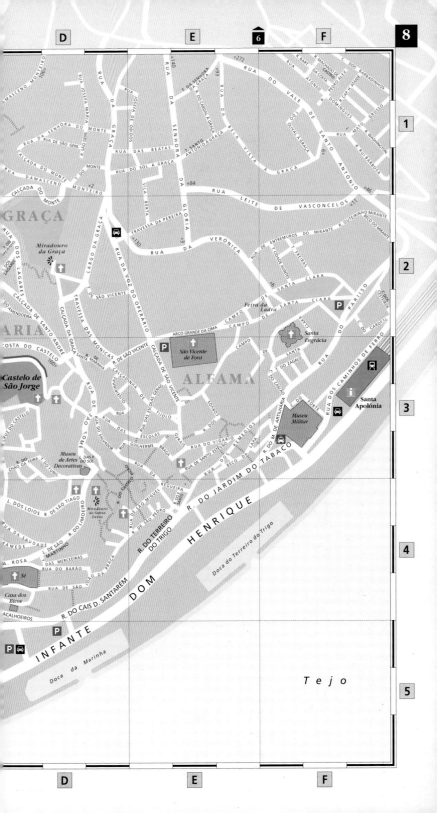

General Index

Page numbers in **bold** type refer to main entries.

A

ABEP (ticket agency) 141
Abrantes, Marquês de 64
ACP (Automóvel Clube de Portugal) 163
Adega Machado 143
Admission charges 146
The Adoration of the Magi (Grão Vasco) 18
Adoration of St Vincent (Gonçalves) 57, 58–9
Afonso I, King
  see Afonso Henriques
Afonso II, King 16, 109
Afonso III, King 13, 16
Afonso IV, King 16
  tomb of 36
Afonso V, King 16
  Monument to the Discoveries 69
  portrait of 59
Afonso VI, King 17, 98
Afonso, Jorge 108
  Apparition of Christ to the Virgin 28
Afonso Henriques (Afonso I), King 16, 34
  Castelo de São Jorge 38–9
  Castelo dos Mouros (Sintra) 97
  Chronica de Dom Afonso Henriques 13, 102
  expels Moors 13
  Palácio Nacional de Sintra 98
  Sé 36
  statue of 38
Age of Discovery 14, 18–19
Água, Museu da
  see Museu da Água
Air France 155
Air travel 154
Airport 154, 163
Alans 13
Albergarias (inns) 112
Albert, Prince Consort 101
Albufeira, Lagoa do 103

Albuquerque, Afonso de
  cenotaph 35
  Praça Afonso de Albuquerque 62, 63
Albuquerque, Brás de 35
Alcácer do Sal **109**
  hotels 118
Alcácer-Quibir, Battle of (1578) 14
Alcântara
  cafés and bars 134
  restaurants 128
Alcochete 89, **103**
Alcohol
  duty-free allowances 146
Alentejo
  wines 125
Alexander the Great 78
Alfama **30–39**
  area map 31
  cafés and bars 134
  restaurants 128
  Street-by-Street map 32–3
Alfarim
  festivals 25
All Saints' Day 24–5
Almada
  restaurants 128
Almeida, Leopoldo de
  statue of João I 45
Alves, Diogo 84
Ambulances 148–9
Amélia, Queen 64, 68
Amoreiras 139
Amoreiras Shopping Centre **74**, 141
Ana Salazar (fashion designer) 139
Antiga Confeitaria de Belém
  Street-by-Street map 63
Antiguidades Moncada 139
Antiques shops 138–9
Antony of Padua, St (Santo António) 36–7
  Museu Antoniano 37
Apparition of Christ to the Virgin (Afonso) 28
Aquariums
  Pavilhão dos Oceanos 81
Aqueduto das Águas Livres 15, **84**

Archaeological Museum
  see Museu Nacional de Arqueologia
Arco do Cego 163
Armazéns do Chiado 136,139
Armed Forces Movement 47
Arqueologia, Museu Nacional de, *see* Museu Nacional de Arqueologia
Arrábida, Serra da
  see Serra da Arrábida
Arrail Gay e Lésbico 23
Arte Antiga, Museu Nacional de
  see Museu Nacional de Arte Antiga
Arte Moderna, Centro de
  see Centro de Arte Moderna
Arte Popular, Museu de
  see Museu de Arte Popular
Arte Rustica 139
Associação Portuguesa de Tradutores 149
Assumption Day 25
Australia
  Embassy 147
  tourist office 147
Auto Jardim 157
Autocoope 157
Automatic teller machines (ATMs) 150
Autumn in Lisbon 24
Avante! (Seixal) 24
Aveiras, Conde de 64
Avenida da Liberdade **44**
Avis, House of 16
Avis Rent-a-Car 157
Azenhas do Mar 93
Azulejos
  Museu Nacional do Azulejo 29, 82–3
Azureira
  festivals 24
Azzolini, Giacomo 64

B

B. Leza (Lisbon club) 141
Bairro Alto and Estrela 14, **48–59**
  area map 49
  cafés and bars 134
  hotels 114
  restaurants 128–9, 130
  Street-by-Street map 50–51

Bairrada
  wines 125
Baixa **40–47**
  area map 41
  cafés and bars 134–5
  hotels 114–15
  restaurants 129
  Street-by-Street map 42–3
Ballet 140–41
  Noites de Bailado
  em Seteais 23
Banking 150–51
Barbizon School 53, 79
Barreiro station 155
Bars and cafés 134–5
Basílica da Estrela **55**
Beaches
  Cascais 102
  Colares 93
  Costa da Caparica 103
  Estoril 102
  Guincho 102
  Península de Tróia 109
  Serra da Arrábida 107
  Sesimbra 106
Beckford, William 95, 105
Beco dos Cruzes
  Street-by-Street map 33
Beer 121, 123
Belém **60–71**
  area map 61
  cafés and bars 135
  restaurants 129–30
  Street-by-Street map 62–3
Belvederes
  Miradouro da Graça 37
  Miradouro de Santa Luzia 34
  Miradouro de São Pedro de
  Alcântara 54
Bernardes, Policarpo de
  Oliveira 108
Best Western (hotels) 113
Birds
  Birds of the Tagus and Sado
  estuaries 109
  Reserva Natural do Estuário
  do Tejo 103
  see also Wildlife
Black Death 14
Boca do Inferno 102
Bocage, Manuel
  Barbosa du 108, 135
  Sétubal 108

Boitac, Diogo
  Ermida de São Jerónimo 71
  Igreja de Jesus (Setúbal) 108
  Mosteiro dos Jerónimos 66
Books
  bookshops 137, 139
  Feira do Livro 22
Bosch, Hieronymus
  *The Temptations of
  St Antony* 56, 58
Boucher, François 79
Bragança dynasty 17, 34
Bragança, Duke of 59
Brazil 18
Breakdowns (cars) 162
Bridges 155
  Ponte 25 de Abril 22, 74
Brique-a-Braque
  São Bento 139
Brisa 163
British Airways 155
British Embassy 147
British Hospital 149
Bullfighting
  beginning of the
  bullfighting season 22
  Campo Pequeno 80
Bureaux de change 150
Burgundy, House of 16
Buses 160
  airport 154
Byron, Lord 95

C

Cabo da Roca 90
  Serra de Sintra Tour 94
Cabo Espichel **103**
  festivals 24
Cabral, Pedro Álvares 18
  Monument to the
  Discoveries 69
Cabral Moncada Leilões 139
Caesar, Julius 13
Caetano regime 47
Café Brasileira 49
Cafés and bars **134–5**
Cais do Sodré station 155
Câmara Municipal
  (Sintra) 96
Camões, Luís de
  cenotaph 35
  Monument to the
  Discoveries 69

Camões, Luís de (cont)
  Os Lusíadas 23, 92
Camões Day 25
Campo Pequeno **80**
  cafés and bars 135
  hotels 115
  restaurants 130
Canadian Embassy 147
Canton 19
Cão, Diogo 18–19, 69
Capuchos Music Festival 23
Carcavelos
  hotels 118
Cardoso, Amadeo de Sousa 80
Carlos I, King 17
  assassination 47
  royal yacht 68
  tomb of 34
Carlos of Évora, Frey 58
Carmelites 52
Carnaval 25
Carol, King of Romania 102
Carrasqueïra 109
Cars
  breakdowns 162
  driving in Lisbon 156
  driving to Lisbon 155
  ferries 163
  hiring 157
  motorways 162
  parking 156–7
  petrol 157
  travelling around the
  Lisbon Coast 162
  see also Tours by car
Carvalho, Santos de 46
Casa do Alentejo
  Street-by-Street map 43
Casa dos Bicos **35**
Casa das Janelas Verdes
  see Museu Nacional
  de Arte Antiga
Casa de pasto 120
Casa Quintão 139
Cascais **102**
  cafés and bars 135
  hotels 118
  restaurants 132
Cascaishopping 139
Cash dispensers 150
Castelo-Melhor, Marquês de 44
Castles
  Castelo dos Mouros 97

Castles (cont)
Castelo de São Filipe
  (Setúbal) 108
  Castelo de São Jorge
  29, **38–9**, 115
  Palmela 106
  Sesimbra 106
Castro Guimarães,
  Conde de 102
Catarina, Queen 67
  tomb of 67
Cathedrals (Sé)
  Lisbon 29, 36
  Setúbal 108
Catherine the Great,
  Empress 76
Cavaco Silva, Aníbal 15, 17
Celeiro Dieta (shop) 137, 139
Cemetery, English 55
Centro Colombo 139
Centro Cultural de
  Belém **68**, 141
Centro de Arte Moderna **80**
Centro Vasco da Gama
  136, 139
Centtures 157
Cerâmica Artística de
  Carcavelos 138–9
Ceramicarte 138–9
Ceramics
  Museu Nacional
  do Azulejo 29, 82–3
  shops 138–9
Cervejarias 120
Cetóbriga 109
Chanterène, Nicolau 66, 101
Chapitô (circus school) 141
Charcutaria Brasil 139
Charcutaria Carvalho &
  Morais 139
Chermayeff, Peter 81
Chiado **52–3**
  fire (1988) 15, 52
  restaurants 130
  Street-by-Street map 50
Children
  in hotels 113
  in restaurants 121
China 19
Choice Hotels Portugal 113
Christmas 25
*Chronica de Dom Afonso
  Henriques* 13, 102

Churches (general)
  opening hours 146
Churches (individual)
  Basílica da Estrela 55
  Ermida de São
  Jerónimo 71
  Igreja do Carmo 51, 52
  Igreja da Graça 37
  Igreja da Memória 71
  Madre de Deus 83
  Nossa Senhora da
  Conceição Velha 47
  Nossa Senhora dos
  Remédios 33
  Santa Cruz do Castelo 39
  Santa Engrácia 35
  Santa Luzia 32
  Santa Maria de Belém 61
  Santo António à Sé 37
  São Domingos 43
  São Miguel 33
  São Roque 51, 52
  São Vicente de Fora 34
Churrasqueira restaurants 120
Cidade, Museu da
  see Museu da Cidade
Ciência, Museu da
  see Museu da Ciência
Cifka, Wenceslau 57
Cima da Conegliano 78
Cinema 140, 141
Cinemateca Portuguesa 141
Circus 24
Citirama (coach tours)
  163
Clement XI, Pope 63
Climate 23–5
Clothes
  shops 138–9
  size chart 138
Coach Museum
  see Museu Nacional
  dos Coches
Coach travel 162–3
Coches, Museu Nacional dos
  see Museu Nacional
  dos Coches
Coelho, Eduardo 54
Coffee 121
Coins 151
Colaço, Jorge 75
Colares 89, **93**
  Serra de Sintra Tour 94

Coliseu dos Recreios 141
Consulates 147
Contemporary Art, National
  Museum of
  see Museu do Chiado
Convento da Arrábida 91, 107
Convento da Madre
  de Deus 82
Convento dos Capuchos
  Serra de Sintra Tour 95
Conversion chart 147
Cook, Sir Francis 95
Corelli, Arcangelo 57
Corpus Christi 25
Corte Real, Gaspar 18
Costa, Jorge da, Archbishop
  of Lisbon 59
Costa, Manuel de 104
Costa da Caparica 89, **103**
  hotels 118
Costa e Silva, José da 53
Costume Museum
  see Museu Nacional do Traje
Crafts shops 138–9
Cranach, Lucas the Elder 58
Credit cards 150
  in restaurants 121
  in shops 136
Crime 148–9
Cristo Rei **74**
Croft (port shippers) 126
Currency 151
Currency exchange 150
Customs and excise 146

D

Da Gama, Vasco 13, 68
  cenotaph 35
  expeditions 14, 18, 19
  Monument to the
  Discoveries 69
  statue of 47
  tomb of 66
Dance 140–41
Dão
  wines 125
Delta Airlines 155
Dia da Restauração 25
Dia da Revolução 22
Dia do Magusto de
  Sao Martinho 24
Dia do Trabalhador 22, 25
Dia 25 de Abril 25

Dialling codes 153
Diana (Houdon) 76, 79
Dias, Bartolomeu 18
Dinis, King 14, 16, 98
Direcção-Geral do Turismo 113
Disabled travellers 146
  in hotels 113
  in restaurants 120
Discounts
  Metro 158
  rail travel 161
  student 146
Douro, River
  Port region 126
  wines 125
Drinks 121
  coffee 121
  local drinks 123
  Story of Port 126–7
  see also Wines
Duarte, Alfredo 143
Duarte, King 16
Durand, Antoine Sébastien 76
Dürer, Albrecht
  St Jerome 56, 58

E

Eanes, Gil 18
Earthquake (1755) **20–21**
Ecce Homo 56
Edward VII, King
  of England 75
Electricity 147
Eleonor of Aragon, Queen 59
Elevador do Carmo
  see Elevador de Santa Justa
Elevador da Glória
  Street-by-Street map 42
Elevador de Santa Justa 29, **46**
  Street-by-Street map 51
Embassies 147
Emergencies 148
Enatur 113
Encontros ACARTE 24
English Cemetery 55
Enrique II, King of Castile 14
Entertainment 140–43
  Fado: the music
  of Lisbon **142–3**
Entrecampos
  hotels 115
  restaurants 130
Epiphany 25

Ericeira **93**
  hotels 118
  restaurants 132
Ermida de São Jerónimo **71**
Eschwege, Baron von 97, 100
Estádio da Luz 141
Estádio José Alvalade 141
Estefânia
  hotels 115–16
  restaurants 130
Estoril **102–3**
  cafés and bars 135
  festivals 23–4
  hotels 118–19
  restaurants 132
Estoril Golf Open 24
Estoril Open Tennis
  Championship 22
Estrada de Escarpa 107
Estrela *see* Bairro Alto
  and Estrela
Estrela, Basílica da 55
Estrela, Jardim da 55
Estremadura
  wines 125
Etiquette 147
Eurocheques 150
Eurodollar 157
European Union 15, 68
EVA (bus company) 163

F

Fabri, Francesco
  Savario 42, 44
Fado: the music of
  Lisbon **142–3**
O Fado (Malhôa) 143
Feira dos Alfarrabistas
  137, 139
Feira dos Alhos 23
Feira de Antiguidades 137
Feira de Artesanato
  (Estoril) 23
Feira de Carcavelos 139
Feira de Cascais 139
Feira Grande de São Pedro
  (Sintra) 23
Feira da Ladra **35**, 139
Feira do Livro 22
Feira da Luz 24
Feira do Mar 22
Feira Numismatica 139
Feira de São Pedro 139

Feira de Todos os Santos
  (Azureira) 24
Felipe I, King
  see Philip II, King of Spain
Felipe II, King
  see Philip III, King of Spain
Felipe III, King
  see Philip IV, King of Spain
Ferdinand of Saxe-Coburg-
  Gotha (Fernando II) **101**
  Castelo dos Mouros
  (Sintra) 97
  Palácio da Pena (Sintra) 100
Fernando I, King 14, 16
Fernando II, King
  see Ferdinand of
  Saxe-Coburg-Gotha
Fernão, Infante 59
Ferries 163
Festa de Imaculada
  Conceição 25
Festa dos Merendeiros 22
Festa da Primavera 22
Festa de Santo António 23
Festa de Senhora de
  Consolação 24
Festa das Vindimas
  (Palmela) 24
Festas da Cidade 23
Festival Estoril Jazz 23
Festival Internacional
  de Teatro (FIT) 23
Festival de Música de Sintra
  (Sintra) 23
Festivals **22–5**
FIA-Lisbon International
  Handicraft Exhibition 23
Fielding, Henry
  tomb of 55
Figueirinha 107
Films *see* Cinema
Fire service 148–9
FNAC (shop) 139
Folk music 140–41
Fonseca, JM da **107**, 139
Fonte Mourisca (Sintra) 96
Fonte da Sabuga (Sintra) 96
Food and drink
  cafés and bars 134–5
  coffee 121
  Mercado 24 de Julho 53, 139
  shops 137, 139
  Story of Port 126–7

Food and drink (cont)
  What to Eat in
  Lisbon 122–3
  Wines of Portugal 124–5
  see also Restaurants
Foz, Marquês de 44
Frágil (club) 141
Fragonard, Jean
  Honoré 79
Francis of Assisi, St 36
Francis Xavier, St 52
Franciscan Order 36
Franco, Francisco 74
Franco, Zé 92
Fronteira, Marquês de 85
Fundação Calouste
  Gulbenkian 141
Funicular railways 160
  Elevador da Glória 42

G

Gainsborough, Thomas 79
Galapos 107
Galerias Monumental 139
Galleries
  see Museums and galleries
Galvão, Duarte 102
Garagem Almeida Navarro 157
Gardens *see* Parks and gardens
Garrafeira (wine
  merchants) 137, 139
Garrett, João Almeida 53
Germain, Thomas 59
Ghirlandaio, Domenico 78
Gilbert of Hastings 13, 36
Gildemeester, Daniel 95
Giusti, Alessandro 92
Goa 18, 19
Gomes, Diogo 18
Gonçalves, Nuno 69
  Adoration of St Vincent 57–9
Good Friday 25
Graça
  cafés and bars 135
  hotels 116
  Miradouro da Graça 37
  restaurants 130
Grão Vasco
  The Adoration of the Magi 18
Gray Line
  (coach company) 163
Greater Lisbon
  map 10–11

Guardi, Francesco
  *View of the Molo with
  the Ducal Palace* 79
Guérin 157
Guincho 102
  hotels 119
  restaurants 132–3
Guitarra 142
Gulbenkian, Calouste **79**
  Museu Calouste
  Gulbenkian 76–9
Gulbenkian Contemporary
  Music Encounter 22
Gulbenkian Foundation
  Planetário Calouste
  Gulbenkian 65
Guterres, António 17

H

Hapsburg dynasty 17
Health 148
Henrique, Infante Dom,
  see Henry the Navigator
Henrique, King 17
Henry the Navigator 19
  cenotaph 35
  Monument to the
  Discoveries 68–9
  Mosteiro dos Jerónimos 68
  portrait of 59
Herculano, Alexandre
  tomb of 67
Hertz 157
Hieronymites (Order of
  St Jerome) 66
Hiring cars 157
História Natural, Museu de
  see Museu de História Natural
History **13–21**
Holbein, Hans the Elder
  *The Virgin and Child
  and Saints* 56
Holidays, public 25
Hotéis Alexandre
  de Almeida 113
Hotéis Tivoli 113
Hotels 112–19
  booking 113
  children in 113
  disabled travellers 113
  gradings 113
  hotel chains 112–3
  Lisbon Coast 118–19

Hotels (cont)
  prices 113
  types of hotel 112
Houdon, Jean-Antoine
  Diana 76, 79

I

Igreja do Carmo **52**
  Street-by-Street map 51
Igreja da Graça 37
Igreja da Memória **71**
Immaculate Conception 25
Impressionists 79
India 19
Inquisition 14, 45
Insect repellent 148
Insurance
  medical 148
  travel 149
Isabel, Queen 59
Islam 18
IVA (Value Added Tax) 136

J

Jardim Agrícola Tropical **65**
  Street-by-Street map 63
Jardim Botânico **44**
Jardim Botânico da Ajuda **71**
Jardim da Estrela **55**
Jardim do Ultramar
  see Jardim Agrícola Tropical
Jardim Zoológico **84**
Jazz 140–41
  Festival Estoril Jazz 23
  Jazz em Agosto 23
Jerome, St
  Mosteiro dos Jerónimos 66–7
Jerónimos monastery
  see Mosteiro dos
  Jerónimos
Jesuits 52
João I, King 14, 16
  Palácio Nacional de Sintra 98
  Palmela 106
  statue of 43, 45
João II, King 16
  maritime expansion 19
  portrait of 59
João III, King 16
  Convento da Madre
  de Deus 82
  tomb of 67
  and Vasco da Gama 68

João IV, King 14, 17
  tomb of 34
João V, King 17, 59
  Aqueduto das
    Águas Livres 84
  building programme 14–15
  Convento da Madre
    de Deus 82
  Palácio de Belém 62, 64
  Palácio de Mafra 92
  Palácio Pimenta 81
  São Roque 52
  Sé 36
João VI, King 17, 105
  Palácio Nacional da Ajuda 71
João of Avis see João I
João de Castilho 66, 67
John Paul II, Pope 37
José (son of Maria I) 55
José I, King 17
  Igreja da Memória 71
  Palácio de Belém 64
  silver tableware 59
  statue of 46, 47
Josefa de Óbidos 58, 102
Juan of Castile, 14

K

Kapital (nightclub) 141
Kings and queens 16–17
Knights of Christ 68
Kremlin (nightclub) 141

L

La Fontaine, Jean de 34
Labels, wine 124
Lalique, René 76
  Lalique Collection 79
Language 146
Lapa
  hotels 116
  restaurants 130–31
Largo do Chafariz de Dentro
  Street-by-Street map 33
Largo do Chiado
  Street-by-Street map 50
Largo das Portas do Sol
  Street-by-Street map 32
Lavatories, public 149
Legal assistance 149
Leo X, Pope 47
Leonor, Dona 82
  statue of 47

Lisboa à Noite 143
Lisbon Coast **87–109**
  cafés and bars 135
  hotels 118–19
  restaurants 132–3
  Serra de Sintra Tour 94–5
  travel 161–3
Lisbon Half Marathon 22
Lisbon Marathon 25
Listings magazines 140
Livraria Bertrand 139
Livraria Buchholz 139
Livraria Olisipo 139
Livraria Portugal 139
Lobo, Felipe 66
Lobo, Silvestre Faria 105
Lodi, Fortunato 45
Loja das Meias 139
Lontra (club) 141
Lopes, Carlos 75
Lopes, Gregório 58
Lopes, Teixeira
  statue of Eça de
    Queirós 50
Ludwig (Ludovice), Johann
  Friedrich 54, 92
Lufthansa 155
Luís I, King 17
  Cascais 102
  Palácio Nacional da Ajuda 71
Luís Felipe, Prince
  assassination 47
  tomb of 34
Luso (mineral water) 143
Lux (nightclub) 141

M

Macau 19
Machado de Castro,
  Joaquim 58
  Basílica da Estrela 55
  São Vicente de Fora 34
  Sé 36
  statue of José I 47
Madre de Deus, Convento
  da 82, 83
Mãe d'Água das
  Amoreiras 84
Mafra
  hotels 119
  Palácio de Mafra 92
Mafra School of
  sculpture 55, 92

Magalhães, Fernão de
  (Ferdinand Magellan) 18
  Monument to the
    Discoveries 69
Magalhães, Teresa 80
Magazines
  entertainments listings 140
Magellan, Ferdinand
  see Magalhães, Fernão
Maia, Manuel da 80
Mail services 153
Malhôa, José 81
  O Fado 143
Malveira 92
Manet, Edouard 79
Manteigaria Londrina 139
Manuel I, King 16
  armillary sphere 18
  Belém 61
  Castelo de São Jorge 38
  maritime expansion 19
  Monument to the
    Discoveries 69
  Mosteiro dos Jerónimos 66
  Palácio Nacional de Sintra
    (Sintra) 98, 99
  Praça do Comércio 47
  statue of (Alcochete) 103
  statue of (Praça do
    Comércio) 47
  tomb of 67
  Torre de Belém 14, 70
Manuel II, King 17
  exile 93
  Palácio da Pena (Sintra) 100
  Palácio de Mafra 92
  tomb of 34
Manueline architecture 14
  see also Mosteiro
    dos Jerónimos
Maps
  Age of Discovery 18–19
  Alfama 31, 32–3
  Bairro Alto 50–51
  Bairro Alto and Estrela 49
  Baixa 41, 42–3
  Belém 61, 62–3
  bus and tram routes 160
  Castelo de São Jorge 38–9
  Europe 10–11
  Further Afield 29, 73
  Greater Lisbon 10–11
  Lisbon 28–9

Maps (cont)
  Lisbon Coast 90–91
  Metro 159
  Port region 126
  Serra da Arrábida 107
  Serra de Sintra Tour 94–5
  Sintra 97
  Street Finder 164–77
  Wines of Portugal 124
Mardel, Carlos 84
Maria, Dona (wife of Manuel I)
  tomb of 67
Maria I, Queen 17, 34, 59, 105
  Basílica da Estrela 55
  Palácio de Queluz 104–5
  royal brig 68
  tomb of 55
Maria II, Queen 17, 45, 101
Maria Pia di Savoia 71, 98
Marinha, Museu da
  see Museu da Marinha
Marioneta, Museu da
  see Museu da Marioneta
Marisqueira restaurants 120
Maritime Museum
  see Museu da Marinha
Markets 137, 139
  Feira da Ladra 35
Measurements
  conversion chart 147
Medical treatment 148
Memling, Hans 58
Mendes, Fernão 68
Menus 120–21
Metro 158–9
Militar, Museu see Museu Militar
Miradouro da Graça 37
Miradouro de Santa Luzia 34
  Street-by-Street map 32
Miradouro de São Pedro
  de Alcântara 54
Miradouro da Vigia (Sintra) 96
Miranda & Ferrão 157
Mobil 157
Moda Lisboa 22
Moluccas 19
Monasteries
  Mosteiro dos Jerónimos 14,
  28, 62, 66–7
Monet, Claude 79
Money 150–51
Monserrate 95
  Serra de Sintra Tour 95

Monte Estoril
  restaurants 133
Monteiro, José Luís 42, 44
Montijo
  festivals 23
Monuments
  Cristo Rei 74
  Monument to the
  Discoveries 68–9
  Praça Marquês de Pombal 75
Moore, Henry 80
Moors 13, 89
Morais, Cristóvão de 58
Morais, Graça 80
Mosteiro dos
  Jerónimos 14, 28, 66–7
  Museu da Marinha 68
  Museu Nacional de
  Arqueologia 65
  Street-by-Street map 62
Motorways 162
Movies see Cinema
Multimedia shops 137, 139
Museums and galleries
  (general)
  opening hours 146
  admission charges 146
Museums and galleries
  (individual)
  Centro Cultural de Belém 68
  Centro de Arte Moderna 80
  Museu da Água 80
  Museu de Arte Moderna
  (Sintra) 96
  Museu Antoniano 37
  Museu de Arqueologia e
  Etnografia (Setúbal) 108
  Museu Arqueológico
  (Alcácer do Sal) 109
  Museu de Arte Popular 69
  Museu de Arte Sacra 51, 52
  Museu de Artes
  Decorativas 32, 34
  Museu do Brinquedo
  (Sintra) 96
  Museu Calouste
  Gulbenkian 76–9
  Museu do Chiado 53
  Museu da Cidade 81
  Museu da Ciência 44
  Museu do Condo de Castro
  Guimaraes (Cascais) 102
  Museu da Ericeira 93

Museums and galleries (cont)
  Museu de História Natural 44
  Museu de Marinha 68
  Museu Militar 35
  Museu Nacional de
  Arqueologia 62, 65
  Museu Nacional de Arte
  Antiga 28, 56–9
  Museu Nacional do
  Azulejo 29, 82–3
  Museu Nacional dos
  Coches 63, 64–5
  Museu da Marioneta 53
  Museu Nacional do
  Teatro 85
  Museu Nacional do
  Traje 85
  Museu Oceanográfico
  (Serra da Arrábida) 107
  Museu da Sociedade de
  Geografia 43, 45
  Museu Tropical 65
Music
  classical music, opera
  and dance 140, 141
  Fado: the music of
  Lisbon 142–3
  Festa da Primavera 22
  Festival Estoril Jazz 23
  Jazz em Agosto 23
  shops 137, 139
  world music, jazz, folk
  and rock 140–41
Muslims 18

N
Napoleão (wine
  merchants) 139
Napoleon I, Emperor 15
National Tile Museum
  see Museu Nacional
  do Azulejo
Natural History Museum
  see Museu de História Natural
Negreiros, José de
  Almada 80
New Year 25
Newspapers 147
Nightclubs 141
Noites de Bailado
  em Seteais 23
Nossa Senhora do Cabo
  Espichel (festival) 24

Nossa Senhora da Conceição
(festival) 25
Nossa Senhora da Conceição
Velha (church) **47**
Nossa Senhora da Luz
(Sampaio) 24
Nossa Senhora dos Remédios
Street-by-Street map 33

O

Oceanário de Lisboa 73
Odysseus 13
Olaias
restaurants 131
Opening hours 146
banks 150
restaurants 120
shops 136
Opera 25, 140–41
Ordem dos Advogados 149
Order of St Jerome
(Hieronymites) 66
Order of Santiago 106

P

Pacheco, Lopo Fernandes
tomb of 36
Paço d'Arcos
restaurants 133
Padrão dos Descobrimentos
see Monument to
the Discoveries
Palácio de Belém **64**
Street-by-Street map 63
Palácio de Brejoeira 124
Palácio Cor de Rosa
see Palácio de Belém
Palácio de Cortes 55
Palácio Foz
Street-by-Street map 42
Palácio Fronteira 73, **85**
Palácio de Mafra **92**
Palácio Nacional da Ajuda 71
Palácio Nacional de Sintra
(Sintra) 96, **98–9**
Palácio da Pena
(Sintra) **100–1**
Palácio Pimenta 81
Palácio de Queluz **104–5**
Palácio de São Bento **55**
Palmela 89, **106**
festivals 24

Palmela (cont)
hotels 119
restaurants 133
Parking 156–7
Parks and gardens
Castelo de São Jorge 39
Jardim Agrícola
Tropical 63, **65**
Jardim Botânico 44
Jardim Botânico da Ajuda 71
Jardim da Estrela 55
Jardim Zoológico 84
Monserrate 95
Palácio Fronteira 85
Palácio de Queluz 105
Parque Eduardo VII 73, **75**
Parque da Liberdade 96
Parque do Monteiro-Mor **85**
Parque das Nações **81**, 137
Parque da Pena 95, 97
Praça do Príncipe Real 54
Parliament
Palácio de São Bento 55
Parque da Pena
Serra de Sintra Tour 95
Parreirinha de Alfama 143
Passports, theft of 149
Paula, Madre 81
Pavilhão Atlântico 141
Pedro I, King 16
Pedro II, King 17
Serra da Arrábida 107
War of Restoration 85
Pedro III, King 17, 104
Pedro IV, King 17, 34
Palácio de Queluz 104
statue of 45
Pedro V, King 17
Penha da França
cafés and bars 135
Peninha
Serra de Sintra Tour 94
Península de Tróia 89, **109**
Pensões (guesthouses) 112
Pereira, Nuno Álvares 52
Perfumes
duty-free allowances 146
Pero Pinheiro 89
Personal security 148–9
Pessoa, Fernando 80
statue of 53
Petrol 157
Pharmacies 148

Philip II, King of Spain
(Felipe I of Portugal) 14, 17
Castelo de São Filipe
(Setúbal) 108
coach 64
Philip III, King of Spain
(Felipe II of Portugal) 17
Philip IV, King of Spain
(Felipe III of Portugal) 17
Piero della Francesca
St Augustine 56, 58
Pius XI, Pope 36
Planetário Calouste
Gulbenkian **65**
Police 148–9
Pombal, Marquês de
Avenida da Liberdade 44
Baixa 41
Jardim Botânico da Ajuda 71
Lisbon earthquake 20–21
mulberry trees 74
Museu Nacional
de Arte Antiga 56
Praça do Comércio 47
Praça da Figueira 45
Praça Marquês de
Pombal 75
rebuilding programme 15
statue of 47
and the Távora family 71
tomb of 71
Ponsard, Raoul Mesnier du 46
Ponte 25 de Abril 15, **74**
Port **126–7**
Solar do Vinho do Porto 54
Portela Airport 154
Portinho da Arrábida 107
restaurants 133
Porto do Abrigo
(Sesimbra) 106
Portrait of an Old Man
(Rembrandt) 77, 78–9
Portugal Tours 163
Post offices 153
Postal services 153
Poste restante 153
Pousadas 112, 120
Praça Afonso de
Albuquerque 62
Street-by-Street map 63
Praça do Comércio 14, 41, **47**
Praça da Figueira **45**
Street-by-Street map 43

Praça do Império
  Street-by-Street map 62
Praça do Príncipe Real **54**
Praça dos Restauradores **44**
  Street-by-Street map 42
Praça Marquês de Pombal **75**
Praça Sony 141
Praia da Adraga 93
Praia Grande (Colares) 93
Praia das Maçãs (Colares) 93
Procissão do Senhor dos
  Passos da Graça 25
Procissão dos Terceiros
  Franciscanos (Mafra) 22
Public conveniences 149
Public holidays 25
Public transport 158–60
Puppets
  Museu da Marioneta 37

Q
Queirós, Eça de
  statue of 50
Queluz
  hotels 119
  Palácio de Queluz 104–5
  restaurants 133
Quinta de Regaleira
  (Sintra) 96

R
Radio 147
Railways *see* Trains
Rainfall 24
Raphael 58
Rato
  cafés and bars 135
  hotels 116
  restaurants 131
Realists 79
Rede Expressos 163
Regionalia (shop) 139
Rego, Paula 80
Rembrandt
  *Portrait of an
  Old Man* 77, 78–9
Renoir, Pierre Auguste 79
Republic Day 24, 25
Reserva Natural do Estuário
  do Sado 108–9
Reserva Natural do Estuário
  do Tejo 103

Restaurants **120–35**
  cafés and bars 134–5
  children in 121
  drinking coffee 121
  eating hours 120
  Lisbon 128–31
  Lisbon Coast 132–3
  menus 120–21
  paying 121
  reservations 120
  smoking in 121
  types of restaurants 120
  vegetarian meals 121
  what to drink 121
  What to Eat in Lisbon 122–3
  see also Food and drink
Retális (car hire) 157
Reverse charge
  telephone calls 153
Ribatejo
  wines 125
Ribeiro, António 52
Ricardo do Espírito Santo
  Silva Foundation *see* Museu
  de Artes Decorativas
Robillion, Jean-Baptiste 104–5
Roch, St (São Roque) 52
Rock music 140–41
Rodin, Auguste 53
Rodoviária de Lisboa 163
Rodrigues, Amália 85, 143
Roman Empire 13
Romaria de São Mamede 23
Romney, George 79
Rosa & Teixeira (shop) 139
Rossio **45**
  Street-by-Street map 43
Rossio station 155, 161
  Street-by-Street map 42
Rotunda
  hotels 116–17
  restaurants 131
Rua Augusta **46**
Rua do Carmo
  Street-by-Street map 51
Rua Garrett
  Street-by-Street map 50
Rua do Norte
  Street-by-Street map 50
Rua das Portas de Santo Antão
  Street-by-Street map 43
Rua de São Pedro
  Street-by-Street map 33

Rua Vieira Portuense
  Street-by-Street map 63
Rubens, Peter Paul 79
Rulers of Portugal 16–17
Rush hours 156

S
Sado, River 89, 109
  Birds of the Tagus and
  Sado estuaries 109
St Catherine (Van der
  Weyden) 76, 78
St Jerome (Dürer) 56, 58
Salazar, António 17
  Belém 62
  Castelo de São Jorge 38
  Cristo Rei 74
  modernization
  programme 15
  Ponte 25 de Abril 74
Saldanha
  hotels 117
  restaurants 131
Salsa Latina (nightclub) 141
Salt 103
Salvi, Nicola 52
Sampaio
  festivals 24
Sanches, Rui 80
Sancho I, King 16
  gold cross 59
  Palmela 106
Sancho II, King 16, 106
Sant'Anna 139
Santo António, festival of 23
Santo António à Sé **37**
Santa Cruz 39
Santa Cruz do Castelo 39
Santa Engrácia **35**
Santa Luzia
  Street-by-Street map 32
Santa Maria de Belém 61
Santos, Argentina 142–3
Santos Oficios 139
São Domingos
  Street-by-Street map 43
São João 23
São Miguel
  Street-by-Street map 33
São Pedro (Montijo) 23
São Roque **52**
  Street-by-Street map 51
São Vicente de Fora **34**

Saxe-Coburg-Gotha, Duke of
see Ferdinand of
Saxe-Coburg-Gotha
Scarlatti, Domenico 57
*Scenes from the Life of the
Virgin* 78
Science Museum
see Museu da Ciência
Scotturb 163
Scoville, Mrs 107
Sé (Lisbon) 29, **36**
Sebastião I, King 17
Battle of Alcácer-Quibir 14
portrait of 58
tomb of 67
Secretariado Nacional de
Reabilitação 113
Security 148–9
Seixal
festivals 24
Senhor Vinho 143
Sequeira, Domingos António
de 58, 85
Serra da Arrábida 89, **106–7**
map 107
Serra de Sintra Tour **94–5**
Serres, JT
*The Torre de Belém
in 1811* 70
Sesimbra 89, 91, **106**
festivals 22, 23, 24
hotels 119
restaurants 133
Seteais
Serra de Sintra Tour 95
Setúbal **108**
hotels 119
restaurants 133
wines 125
A Severa (*fado* house)143
Severa, Maria 142
Shopping 136–9
antiques 138–9
bookshops 137, 139
ceramics 138–9
clothes 138–9
food shops 137, 139
markets 137, 139
music and
multimedia 137, 139
opening hours 136
regional crafts 138–9
shopping centres 136, 139

Shopping (cont)
size chart 138
VAT and taxes 136
wines and spirits 137, 139
Silva, Ricardo do Espírito
Santo 32
Silves, Diogo de 18
Sintra 90, **96–101**
cafés and bars 135
festivals 23
hotels 119
map 97
Palácio da Pena 100–1
Palácio Nacional de
Sintra 98–9
restaurants 133
Serra de Sintra tour 95
Sintra Bazar 139
Size chart 138
Smoking, in restaurants 121
Soares, Mário 17
Sobreiro 92
Sociedade de Geografia,
Museu da *see* Museu da
Sociedade de Geografia
Solar do Vinho
do Porto **54**, 139
Speakeasy (club) 141
Spice trade 19
Spirits
shops 137, 139
Sports 141
Spring in Lisbon 22
Sri Lanka 19
Stoop, Dirk
Terreiro do Paço 81
Street Finder 164–77
Student discounts 146
Suevi tribe 13
Summer in Lisbon 23
Sunshine 23

T

Tagus, River 15
Birds of the Tagus and
Sado estuaries 109
ferries 163
TAP-Air Portugal 155
Tascas (taverns) 120
Tavares (restaurant)
Street-by-Street
map 50
Távora family 71

Taxation
Value Added Tax (VAT) 136
Taxis 157
airport 154
Teatro Nacional Dona
Maria II 45, 141
Street-by-Street map 43
Teatro Nacional de
São Carlos **53**, 141
Teatro da Trindade 141
Street-by-Street map 51
Telecom card phones 152
Telephones 152–3
Television 147
Temperatures 25
The Temptations of St Antony
(Bosch) 56, 58
Tennis
Estoril Open Tennis
Championship 22
Terreiro do Paço 14
see also Praça do
Comércio
Terreiro do Paço (Stoop) 81
Terzi, Filippo 34
Theatre 140–41
Festival Internacional
de Teatro (FIT) 22
Theatres
Museu Nacional do
Teatro 85
Teatro Nacional
Dona Maria II 45
Teatro Nacional
de São Carlos 53
"Thieves' Market" 35
Tiles *see* Azulejos
Time zone 147
Tipping 121
Tobacco
duty-free allowances 146
Todi, Luísa 108
Toilets 149
Torre de Belém 14, 28, **70**
The Torre de Belém in 1811
(Serres) 70
Tourist information 146–7
Tours by car
Serra de Sintra Tour 94–5
Toys
Museu do Brinquedo
(Sintra) 96
Trains 155, 161

Trams 159–60

Transtejo
(ferry operator) 163

Travel **154–63**
air 154
buses 160
cars 155, 156–7, 162
coaches 162–3
ferries 163
funiculars 160
getting around
the city 156–7
Lisbon coast 91, 161–3
Metro 158–9
public transport 158–60
taxis 157
trains 155, 161
trams 159

Traveller's cheques 150

Trindade, Cervejaria 134

Troia International Film
Festival 23

Tróia peninsula *see*
Península de Tróia

TST (coach operator) 163

Turner, JMW 79

TWA 155

U

Ulysses 13

Umberto II,
King of Italy 102

UNESCO World Heritage
sites (Sintra) 96

United Kingdom
Consular office 147
Embassy 147
tourist office 147

University of Lisbon 14

V

Vaccinations 148

Valentim de Carvalho 139

Value Added Tax (VAT) 136

Vanvitelli, Luigi 52

Varig (national
airline) 155

Verao Em Sesimbra
(festival) 23

Viana, Eduardo 80

Vicente, Gil, statue of 45

Vicente, Mateus (architect)
37, 104

Victoria, Queen of
England 101

Vieira, Alváro Siza 15, 52

*View of the Molo with the
Ducal Palace* (Guardi) 79

Vila Fresca de Azeitão
restaurants 133

Vila Nogueira de
Azeitão 107

Vila Nova de Gaia 126

Vilalobos, Maria
tomb of 36

Vincent, St 34
Adoration of St Vincent
58–9
statue of 32

Vineyards
Story of Port **126–7**
Wines of Portugal **124–5**

Vinhos verde 124–5

Vintage port 127

*The Virgin and Child and
Saints* (Holbein) 56

Visigoths 13

Vista Alegre (shop) 139

Viúva Lamego (shop) 139

Voltaire 21

W

W (nightclub) 141

Walking around Lisbon 156

War of Restoration
(1640–68) 42, 85

Water
bottled 121, 123
safety 148

Watteau, Antoine 79

Weather 23–5

Weyden, Rogier Van der
St Catherine 76, 78

Wildlife
Birds of the Tagus and
Sado estuaries 109
Reserva Natural do
Estuário do Sado 108–9
Reserva Natural do
Estuário do Tejo 103
Serra da Arrábida 107

Winery JM da Fonseca
(serra da Arrábida) **107**

Wines **124–5**
Colares 93
in restaurants 121
shops 137, 139
tasting 107
see also Port

Winter in Lisbon 25

World music 140–41

X

Xabregas
restaurants 131

Z

Zoos
Jardim Zoológico 84

Acknowledgments

DORLING KINDERSLEY would like to thank the following people whose contributions and assistance have made the preparation of this book possible.

CONTRIBUTORS

SUSIE BOULTON studied History of Art at Cambridge University. A freelance travel writer, she is the author of *Eyewitness Venice and the Veneto*.

SARAH MCALISTER is a freelance writer and editor for the *Time Out* guides. Her knowledge of Lisbon and the surrounding area is a result of extensive visits to the country.

CONSULTANT

MARTIN SYMINGTON was born in Portugal and is a freelance travel writer. He contributes to numerous British newspapers including the *Daily Telegraph* and the *Sunday Telegraph*. He is the author of guides to *The Loire Valley* (Hodder and Stoughton), *Portugal* (AA) and *Denmark* (AA/Thomas Cook). He has also contributed to *The Algarve and Southern Portugal* (AA/Thomas Cook), *Portugal* (Insight), *Eyewitness Great Britain* and *Eyewitness Seville and Andalusia*.

ADDITIONAL CONTRIBUTORS

Paul Vernon, Edite Vieira.

DESIGN AND EDITORIAL ASSISTANCE

Gillian Allan, Douglas Amrine, Gillian Andrews, Andrew Costello, Angela Marie Graham, Paul Hines, Esther Labi, Kathryn Lane, Michelle de Larrabeiti, Adam Moore, Naomi Peck, Andrea Powell, Tom Prentice, Jake Reimann, Amanda Tomeh, Tomas Tranaeus, Ingrid Vienings, Fiona Wild.

INDEXER

Hilary Bird.

ADDITIONAL PHOTOGRAPHY

Steve Gorton, John Heseltine, Dave King, Martin Norris, Roger Philips, Clive Streeter.

PHOTOGRAPHIC AND ARTWORK REFERENCE

Joy FitzSimmons, Veronica Wood.

PHOTOGRAPHY PERMISSIONS

DORLING KINDERSLEY would like to thank the following for their assistance and kind permission to photograph at their establishments: Instituto Português do Património Arquitectónico e Arqueológico (IPPAR), Lisboa; Instituto Português de Museus (IPM), Lisboa; Museu do Mar, Cascais; Museu da Marinha, Lisboa; Fundação da Casa de Alorna, Lisboa, and all other churches, museums, parks, hotels, restaurants and sights too numerous to thank individually.

SPECIAL ASSISTANCE

Emília Tavares, Arquivo Nacional de Fotografia, Lisboa; Luísa Cardia, Biblioteca Nacional e do Livro, Lisboa; Marina Gonçalves and Aida Pereira, Câmara Municipal de Lisboa; Caminhos de Ferro Portugueses; Carris; Enatur, Lisboa; Karen Ollier-Spry, John E. Fells and Sons Ltd; Maria Helena Soares da Costa, Fundação Calouste Gulbenkian, Lisboa; Pilar Serras and José Aragào, ICEP, London; Instituto do Vinho de Porto, Porto; Simoneta Afonso, IPM, Lisboa; Mário Abreu, Dulce Ferraz, IPPAR, Lisboa; Pedro Moura Bessa and Eduardo Corte-Real, Livraria Civilização Editora, Porto; Metropolitano de Lisboa; Raquel Florentino and Cristina Leite, Museu da Cidade, Lisboa; Joao Castel Branco G. Pereira, Museu Nacional do Azulejo; and the staff at all the other tourist offices and town halls in Portugal.

PICTURE CREDITS

t = top; tl = top left; tlc = top left centre; tc = top centre; tr = top right; cla = centre left above; ca = centre above; cra = centre right above; cl = centre left; c = centre; cr = centre right; clb = centre left below; cb = centre below; crb = centre right below; bl = bottom left; b = bottom; bc = bottom centre; bcl = bottom centre left; br = bottom right; d = detail.

Works of art have been reproduced with the permission of the following copyright holders: The work illustrated on page 80tl, *Reclining Figure*, 1982, is reproduced by kind permission of the Henry Moore Foundation; *Terreiro do Paço* by Dirk Stoop 81b is reproduced by kind permission of the Museu da Cidade, Lisboa.

DORLING KINDERSLEY would like to thank the following individuals, companies and picture libraries for permission to reproduce their photographs:
AISA: 16tr, 17tc/br, 66b; ARQUIVO NACIONAL DE FOTOGRAFIA-INSTITUTO PORTUGUÊS DE MUSEUS: Museu Conde de Castro Guimarães/Manuel Palma 12; Biblioteca da Ajuda/José Pessoa 14c; Museu Grao Vasco/José Pessoa 18bl; Museu Nacional dos

Coches/José Pessoa 17bc, 63bl; Henrique Ruas 64b; Igreja São Vicente de Fora/Carlos Monteiro 17bl; Museu Nacional de Arte Antiga/Luís Pavão 28t, 56bl/br, 57t/c/b, 59c; Francisco Matias 19tl, José Pessoa 19tr, 56tl/tr, 58b, 59b; Pedro Ferreira 58t, 59t; Museu Nacional de Arqueologia/ José Pessoa 65c; Arnaldo Soares 142tr, 143tl; Museu Nacional do Teatro/Arnaldo Soares 142cl; Luisa Oliveira 143tr; José Pessoa 142b, 20–21t; San Payo 17tr; Tony Arruza: 16c, 20–21lc.

Instituto da Biblioteca Nacional e do Livro, Lisboa: 13b, 14b, 105bl; © Trustees of the British Museum, London: 18br; Boutinot Prince Wine Shippers, Stockport: 126br.

Câmara Municipal de Oeiras: 15c; Câmara Municipal de Lisboa: Antonio Rafael 20cl; Cephas: Peter Stowell 24b; Mick Rock 124cb, 125c, Peter Stowell 24b; Chapitô: 140tr; Cockburn Smithes & cia, S. A. – an Allied Domecq Company: 126crb.

Dow's Port 229cra.

Mary Evans Picture Library: 21tr, 101b.

Fototeca Internacional, Lisboa: César Soares 16bl; Luís Elvas 25b/t; Fundação Ricardo do Espírito Santo Silva: Museu-Escola de Artes Decorativas Portuguesas 34c.

Giraudon: 18cl; Calouste Gulbenkian Foundation, Lisboa: 140b.
Ideal Photo: N. Adams 116cl; The Image Bank:

José Manuel 4b, 23b; Moura Machado 24c. Lusa: Luís Vasconcelos 52b; André Kosters 53t; António Cotrim 143c.

José Manuel: 21br; Museu Calouste Gulbenkian, Lisboa: Enamelled Silver Gilt Corsage Ornament, Rene Lalique, © ADAGP, Paris and DACS, London 1997, 76ca; 76t/ca/cb/b, 77t/ca/cb/b, 78c/b/t,79b/t/c; Museu da Cidade, Lisboa: Antonio Rafael 20tl/cl/bl/br, 21c/bl; Museu da Marinha, Lisboa: 16br, 68b.

Nationalmuseet, Copenhagen: 18tr; Naturpress: Juan Hidalgo-Candy Lopesino 22t.

Oronoz, Madrid: 16bc.

RCL, Parede: Rui Cunha 141t; Dias dos Reis: 81tl, Rex Features: Sipa Press, Michel Ginies 15b.

Science Photo Library/CNES 1993, Distribution Spot Image: 10.

Symington Port & Madeira Shippers: Claudio Capone 125cl, 127t, cla, bc.

Peter Wilson: 30 (front endpaper tr), 44tl, 53b, 136b, 137c, 138c, 47br; Woodfall Wild Images: Mike Lane 109b; World Pictures: 23t.

Jacket
Front – DK Picture Library: Clive Streeter cb; Peter Wilson bca, bl; Getty Images: Simeone Huber main image. Back – DK Picture Library: Linda Whitwam b; Peter Wilson t.
Spine – Getty Images: Simeone Huber.

Phrase Book

IN EMERGENCY

Help!	Socorro!	soo-**koh**-roo
Stop!	Pare!	pahr'
Call a doctor!	Chame um médico!	**shahm**' ooñ **meh**-dee-koo
Call an ambulance!	Chame uma ambulância!	**shahm**' oo-muh añ-boo-**lañ**-see-uh
Call the police!	Chame a polícia!	**shahm**' uh poo-**lee**-see-uh
Call the fire brigade!	Chame os bombeiros!	**shahm**' oosh bom-**bay**-roosh
Where is the nearest telephone?	Há um telefone aqui perto?	ah ooñ te-le-**fon**' uh-**kee pehr**-too
Where is the nearest hospital?	Onde é o hospital mais próximo?	ond' eh oo **ohsh**-pee-**tahl' mysh pro**-see-moo

COMMUNICATION ESSENTIALS

Yes	Sim	seeñ
No	Não	nowñ
Please	Por favor/ Faz favor	poor fuh-**vor** fash fuh-**vor**
Thank you	Obrigado/da	o-bree-**gah**-doo/duh
Excuse me	Desculpe	dish-**koolp**'
Hello	Olá	oh-**lah**
Goodbye	Adeus	a-**deh**-oosh
Good morning	Bom-dia	boñ **dee**-uh
Good afternoon	Boa-tarde	boh-uh **tard**'
Good night	Boa-noite	boh-uh **noyt**'
Yesterday	Ontem	oñ-**tayñ**
Today	Hoje	ohj'
Tomorrow	Amanhã	ah-mañ-**yañ**
Here	Aqui	uh-**kee**
There	Ali	uh-**lee**
What?	O quê?	oo keh
Which?	Qual?	kwahl'
When?	Quando?	**kwañ**-doo
Why?	Porquê?	poor-**keh**
Where?	Onde?	oñd'

USEFUL PHRASES

How are you?	Como está?	koh-moo shtah
Very well, thank you.	Bem, obrigado/da.	bayñ o-bree-**gah**-doo/duh
Pleased to meet you.	Encantado/a.	eñ-kañ-**tah**-doo/duh
See you soon.	Até logo.	uh-**teh loh**-goo
That's fine.	Está bem.	shtah bayñ
Where is/are . . . ?	Onde está/estão . . . ?	ond' shtah/shtowñ
How far is it to . . . ?	A que distância fica . . . ?	uh kee dish-**tañ**-see-uh **fee**-kuh
Which way to . . . ?	Como se vai para . . . ?	koh-moo seh vy **para**
Do you speak English?	Fala inglês?	**fah**-luh eeñ-**glehsh**
I don't understand.	Não compreendo.	nowñ kom-pree-**eñ**-doo
Could you speak more slowly please?	Pode falar mais devagar por favor?	pohd' fuh-**lar** mysh d'-va-**gar** poor fuh-**vor**
I'm sorry.	Desculpe.	dish-**koolp**'

USEFUL WORDS

big	grande	**grañd**'
small	pequeno	pe-**keh**-noo
hot	quente	**keñt**'
cold	frio	**free**-oo
good	bom	boñ
bad	mau	**mah**-oo
quite a lot/enough	bastante	bash-**tañt**'
well	bem	bayñ
open	aberto	a-**behr**-too
closed	fechado	fe-**shah**-doo
left	esquerda	**shkehr**-duh
right	direita	dee-**ray**-tuh
straight on	em frente	ayñ **freñt**'
near	perto	**pehr**-too
far	longe	**loñj**'
up	suba	**soo**-buh
down	desça	**deh**-shuh
early	cedo	**seh**-doo
late	tarde	**tard**'
entrance	entrada	eñ-**trah**-duh
exit	saída	sa-**ee**-duh
toilets	casa de banho	**kah**-zuh d' **bañ**-yoo
more	mais	mysh
less	menos	**meh**-noosh

MAKING A TELEPHONE CALL

I'd like to place an international call.	Queria fazer uma chamada internacional.	**kree**-uh fuh-**zehr** oo-muh sha-**mah**-duh in-ter-na-**see**-oo-nahl'
a local call.	uma chamada local.	oo-muh sha-**mah**-duh loo-**kahl**'
Can I leave a message?	Posso deixar uma mensagem?	**poh**-soo day-**shar** oo-muh meñ-**sah**--jayñ

SHOPPING

How much does this cost?	Quanto custa isto?	**kwañ**-too **koosh**-tuh **eesh**-too
I would like . . .	Queria . . .	**kree**-uh
I'm just looking.	Estou só a ver obrigado/a.	**shtoh** soh uh vehr o-bree-**gah**-doo/uh
Do you take credit cards?	Aceita cartões de crédito?	uh-**say**-tuh kar-**toinsh** de **kreh**-dee-too
What time do you open?	A que horas abre?	uh **kee oh**-rash **ah**-bre
What time do you close?	A que horas fecha?	uh **kee oh**-rash **fay**-shuh
This one	Este	ehst'
That one	Esse	ehss'
expensive	caro	**kah**-roo
cheap	barato	buh-**rah**-too
size (clothes/shoes)	tamanho	ta-**man**-yoo
white	branco	**brañ**-koo
black	preto	**preh**-too
red	roxo	**roh**-shoo
yellow	amarelo	uh-muh-**reh**-loo
green	verde	**vehrd**'
blue	azul	uh-**zool**'

TYPES OF SHOP

antique shop	loja de antiguidades	**loh**-juh de añ-tee-gwee-**dahd'sh**
bakery	padaria	pah-duh-**ree**-uh
bank	banco	**bañ**-koo
bookshop	livraria	lee-vruh-**ree**-uh
butcher	talho	**tah**-lyoo
cake shop	pastelaria	pash-te-luh-**ree**-uh
chemist	farmácia	far-**mah**-see-uh
fishmonger	peixaria	pay-shuh-**ree**-uh
hairdresser	cabeleireiro	kab'-lay-**ray**-roo
market	mercado	mehr-**kah**-doo
newsagent	kiosque	kee-**yohsk**'
post office	correios	koo-**ray**-oosh
shoe shop	sapataria	suh-puh-tuh-**ree**-uh
supermarket	supermercado	soo-**pehr**-mer-**kah**-doo
tobacconist	tabacaria	tuh-buh-kuh-**ree**-uh
travel agency	agência de viagens	uh-jen-see-uh de vee-**ah**-jayñsh

SIGHTSEEING

cathedral	sé	seh
church	igreja	ee-**gray**-juh
garden	jardim	jar-**deeñ**
library	biblioteca	bee-blee-oo-**teh**-kuh
museum	museu	moo-**zeh**-oo
tourist information office	posto de turismo	**posh**-too d' too-**reesh**-moo
closed for holidays	fechado para férias	fe-**sha**-doo puh-ruh **feh**-ree-ash
bus station	estação de autocarros	shta-**sowñ** d' oh-too-**kah**-roosh
railway station	estação de comboios	shta-**sowñ** d' koñ-**boy**-oosh

STAYING IN A HOTEL

Do you have a vacant room?	Tem um quarto livre?	tayñ ooñ **kwar**-too **leevr**'
room with a bath	um quarto com casa de banho	ooñ **kwar**-too koñ **kah**-zuh d' **bañ**-yoo
shower	duche	doosh
single room	quarto individual	**kwar**-too een-dee-vee-doo-**ahl**'
double room	quarto de casal	**kwar**-too d' kuh-**zahl**'
twin room	quarto com duas camas	**kwar**-too koñ **doo**-ash **kah**-mash
porter	porteiro	poor-**tay**-roo
key	chave	**shahv**'
I have a reservation.	Tenho um quarto reservado.	**tayñ**-yoo ooñ **kwar**-too-re-ser-**vah**-doo

Eating Out

Have you got a table for . . . ?	Tem uma mesa para . . . ?	tayñ oo-muh meh-zuh puh-ruh
I want to reserve a table.	Quero reservar uma mesa.	keh-roo re-zehr-var oo-muh meh-zuh
The bill please.	A conta por favor/ faz favor.	uh kohn-tuh poor fuh-vor/ fash fuh-vor
I am a vegetarian.	Sou vegetariano/a.	Soh ve-je-tuh-ree-ah-noo/uh
Waiter!	Por favor!/ Faz favor!	poor fuh-vor/ fash fuh-vor
the menu	a lista	uh leesh-tuh
fixed-price menu	a ementa turística	uh ee-mehñ-tuh too-reesh-tee-kuh
wine list	a lista de vinhos	uh leesh-tuh de veeñ-yoosh
glass	um copo	ooñ koh-poo
bottle	uma garrafa	oo-muh guh-rah-fuh
half bottle	meia-garrafa	may-uh guh-rah-fuh
knife	uma faca	oo-muh fah-kuh
fork	um garfo	ooñ gar-foo
spoon	uma colher	oo-muh kool-yair
plate	um prato	ooñ prah-too
napkin	um guardanapo	ooñ goo-ar-duh-nah-poo
breakfast	pequeno-almoço	pe-keh-noo-ahl-moh-soo
lunch	almoço	ahl-moh-soo
dinner	jantar	jan-tar
cover	couvert	koo-vehr
starter	entrada	eñ-trah-duh
main course	prato principal	prah-too prin-see-pahl
dish of the day	prato do dia	prah-too doo dee-uh
set dish	combinado	koñ-bee-nah-doo
half portion	meia-dose	may-uh doh-se
dessert	sobremesa	soh-bre-meh-zuh
rare	mal passado	mahl puh-sah-doo
medium	médio	meh-dee-oo
well done	bem passado	bayñ puh-sah-doo

Menu Decoder

abacate	uh-buh-kaht'	avocado
açorda	uh-sor-duh	bread-based stew (often seafood)
açúcar	uh-soo-kar	sugar
água mineral	ah-gwuh mee-ne-rahl'	mineral water
(com gás)	koñ gas	sparkling
(sem gás)	sayñ gas	still
alho	ay-oo	garlic
alperce	ahl'-pehrce	apricot
amêijoas	uh-may-joo-ash	clams
ananás	uh-nuh-nahsh	pineapple
arroz	uh-rohsh	rice
assado	uh-sah-doo	baked
atum	uh-tooñ	tuna
aves	ah-vesh	poultry
azeite	uh-zayt'	olive oil
azeitonas	uh-zay-toh-nash	olives
bacalhau	buh-kuh-lyow	dried, salted cod
banana	buh-nah-nuh	banana
batatas	buh-tah-tash	potatoes
batatas fritas	buh-tah-tash free-tash	french fries
batido	buh-tee-doo	milk-shake
bica	bee-kuh	espresso
bife	beef	steak
bolacha	boo-lah-shuh	biscuit
bolo	boh-loo	cake
borrego	boo-reh-goo	lamb
caça	kah-ssuh	game
café	kuh-feh	coffee
camarões	kuh-muh-roysh	large prawns
caracóis	kuh-ruh-koysh	snails
caranguejo	kuh-rañ-gay-joo	crab
carne	karn'	meat
cataplana	kuh-tuh-plah-nuh	sealed wok used to steam dishes
cebola	se-boh-luh	onion
cerveja	sehr-vay-juh	beer
chá	shah	tea
cherne	shern'	stone bass
chocolate	shoh-koh-laht'	chocolate
chocos	shoh-koosh	cuttlefish
chouriço	shoh-ree-soo	red, spicy sausage
churrasco	shoo-rahsh-coo	on the spit
cogumelos	koo-goo-meh-loosh	mushrooms
cozido	koo-zee-doo	boiled
enguias	eñ-gee-ash	eels
fiambre	fee-añbr'	ham
fígado	fee-guh-doo	liver
frango	frañ-goo	chicken
frito	free-too	fried
fruta	froo-tuh	fruit
gambas	gam-bash	prawns
gelado	je-lah-doo	ice cream
gelo	jeh-loo	ice
goraz	goo-rash	bream
grelhado	grel-yah-doo	grilled
iscas	eesh-kash	marinated liver
lagosta	luh-gohsh-tuh	lobster
laranja	luh-rañ-juh	orange
leite	layt'	milk
limão	lee-mowñ	lemon
limonada	lee-moo-nah-duh	lemonade
linguado	leeñ-gwah-doo	sole
lulas	loo-lash	squid
maçã	muh-sañ	apple
manteiga	man-tay-guh	butter
mariscos	muh-reesh-koosh	seafood
meia-de-leite	may-uh-d' layt'	white coffee
ostras	osh-trash	oysters
ovos	oh-voosh	eggs
pão	powñ	bread
pastel	pash-tehl'	cake
pato	pah-too	duck
peixe	paysh'	fish
peixe-espada	paysh'-shpah-duh	scabbard fish
pimenta	pee-meñ-tuh	pepper
polvo	pohl'-voo	octopus
porco	por-coo	pork
queijo	kay-joo	cheese
sal	sahl'	salt
salada	suh-lah-duh	salad
salsichas	sahl-see-shash	sausages
sandes	sañ-desh	sandwich
santola	sañ-toh-luh	spider crab
sopa	soh-puh	soup
sumo	soo-moo	juice
tamboril	tañ-boo-ril'	monkfish
tarte	tart'	pie/cake
tomate	too-maht'	tomato
torrada	too-rah-duh	toast
tosta	tohsh-tuh	toasted sandwich
vinagre	vee-nah-gre	vinegar
vinho branco	veeñ-yoo brañ-koo	white wine
vinho tinto	veeñ-yoo teeñ-too	red wine
vitela	vee-teh-luh	veal

Numbers

0	zero	zeh-roo
1	um	ooñ
2	dois	doysh
3	três	tresh
4	quatro	kwa-troo
5	cinco	seeñ-koo
6	seis	saysh
7	sete	set'
8	oito	oy-too
9	nove	nov'
10	dez	desh
11	onze	oñz'
12	doze	doz'
13	treze	trez'
14	catorze	ka-torz'
15	quinze	keeñz'
16	dezasseis	de-zuh-saysh
17	dezassete	de-zuh-set'
18	dezoito	de-zoy-too
19	dezanove	de-zuh-nov'
20	vinte	veent'
21	vinte e um	veen-tee-ooñ
30	trinta	treeñ-tuh
40	quarenta	kwa-reñ-tuh
50	cinquenta	seen-kweñ-tuh
60	sessenta	se-señ-tuh
70	setenta	se-teñ-tuh
80	oitenta	oy-teñ-tuh
90	noventa	noo-veñ-tuh
100	cem	sayñ
101	cento e um	señ-too-ee-ooñ
102	cento e dois	señ-too ee doysh
200	duzentos	doo-zeñ-toosh
300	trezentos	tre-zeñ-toosh
400	quatrocentos	kwa-troo-señ-toosh
500	quinhentos	kee-nyeñ-toosh
700	setecentos	set'-señ-toosh
900	novecentos	nov'-señ-toosh
1,000	mil	meel'

Time

one minute	um minuto	ooñ mee-noo-too
one hour	uma hora	oo-muh oh-ruh
half an hour	meia-hora	may-uh-oh-ruh
Monday	segunda-feira	se-goon-duh-fay-ruh
Tuesday	terça-feira	ter-sa-fay-ruh
Wednesday	quarta-feira	kwar-ta-fay-ruh
Thursday	quinta-feira	keen-ta-fay-ruh
Friday	sexta-feira	say-shta-fay-ruh
Saturday	sábado	sah-ba-doo
Sunday	domingo	doo-meen-goo

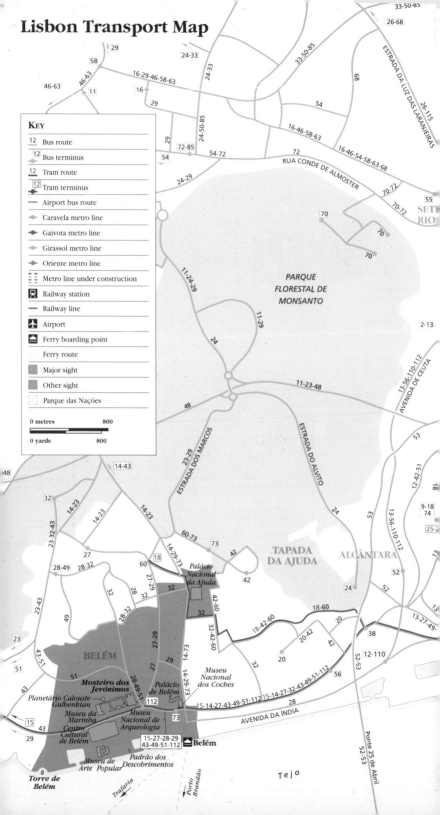

Lisbon Transport Map